THE TEMPLE
OF JERUSALEM

THE TEMPLE
OF JERUSALEM

JOAN COMAY

HOLT, RINEHART AND WINSTON
New York

Library of Congress Cataloging in Publication Data

Comay, Joan.
  The Temple of Jerusalem.
    1. Jerusalem. Temple. I. Title.
DS109.3.C64 956.94'4 75-5453
ISBN 0-03-012706-8   *Jan 25'78*

Designed by Freda Harmer

Photoset in Great Britain by Keyspools Ltd, Golborne, Lancashire
Printed in Great Britain by Morrison & Gibb Ltd,
Edinburgh and London.

The Scripture quotations in this publication are from the
Revised Standard Version Bible, copyrighted 1946, 1952 and 1971 by
the Division of Christian Education of the National Council of the
Churches of Christ in the USA and used by permission.

Contents

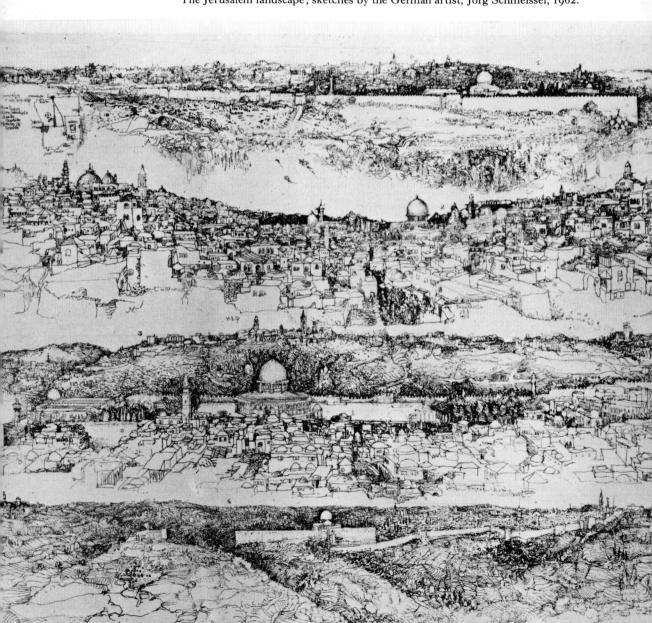

The Jerusalem landscape; sketches by the German artist, Jörg Schmeissel, 1962.

Introduction

Jerusalem is on the watershed of the Judean hills, and exactly on the frontier between the Mediterranean basin and the Asian desert. On the western side of the city limestone hills drop down 2600 feet to the coastal plain, their terraces worn bare or dotted with clumps of trees and patches of red earth. To the east the Judean wilderness of dun-coloured chalk and sandstone plunges 4000 feet to the Jordan valley and the Dead Sea.

The ancient landscape round the city has a bleak and indefinable beauty. The light is incredibly sharp and clear, the sky luminous except when shrouded by the winter rains. At sunset the harshness melts into soft shades of orange and mauve, before the swift dark comes and the rush of stars. These hills have a brooding quality, and one can believe that here the Hebrew prophets of old talked to God.

Yet the air of serenity is belied by thirty-three centuries of turbulent history. At times Jerusalem's buildings and ramparts burgeoned into splendour, under Solomon, Herod, Constantine and Suleiman. At other times the city was reduced to rubble, with the blood of its slaughtered citizens flowing down the gutters. The Jewish sages said: 'Ten parts of beauty were allotted the world at large, and of these Jerusalem assumed nine measures and the rest of the world but one . . . ten parts of suffering were visited upon the world – nine for Jerusalem and one for the world.'

Many different men other than Jews have sat here in the seat of power – Jebusites, Egyptians, Babylonians and Persians; Hellenist Greeks and Romans; Byzantines, Arabs, Crusaders, Mamelukes, Turks and British. But throughout the flux of these thousands of years there runs one constant thread – the unique attachment of the Jewish people to Jerusalem and the site of their holy Temple. History has no parallel to this mystic bond, and without it there would have been no state of Israel today.

One of the finest modern writers on the Holy Land, the Reverend

George Adam Smith, observed in the introduction to his book, *Jerusalem* (1908): 'Left alone by the main currents of the world's history, Jerusalem had been but a small highland township, her character compounded of the rock, the olive and the desert. ... But she became the bride of Kings and the Mother of Prophets. ...' The human strife in which the city was involved, he wrote, was one side of the more awful contest through the ages between the spirit of God and the spirit of man. Nowhere else has this universal struggle been waged so consciously, so articulately as in Jerusalem.

For a thousand years the focus of Jewish fervour was the Temple of Jerusalem, and its memory has remained potent for the nineteen centuries that have passed since it was finally destroyed. The Temple was as much a concept as a building, expressing the unique conjunction of a people, a faith, a land and a city. To understand what the sanctuary meant to its worshippers its background must first be noted – how the Hebrew people was shaped; how its faith was born; how it took root in the Promised Land; and how Jerusalem became its national centre.

PART I

BEFORE THE TEMPLE

1 *The Sinai Covenant*

The Patriarchs   According to the Book of Genesis, Abraham and his family came originally from the city of Ur, in southern Mesopotamia, near the head of the Persian Gulf. They moved northwards up the Euphrates valley and settled in the area of Haran, a trading town in northern Syria. The first eleven chapters of Genesis, describing the Creation, the Flood, the Tower of Babel, reflect this Mesopotamian background and there are striking parallels in Sumerian and Babylonian mythology. Some of the names the Bible gives to Abraham's relatives, such as his father Terah, his brothers Nahor and Haran, his wife Sarai and his sister-in-law Milcah, have been connected by scholars with place names in the Haran region or the moon-worship of which Ur and Haran were centres.

At an age given as seventy-five, Abraham migrated south-west and reached the land of Canaan. Here the biblical patriarchs are seen as clans of tent-dwelling herdsmen, moving slowly from place to place in search of grazing and water, with their wives, concubines and servants, and their cattle, sheep and goats. They avoided the fertile, settled plains and kept to the more sparsely populated hill-country.

The patriarchs remained in touch with their kinsmen in Haran. Abraham had a bride brought from there for his son Isaac, and Jacob fled there to his uncle Laban to escape the anger of his half-brother Esau. But the Mesopotamian past began to fade out. Henceforth the external cultural influence on the Hebrews would be that of the Canaanite people among whom they lived, and of Egypt, to which they trekked across the desert when driven by drought and famine.

The Near East of some four thousand years ago saw a general migration of nomads. There was nothing to distinguish this tiny Hebrew group of Semites from the rest, except for its distinctive religion. The patriarchs were peaceful people and seem to have lived on good terms with their local Canaanite neighbours. Inevitably they started to assimilate certain Canaanite religious customs, such as the altars,

animal sacrifices, sacred trees and pillars. But there was this fundamental difference: theirs was a single, invisible deity quite unlike
the pagan Baals of the Canaanite nature cults. The Hebrew *Yahweh*
(Jehovah) had no priests, no sanctuaries, no images, no fertility rites or
magic practices. *Yahweh* had no birth, no death, no family, no progeny.

The patriarchs lived in intimate personal communion with *Yahweh*.
He spoke to them directly or through angel messengers, like the three
strangers who came to Abraham at Mamre or the spirit who wrestled
with Jacob at the Jabbok river ford. *Yahweh* made Abraham a promise
(reaffirmed to Isaac and Jacob) that 'all the land which you see I will
give to you and to your descendants for ever' (Genesis 13: 14). This
covenant was sealed by an ancient ritual in which the carcasses of
sacrificial animals were severed and God passed between the halves in
the form of 'a smoking fire pot and a flaming torch' (Genesis 15: 17).

It is difficult now to imagine what precisely were the beliefs of the
patriarchs, and what stage of development they had reached. The old
traditions dating from their time were first recorded a thousand or so
years later. They then went through a lengthy process of editing and
re-editing before the Old Testament took the form it has today. The
priestly scribes may have tended to attribute to their forefathers religious
concepts and institutions that matured much later. However that may
be, in the patriarchal period as described in Genesis we can see the
embryo of a Hebrew people with a unique monotheistic idea of God,
and a bond with the land of Canaan consecrated by divine covenant.

The Exodus

After Jacob and his sons had settled in the Egyptian district of
Goshen, at the eastern edge of the Nile delta, there is a blank in the
record for the next four centuries. When it resumes the Israelite community is being used by the Pharaoh Seti I (1303–1290 BC) and his son
Pharaoh Rameses II (1290–1223 BC) as slave labour in the building of
two royal store-cities, Pithom and Rameses. In the reign of Rameses II
there emerges the most towering figure in the Old Testament – Moses
the liberator, lawgiver and founding father of Israelite nationhood.

The story is a familiar one, retold by Jews yearly at Passover. It
recounts how the Lord forced Pharaoh by a series of plagues to 'let my
people go', and how Moses led them out eastward into the Sinai desert,
on the long and perilous journey to the ancestral land. At Mount Sinai,
also called Mount Horeb (the locality is uncertain), a new covenant
was concluded between the Lord and the Children of Israel. It has been
pointed out that this covenant resembles in form the type of treaty
made by the rulers of the ancient Hittite empire with their vassals. By
such pacts the subject peoples would render loyalty and tribute in
return for the protection they would be given by their powerful overlord. With the Israelites, the protector was God himself, and in return
for his favour they undertook to observe the moral code made known to

The Law

them at Sinai. This unique concept of a treaty relationship between God and man has been the central idea in the history of the Jewish faith.

The making of the Sinai covenant is vividly described in the Book of Exodus. Moses went alone to the top of the desolate mountain, and the Lord instructed him to say to the people: '. . . if you will obey my voice and keep my covenant, you shall be my own possession among all peoples; for all the earth is mine, and you shall be to me a kingdom of priests and a holy nation' (Exodus 19: 5–6). Moses came down to report this to the people encamped near the foot of the mountain. They expressed their acceptance by answering in unison: 'All that the Lord has spoken we will do' (Exodus 19: 8). For the next two days they cleansed and prepared themselves. On the morning of the third day there was an awesome scene, with the mountain top enveloped in cloud, lightning, fire and smoke, the rumble of the thunder mingling with blasts of the *shofar* (ram's horn) and the quaking of the earth. The voice of the Lord then proclaimed the Ten Commandments and human thought took a revolutionary leap forward.

The first three commandments demand a total break with pagan cults and a total adherence to monotheism:

I am the Lord your God, who brought you out of the land of Egypt, out of the house of bondage. You shall have no other gods before me.

You shall not make for yourself a graven image . . . you shall not bow down to them or serve them; . . .

You shall not take the name of the Lord your God in vain; . . .
[Exodus 20: 2–7].

The incident of the golden calf was a warning that it would be a hard struggle to keep these precepts intact in the centuries to come.

The remaining seven commandments deal with human conduct – a compulsory day of rest on the weekly Sabbath; honouring one's parents; and prohibitions against killing, adultery, stealing, bearing false witness and coveting one's neighbour's possessions.

The Sinai covenant was reduced to written form by engraving the Ten Commandments on two stone tablets. Moses smashed them in anger and disappointment when he returned from a long sojourn on the mountain and found his people dancing round the golden calf. His action signified that the newly formed covenant had already been broken by a relapse into pagan practices. After Moses had taken stiff measures to restore discipline he disappeared again up the barren slopes of the mountain and returned forty days later with fresh tablets.

The brief guide-lines of the commandments were expanded into a detailed series of regulations, in what is known as the Covenant Code, set out in chapters 21 to 23 of the Book of Exodus. Some of its provisions were doubtless evolved later, when the Israelites were settled on the

Moses receives the Sinai Covenant from the hand of the Lord and expounds the Law to the Israelites; from the ninth-century Alcuin Bible.

Moses returned to his people from Mount Sinai to find they had reverted to the pagan worship of the golden calf. A nineteenth-century engraving after a painting by Nicolas Poussin.

land in Canaan, and the Jerusalem Temple was the focus of their religion. This applied, for instance, to the observance of the three pilgrim festivals – Passover, the Feast of Weeks and Tabernacles – which are rooted in the cycle of the agricultural year; and to the requirement that the first fruits should be brought to the 'House of the Lord'. But there is no reason for doubt that the general spirit of the Covenant Code and most of its precepts date from the formative period of the Hebrew faith in the time of Moses.

The Mosaic code represents social legislation of a remarkably progressive and humane kind. For instance there are the ordinances calling for justice and compassion for the poor:

If you lend money to any of my people with you who is poor, you shall not be to him as a creditor, and you shall not exact interest from him. If ever you take your neighbour's garment in pledge, you shall

restore it to him before the sun goes down; for that is his only covering, it is his mantle for his body; in what else shall he sleep? And if he
cries to me, I will hear, for I am compassionate [Exodus 22: 25–27].

Other provisions protect widows, orphans and slaves, and require that
fields and vineyards shall lie fallow every seventh year, with whatever
grows in them during that period being made available to the needy.

**The Ark and
the Tabernacle**

In their wandering desert life the Israelites were shaped into a
distinctive and well-organized community under Moses' leadership.
They had a defined relationship with the Lord, a system of laws and a
priesthood headed by Moses' brother Aaron and his two sons. The
Shechinah, the Divine Presence, travelled with them, and was associated with two sacred objects – the Ark of the Covenant and the Tabernacle – that together formed a portable sanctuary.

The Ark was the container for the Tablets of the Law, and was also
called the Ark of the Law. It was put into the care of the tribe of Levi,
which was exempted from military duties. The Ark was an acacia-wood
box about 4 feet long and $2\frac{1}{2}$ feet in width and height, covered inside and
outside with gold, and with four rings fixed to its sides, through which
two carrying poles were passed. On top of the Ark was a 'mercy seat'
that had two golden cherubim with outstretched wings at its ends.
These winged creatures, possibly related to the Egyptian sphinx, were
regarded as a species of angel that served as God's chariot, and here
guarded the throne of the Divine Presence. (The cherubim were to
reappear on a much larger scale in Solomon's Temple.) In instructing
Moses how to make the Ark the Lord said: 'There I will meet with you,
and from above the mercy seat, from between the two cherubim that are
upon the ark of the testimony, I will speak with you of all that I will give
you in commandment for the people of Israel' (Exodus 25: 22).

Precise directions were given for constructing a huge, elaborate
Tabernacle (in Hewbrew, *mishkan*) enclosed within a tent made from the
skins of rams and goats. The Tabernacle and its outer court consisted
of curtains of richly decorated linen hung on upright frames of acacia
wood covered with gold. A veil of fine linen separated the Holy of
Holies, in which the Ark was kept. The directions also covered an altar
and its utensils, a table, a laver, splendid priestly vestments and even
recipes for the anointing oil and the incense.

When the Israelites were encamped the tribes were arranged in a
square, with the Tabernacle in its centre, surrounded by the tents of the
Levites. When they moved off the Tabernacle was dismantled and
carried, and the furnishings were carried on poles like the Ark.

Although designed to be a portable shrine, the plan and contents of the
Tabernacle have a striking resemblance to that of Solomon's Temple,
which was built about three centuries after the Exodus. It was usually

OPPOSITE The Tabernacle surmounted by the pillar of cloud; the veil of linen is drawn
aside to reveal the Ark in the Holy of Holies. A nineteenth-century engraving.

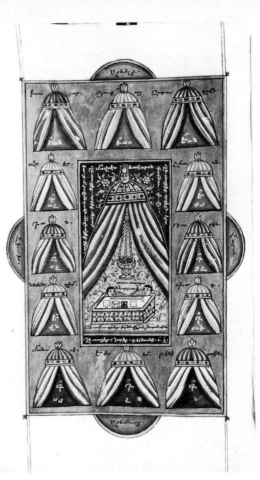

The encampment of the Israelites; the tents of the twelve tribes surround the Tabernacle containing the Ark. An illustration from an Armenian manuscript of the seventeenth century.

assumed by Bible students that the Tabernacle was the prototype for the Temple. But modern scholars are inclined to think that the description of the Tabernacle in the Book of Exodus is of more recent origin, based on post-exilic recollections of the destroyed Temple. It is a puzzling fact that in the same chapters of Exodus there is a passage referring to a simple tent of meeting (in Hebrew, *ohel mo'ed*): 'Now Moses used to take the tent and pitch it outside the camp. . . . And everyone who sought the Lord would go out to the tent of meeting . . .' (Exodus 33: 7). When Moses went alone to this tent, watched by the Israelites from afar, the pillar of cloud would descend to it and the Lord 'used to speak to Moses face to face, as a man speaks to his friend' (Exodus 33: 11). This passage is probably a surviving fragment of an earlier tradition concerning the tent-sanctuary in the wilderness.

Moses died before reaching the Promised Land, of which he was given only a distant glimpse from a mountain top. It was his faithful lieutenant Joshua who led the Israelites across the River Jordan from the east, and launched the conquest, in the latter half of the thirteenth century BC.

2 *In the Promised Land*

The Tribes
The conquest was followed by the period of the Judges (about two centuries), in which the Israelites were a loose confederacy of tribes, settled mainly in the hill areas of the country, each in its own territory. They had no common leader or central authority. Each tribe was made up of sprawling patriarchal families, grouped in clans. The Judges held no formal position but were charismatic individuals who emerged spontaneously to save their tribes from hostile neighbours, or to settle disputes. They were varied personalities: fighters like Gideon, Ehud and Barak; Deborah, a woman of strong character and moral authority; Othniel, a clan head; Samson, a legendary strong man; and prophet-priests like Eli and Samuel.

The cohesive bond between the tribes was their common religion. But the purity of the Mosaic code started to be eroded in the new environment. When the Israelites settled down as peasant cultivators instead of desert nomads, they were repeatedly tempted by the seductions of the local Canaanite nature-cults, and were as repeatedly in trouble with the Lord for this backsliding:

> And the people of Israel did what was evil in the sight of the Lord and served the Baals; and they forsook the Lord, the God of their fathers, who had brought them out of the land of Egypt; they went after other gods, from among the gods of the peoples who were round about them, and bowed down to them; . . . So the anger of the Lord was kindled against Israel, and he gave them over to plunderers, who plundered them . . . [Judges 2: 11–14].

Indeed it is surprising that the Israelite tribes did not disappear by absorption into the Canaanite population, as happened to other groups of desert nomads that erupted into settled communities. Except for their religious and moral code, the Hebrew tribesmen were relatively poor and backward. In political organization, architecture, craftsmanship and agricultural skills their Canaanite fellow-Semites were more advanced. The Israelites could neither build walled cities of their own, nor subdue those of their enemies by direct assault.

Thus, as appears from the Book of Judges, in spite of Joshua's dramatic victories the establishment of Israelite control over Canaan was a slow and incomplete process. It was only under David, two centuries after Joshua, that the Hebrews became the dominant power in the country. Until then there was a struggle for survival against formidable foes – the Canaanites who retained control of fortified cities like Jerusalem and Gezer; the Moabites and Ammonites in Trans-Jordan; the Arameans to the north in Syria; and above all the Philistines, a skilled people who originated in the Aegean and settled on the southern coastal plain of Canaan. There were also feuds between the Israelite tribes themselves; at one point the others aligned themselves against the small tribe of Benjamin, and nearly wiped it out.

Without the special nature of their faith the Israelites might well have lost their identity. It is true that there were local lapses into paganism. Yet the Mosaic creed kept a potent hold on the Hebrew people. That creed differed profoundly from the surrounding religions in Canaan and throughout the Near East. As the renowned archaeologist Professor W.F.Albright put it:

> The Canaanites, with their orgiastic nature-worship, their cult of fertility in the form of serpent symbols and sensuous nudity, and their gross mythology were replaced by Israel, with its pastoral simplicity and purity of life, its lofty monotheism, and its severe code of ethics [*From the Stone Age to Christianity*, 1940].

All ancient religions seem to have identified their deities with the tops of hills and mountains. Such spots were closer to the heavens, relatively isolated and inaccessible and often shrouded in cloud and mist. Climbing up to them induced a feeling of elevation above the humdrum concerns of men in the valleys and plains below, and of closer communion with the elemental forces of nature. The abode of the chief Canaanite god, Baal Hadad, was on Mount Tsafon in northern Syria, just as the Greek gods dwelt on Mount Olympus. In the flat river basins of Mesopotamia and the Nile valley men built ziggurats, pyramids or elevated platforms to simulate sacred mountains for temples or royal tombs. The Tower of Babel in the Old Testament was one such effort.

The new Hebrew owners of the shrines retained some Canaanite practices and cult objects, such as the stone pillars of Baal and the wooden poles of the fertility goddess Asherah (also Asheroth, or Asherim). Shechem, Shiloh, Bethel, Dan, Gilgal, Gibeah and Nob were all examples of Hebrew sanctuaries with a Canaanite past. A

Baal Hadad, the chief god of the
Canaanites; from a stone stele of
the second millennium BC, found
at Ras Shamra in Syria.

common feature of all these 'high places', whether Canaanite or Israelite, was the erection of altars for animal sacrifices.

Though the Israelite tribes were not ruled from a common centre they were accustomed to come together at one place for special religious ceremonies. In Joshua's time, on two important occasions he assembled them at Shechem (later called Nablus), the main town in the Samarian hills about 30 miles north of Jerusalem, then still a Jebusite (Canaanite) city. Shechem was an ancient sanctuary city, figuring in the story of Abraham. During the conquest Joshua gathered the Israelites here, erected an altar and offered a sacrifice, with the priests carrying the Ark of the Covenant. He then read out in public 'all the words of the law' (Joshua 8: 34). Before his death Joshua summoned to Shechem the notables from the tribes, and reaffirmed the Mosaic covenant. There is a theory that Shechem and the surrounding area was inhabited by the descendants of Israelites who had remained behind when the rest of the tribes migrated to Egypt at the end of the patriarchal period. Joshua and his followers therefore found themselves here among their own kin, and merged peacefully with them.

Later Joshua had the Ark placed in the tent of meeting, which he set up at Shiloh, 12 miles south of Shechem in the direction of Jerusalem. It was here he had a survey made of the conquered areas not yet settled and distributed them by lot among seven of the tribes who had not received territory. The Levitical cities were scattered among the tribal lands, since the tribe of Levi carried out religious functions and had no separate territory of its own.

In the later period of the Judges Shiloh was recognized as a central sanctuary and place of pilgrimage and had a priestly order. The young Samuel was reared under the high priest Eli. This sanctuary was the forerunner of the Temple in Jerusalem.

The Monarchy   From the middle of the eleventh century BC the Philistines occupying the southern coastal region started pushing against the hill terrain inhabited by the Israelites. They were a formidable foe. Their five capital cities – Gaza, Ashkelon, Ashdod, Gath and Ekron – formed an alliance, deploying an effective army equipped with iron chariots and weapons. Against them the Israelites could throw only a militia of peasants and herdsmen; what is more, they had not acquired the art of iron smelting. For more than a century, until it was neutralized by David, the pressure of the Philistines dominated the lives of the Hebrew tribes, and put their very existence in jeopardy. The exploits of Samson, and the famous single combat between David and Goliath, were incidents in the struggle for control of the Shefelah (foothills) in the border area between Philistia and Judea. In 1050 BC the Israelites were disastrously defeated in a battle near Aphek, the northernmost Philistine town at the source of the river Yarkon. Among the slain were Eli's

ABOVE The remains of the temple-fortress excavated at Shechem (Nablus).

BELOW Shiloh; Byzantine ruins on the site of the ancient sanctuary city.

two sons, both priests, who had been sent from Shiloh with the Ark of the Covenant to lend the support of the Divine Presence on the battlefield. The Ark was captured and carried off in triumph by the Philistines. When a runner brought the dreadful tidings to the aged Eli he fell backwards with shock and died of a broken neck. Archaeological evidence indicates that the Shiloh sanctuary was destroyed about this time, presumably by the Philistine forces advancing across the hills after the battle.

Samuel, who had emerged as the leading Israelite figure, settled down at Rama, a few miles north of Jerusalem, and from there dispensed justice. Alarmed by the Philistine menace, the tribes were now prepared to form a united front under a single leader for the first time since Joshua. Their elders came to Samuel and said: '. . . now appoint for us a king to govern us like all the nations' (1 Samuel 8: 5). For the prophet the idea was repugnant. Until then the Israelites had had no earthly ruler; God was their king, and his commandments were their law. Samuel warned the people against royal despots who would exploit them. They persisted, and he yielded to them. His choice fell upon Saul, a young man from Gibeah in the territory of Benjamin. He was of imposing height and appearance, and had already shown military capacity by leading a successful expedition to relieve an Israelite town across the Jordan, besieged by the Ammonites. Samuel assembled the people, and Saul was anointed as king in a public ceremony.

After two years Saul was able to take the offensive and push the Philistines out of the places they had captured in the hills. However Samuel bitterly resented the independent authority and prestige of the monarch he had installed. The conflict lasted until the prophet's death. It provides an early example of the perennial tension between Church and State.

During his twenty-year reign Saul succeeded in keeping the Philistine power at bay, and in holding together the Israelite tribes under his leadership. Samuel had been shrewd in selecting a king from the tribe of Benjamin. It was one of the smaller tribes, and the strip of territory it held just north of Jerusalem served as a buffer-state between the confederacy of the northern tribes grouped together as Israel, and the large and powerful southern tribe of Judah.

A Philistine force marched up the Jezreel valley and defeated the Israelites in the battle of Mount Gilboa, where Saul and three of his sons were slain, including David's close friend Jonathan. The united monarchy fell apart and the tribe of Judah seceded.

David had been Saul's brilliant protégé and son-in-law. He had then fled from Saul's jealousy, and had survived for years as leader of a band of outlaws. After Saul's death David became king of Judah, with his capital at Hebron. In the north the veteran General Abner escaped across the river Jordan with Saul's weak son Ishboshet, whom he proclaimed as 'king of all Israel'. There followed two years of a confused power struggle. By then both Ishboshet and Abner had been murdered, and the northern leaders came to pledge their allegiance to David. The breach in the kingdom had been closed – but this unity would last only for the reigns of David and his son Solomon.

Jerusalem

In the eighth year of David's rule in Hebron he took the Jebusite stronghold of Jerusalem by an assault led by his nephew and army commander, Joab. Through an astute stroke of statecraft David promptly made the city his new capital. It was not identified with any of the tribes, but had remained a neutral Canaanite enclave wedged between Israel and Judah. It lay at the strategic crossroads of the central hill country, where the north–south hill road intersected the east–west route from the coast over the Judean range and down to Jericho and the river Jordan and fords. It was easily defended, being built on a narrow spur surrounded on three sides by steep ravines. The Philistines made two attempts to take Jerusalem from the Israelites, but were repulsed.

To consolidate the central authority of the monarchy, David realized that Jerusalem must be made the religious as well as the political centre. He decided to install in the city the most sacred object of the Hebrew faith, the Ark of the Covenant. The Ark had gone through a strange odyssey since the Philistines had captured it. According to the account

The sacred Ark of the Covenant, containing the Tablets of the Law; from an illuminated Latin manuscript of the twelfth century.

David escorts the Ark into Jerusalem. A fifteenth-century miniature.

in the First Book of Samuel, it turned out to be such a troublesome booty that the Philistines were relieved to get rid of it again. When they had placed it in the temple of the chief Philistine god Dagon at Ashdod, the image of the divinity fell over and was smashed. A plague then broke out. The Ark was hurriedly sent off in a cart drawn by oxen and handed over to the Israelites at Bet Shemesh in the Judean foothills. From there it was brought to the sanctuary of Kiriath Jearim, eight miles west of Jerusalem. It was kept at this hilltop locality for twenty years, until David sent a procession to escort it into Jerusalem. On the way one of the escort grabbed at the Ark to steady it when the cart jolted, and was struck dead. For fear that he had displeased the Lord, David cautiously left the Ark in the nearest house for three months. When he heard the house had been blessed he fetched the Ark to Jerusalem. Here he placed it in a great tent, and danced before it, wearing an ephod, a sacred priestly garment. The king then offered sacrifices and blessed the crowd in the name of the Lord.

The dual intent of these ceremonial acts seems plain. The Ark, and the Divine Presence with it, were now linked both with the new capital and with the Davidic throne. Doubtless remembering the schism between King Saul and the prophet Samuel, David also made sure that there should not be any religious authority in the kingdom independent of the palace. The two high priests, Zadok and Abiathar, were appointed by the king and were expected to be loyal to him. Their reliability as 'king's men' stood the test when a revolt broke out against David, led by his son Absalom. The two high priests fled from Jerusalem with David, but were ordered to go back and work for his return to power.

In one successful campaign after another David built up an empire that extended northwards to the river Euphrates in Upper Syria, southwards through the Negev to the head of the Gulf of Akaba and across from the Mediterranean coastline to the desert beyond the Trans-Jordan plateau. Israel had become the dominant state in the region between the Nile valley and Mesopotamia. The kingdoms of Edom, Moab, Ammon and Aram were conquered and incorporated into the empire. The Philistines were defeated and confined to a small coastal strip; and they soon disappeared altogether as a people with a separate identity. The Phoenician people, along the coastline of what is now Lebanon, were unconquered but friendly neighbours. They were a nation of skilful seafarers and traders with an advanced culture. David made a treaty of alliance with their leading ruler, Hiram, King of Tyre, who provided David with materials and craftsmen for his building construction, and was to do the same for Solomon.

3 The Site is Chosen

It would have been logical for David to build a temple in Jerusalem that would serve as a permanent national sanctuary and embellish the capital of his growing empire. That he intended to do so appears from his remark to Nathan, the court prophet: 'See now, I dwell in a house of cedar, but the ark of God dwells in a tent' (2 Samuel 7: 2). Nathan agreed at first, but he came back the following morning with a negative reaction from the Lord. Since the Exodus, said the Lord, 'I have been moving about in a tent for my dwelling' (2 Samuel 7: 6). Had he ever asked for a house of cedar? One senses in this passage a note of nostalgia for the simple nomadic past at a moment of transition to statehood. The text has a play on the word *bayit* (house). The Lord does not need a 'house', a temple, for himself, but he will make David a 'house', a royal dynasty. At the same time, there is a puzzling contradiction in the passage. David's son and successor, it is promised, 'shall build a house for my name, and I will establish the throne of his kingdom for ever' (2 Samuel 7: 13). If the Lord preferred to have a tent as a dwelling, why should Solomon be allowed to build him a temple at all?

A later version in the First Book of Chronicles gives an objective reason why the Temple should be built not by David but by Solomon. In his final address to the nation before his death, David said: 'Hear me, my brethren and my people. I had it in my heart to build a house of rest for the ark of the covenant of the Lord, and for the footstool of our God; and I made preparations for building. But God said to me, "You may not build a house for my name, for you are a warrior and have shed blood"' (1 Chronicles 28: 2–3). The chronicler nevertheless gives David much of the credit for the Temple. It is stated in the same chapter that David handed over to Solomon a detailed plan for the building, together with the gold, silver, precious stones and materials required for its decoration and equipment.

Moreover it was David who acquired the site for the Temple. He had

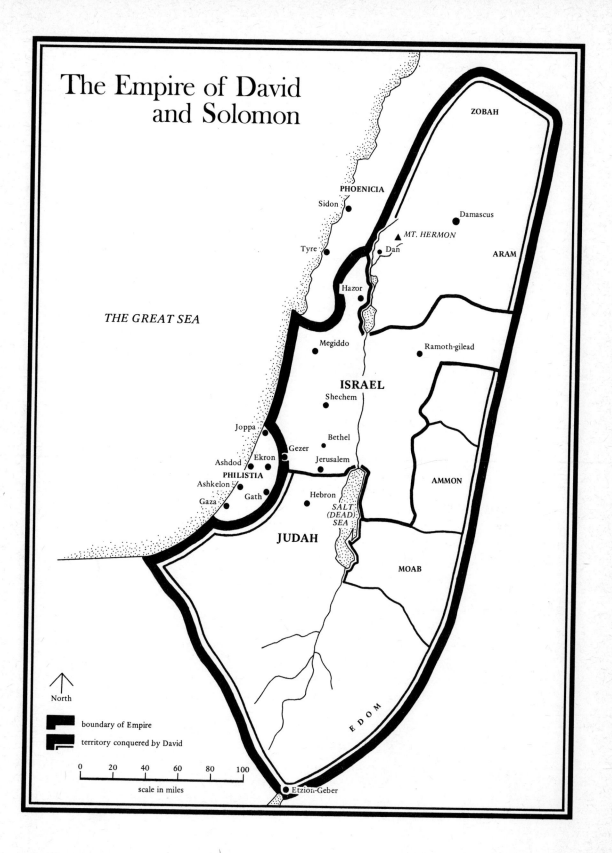

The Empire of David and Solomon

ZOBAH

PHOENICIA

Sidon

MT. HERMON

Damascus

Tyre

Dan

ARAM

Hazor

THE GREAT SEA

Megiddo

Ramoth-gilead

ISRAEL

Shechem

Joppa

Bethel

Gezer

Ashdod

Ekron

Jerusalem

PHILISTIA

AMMON

Ashkelon

Gaza

Gath

Hebron

SALT (DEAD) SEA

JUDAH

MOAB

E D O M

North

boundary of Empire

territory conquered by David

0   20   40   60   80   100

scale in miles

Etzion-Geber

ordered Joab and his army officers to carry out a census in the kingdom. It took over nine months, and produced a tally of all the 'valiant men who drew the sword' (2 Samuel 24: 9). But head-counting was considered unholy, and a serious pestilence at the time was seen as a punishment by the Lord. On the advice of the prophet Gad, David bought the threshing floor of a Jebusite farmer, Araunah, for 50 shekels of silver, erected an altar on it and offered sacrifices. Araunah's oxen were included in the price and killed for the sacrifices, while his sledges and the yokes for the oxen provided wood for the altar fire. The pestilence came to an end.

David's city was on the lower part of the Ophel spur. Araunah's threshing floor was above it to the north, on the flat top of the same ridge. Later the city was to spread westward from the threshing floor and to cover the low plateau between the valleys of Hinnom and Kidron. This Old City plateau is itself contained within a natural bowl or amphitheatre. If one stands on the Temple Mount one's eye can travel along the rim of high ground: Mount Scopus, the Mount of Olives, Abu Dis, the Mount of Evil Counsel, Talpioth, the watershed ridge to the west and north-west, and French Hill.

OPPOSITE The sacred rock on Mount Moriah where David built his altar, now inside the Dome of the Rock. The stone has been associated with the main sacrificial altar of the Temple and with the ascension of the prophet Mohammed.

BELOW The ancient method of threshing corn using wooden sledges, studded with basalt stones, and teams of oxen. An illustration from Sir Charles Wilson's *Picturesque Palestine* published in 1882.

Once Araunah's threshing floor became the site for the Temple it was natural that it should also be linked with Hebrew traditions harking back to the patriarchal age. The hilltop came to be identified with the dramatic episode of the *Akedah*, the sacrifice Abraham was called upon to make of his son Isaac (the Hebrew word *akedah* means binding, since Isaac's limbs were bound like those of a sacrificial animal). The Book of Genesis recounts that Abraham travelled three days from Beersheba to the place of the sacrifice, a hilltop in the land of Moriah that he saw from a distance. It is improbable that this chosen spot would be next to an existing Jebusite city; and in any case the Temple site is not visible from afar because of the ridges round Jerusalem. According to Samaritan tradition the *Akedah* took place on Mount Gerizim at Shechem. The Second Book of Chronicles, which is much later in date than the account in Genesis, simply states that Solomon built the Temple on Mount Moriah, thereby accepting the link with the *Akedah* as a fact.

On the hill there was an outcrop of rock forming a natural platform about 50 by 40 feet, and from 5 to 6 feet high. It was doubtless on this unusual feature that David erected his altar and made his sacrifice to the Lord. It is generally accepted that the great altar of burnt offering in the courtyard of the Temple was based on this rock, and it is the Moslem Sakhra over which the Dome of the Rock Mosque was later built. Visitors today peer at it through a grill introduced in the time of the Crusader kingdom of Jerusalem to stop Christian pilgrims chipping off pieces to carry home as souvenirs. At that time the mosque had become the Church of Templum Domini. It would appear, therefore, that the same slab of rock acquired sacred associations for Jews, Moslems and Christians, according to which religion possessed the hilltop.

PART II

THE FIRST TEMPLE

4 The Royal Builder

Solomon fought no military campaigns and occupied no more territory. He was content to safeguard and consolidate the extensive empire he had inherited from his father. The forty years of his reign were a period of unusual peace and prosperity in the turbulent history of the Hebrews. His very name, Shlomo in Hebrew, derived from *shalom*, meaning peace.

He was the second child of the beautiful Bathsheba, with whom David fell in love when he saw her taking a bath in the moonlight, on a rooftop below the palace. David's eldest son Amnon was murdered by his half-brother Absalom, in revenge for the rape of Absalom's sister Tamar. Absalom himself was defeated and killed, after leading a revolt against his father. When David was nearing the end of his life, Adonijah, the eldest surviving son, made a bid to seize the throne. But, under the influence of Bathsheba and Nathan the prophet, David nominated Solomon, then only a youth, as his successor. After a brief power-struggle Solomon established his rule. It lasted from 970 BC to 931 BC.

Next to David, Solomon is the most celebrated of all the Israelite kings. His sagacity became a legend, as did the splendour of his court and the great number and variety of the women in the royal harem. Yet Solomon's personality emerges in the biblical account with less vividness and human interest than that of his father, and his life was uneventful compared to the drama and struggle of David's rise to power, from his humble beginnings as a Bethlehem shepherd boy.

Solomon continued the process of concentrating central authority – political, military and religious – in the hands of the monarchy in Jerusalem. He retained the services of some of David's seasoned ministers and councillors, or gave appointments to their sons. The kingdom was divided into twelve districts for administrative and tax purposes, and this internal map corresponded only partially to the old tribal boundaries. Each district was governed by a commissioner, who had to collect the grain, oil and other products that served as taxes and provide food for the palace for one month a year. The tribe of Judah, to which the royal family belonged, was governed directly from Jerusalem.

With the territory of the kingdom stabilized, Solomon developed diplomatic alliances and trade with neighbouring countries. In some cases he cemented these political ties by marrying foreign princesses, notably the daughter of the Egyptian Pharaoh.

At a time of relative security in the Near East region, Israel derived lucrative revenues from its position astride the great caravan routes that linked the Nile valley with Mesopotamia and Asia Minor. For instance: 'A chariot could be imported from Egypt for six hundred shekels of silver and a horse for a hundred and fifty; and so through the king's traders they were exported to all the kings of the Hittites and the kings of Syria' (1 Kings 10: 29). (Actually the main supply of horses was from Cilicia in Asia Minor, which the Bible calls Kue.)

Solomon also opened up important trade routes. He had maintained his father's close partnership with Hiram, king of the Phoenician port city of Tyre on the Mediterranean coast. With Phoenician help Solomon constructed a fleet of trading vessels that plied from Etzion-Geber at the tip of the Gulf of Akaba (near modern Eilat) through the Red Sea to south-western Arabia, Yemen and the Horn of Africa (present-day Somaliland). These voyages figure in John Masefield's poem 'Cargoes':

> Quinquireme of Nineveh from distant Ophir
> Rowing home to haven in sunny Palestine,
> With a cargo of ivory,
> and apes and peacocks,
> Sandalwood, cedarwood and sweet white wine.

Etzion-Geber was the port for the copper mines of Timna. A modern copper extraction plant now operates at this spot, with the remains of ancient smelting furnaces built of stones still standing in the nearby wadis.

Somewhere near the lower entrance to the Red Sea was the small trader-state of Sheba. Its dusky queen made the long journey to visit King Solomon in Jerusalem, bearing rich gifts. It may be presumed that the purpose of the journey was not so much romance as trade promotion.

The Building Programme

The palace coffers were swelled by the state control of foreign trade, the tolls on caravans in transit through the kingdom, the tribute from vassal states and the taxes derived from the rising standards of living of the local Israelite population. Much of this wealth was diverted into an ambitious and costly building programme. A chain of fortresses was erected at strategic points on the periphery of the kingdom, or on the main highways to protect the trade caravans. Chariot forces were maintained at three fortified regional centres that have been the sites of archaeological digs: Hazor, north of the Sea of Galilee, commanding

RIGHT Sinai, where Moses received the new Covenant of the Lord.
OVERLEAF The high priest with a censer of incense before the altar in the Tabernacle; behind him, the twelve loaves of shewbread on a golden table and the seven-branched lamp. A fourteenth-century French manuscript illumination.

the Damascus road; Megiddo, controlling the pass from the coastal plain into the Jezreel valley; and Gezer, astride the road from the port of Joppa (now Jaffa) to Jerusalem. The fortifications in these three chariot-cities were of identical design, with wide casement walls and elaborate gateways flanked by square towers.

Solomon's main construction effort lay in enlarging and embellishing Jerusalem. On the rising ground above David's city, a complex of buildings was laid out on terraces. At the top was the Temple, on the site of the threshing floor that David had bought from Araunah the Jebusite. It took seven years to build. The palace compound below and to the south of the Temple took another thirteen years. It contained the royal quarters for the king and the harem, with a separate palace for Pharaoh's daughter; also other buildings for public functions and administrative offices. Important among them were the 'House of the Forest of Lebanon', so called because of its rows of massive cedar pillars, and the Judgement Hall, which held the great ivory throne.

ABOVE Solomon directs the unloading of materials for the building of the Temple. The stone and timber actually had to be brought by land from the port of Joppa. An eighteenth-century engraving from a Bible story book dedicated to the Prince of Condé.

LEFT Jerusalem from the south; the walls of the city in David's time followed the contours of the Ophel spur in the foreground.

The strange rock formation known as the 'pillars of Solomon' near the Timna copper mines north of Etzion-Geber.

The timber for Solomon's building operations was acquired mainly from Hiram. Ten thousand men were said to have been occupied each month in cutting the trees in the cedar and pine forests of the Lebanese mountains, transporting them to the coast of Tyre, floating them in long rafts down to Joppa and hauling them from there to Jerusalem. For this timber, together with the supply of some gold and precious stones and the loan of skilled masons and carpenters, Solomon paid Hiram in wheat and oil exports. During the years the debt to Hiram grew so large that the deficit was made up by cession of a strip of territory known as Cabul along the Acre plain in western Galilee, holding twenty villages.

The labour force engaged on the buildings and in quarrying and hauling the stone was said to total eighty thousand men. They were to a large extent slave labour from the Canaanite territories occupied by David and annexed to the kingdom. However Solomon's chronic shortage of workers and funds drove him to impose the corvée, a compulsory labour levy, on the Israelite population as well.

In the seventy years spanned by their two reigns David and Solomon

ABOVE The timber for Solomon's building projects was brought down from Tyre in long rafts as in this eighth-century BC relief from the palace of Sennacherib at Nineveh. BELOW The island of Jezirat Faraun ('the isle of Pharaoh') identified by a few scholars as Solomon's port of Etzion-Geber.

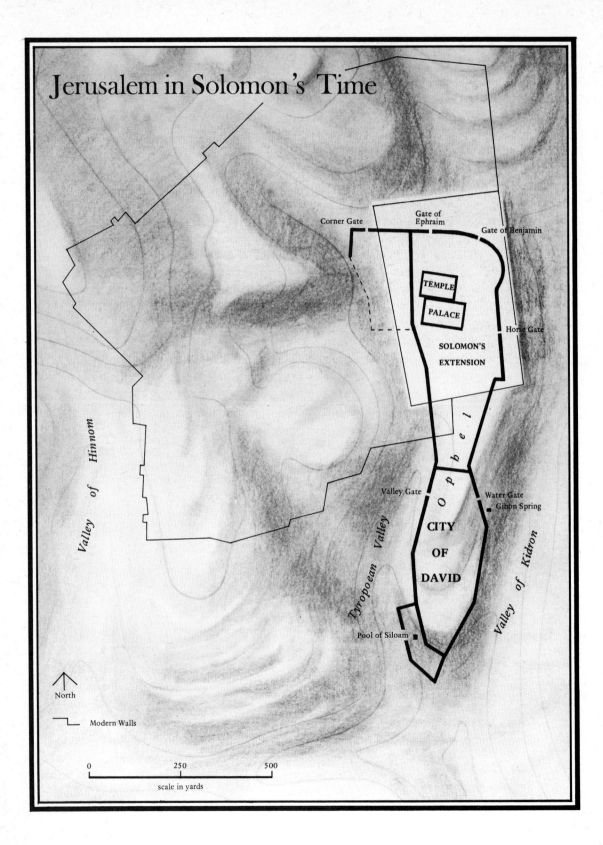

Jerusalem in Solomon's Time

Corner Gate

Gate of Ephraim

Gate of Benjamin

TEMPLE

PALACE

Horse Gate

SOLOMON'S
EXTENSION

Valley of Hinnom

Ophel

Valley Gate

Water Gate
Gihon Spring

CITY
OF
DAVID

Tyropoean Valley

Valley of Kidron

Pool of Siloam

North

Modern Walls

0   250   500

scale in yards

built up a united and prosperous kingdom, with a strong central regime, a religious focus in the Temple and dominion over the surrounding nations – except for their Phoenician ally. The number of their Israelite subjects about doubled (according to Professor Albright, roughly from 400,000 to 800,000). On the material level they were no longer just poor rural communities of peasants and herdsmen; there had been notable advances in trade, building and communications, and a movement from the villages into the growing towns. With relative affluence, and wider contact with the outside world, there also came an intellectual and cultural flowering fostered by these two enlightened monarchs – particularly in literary and poetic expression, music and the visual arts. The latter was much influenced by Phoenician culture, as was evident in the building and adornment of the Temple.

Towards the end of Solomon's reign it was reasonable to believe that the kingdom would remain stable and enduring. But beneath the benign surface there were unresolved strains and tensions. The exactions and burdens on the people became steadily heavier in order to maintain the sumptuous life-style of the court and Solomon's extensive building programmes. The royal coffers were chronically depleted. The corvée was extremely unpopular. The orthodox worshippers were offended by the tolerance at the palace of the pagan cults brought with them by the foreign princesses in the harem. The separatism and regional autonomy of the tribal system that had antedated the monarchy remained submerged under the splendours and successes of David's and Solomon's reigns, but had by no means disappeared. The identification of the northern tribes with the Davidic dynasty, drawn from the southern tribe of Judah, was less than wholehearted.

In retrospect, there had been an ominous warning in an episode that Solomon had dealt with without much bother and then disregarded. One Jeroboam, from the northern tribe of Ephraim, was placed by Solomon in charge of the forced labour from that tribe working in Jerusalem. He organized an abortive revolt against the throne and fled for his life to Egypt, where he was given political asylum.

5 Solomon's Temple

The Temple was started in the fourth year of Solomon's reign and completed in the eleventh year. A great crowd attended the dedication ceremony, including the tribal elders, heads of clans and other notables from all over the country, 'from the entrance of Hamath to the Brook of Egypt' (1 Kings 8: 65). In solemn procession the priests carried the Ark from David's tent to the new sanctuary to the sound of trumpets and cymbals. It was deposited in the Holy of Holies, under the wings of the cherubim. The biblical account states that the glory of the Lord filled the building in the form of a cloud. In the courtyard outside the king blessed the crowd, then knelt at the altar, stretched his arms upwards and made a supplication to the Lord. In his prayer God's endorsement of the royal dynasty was stressed. A great number of sacrifices followed and the inaugural feast lasted for seven days.

The theological paradox concerning the Temple emerged in Solomon's prayer. Pagan gods had local abodes; but how could this apply to the single, invisible deity of the Israelite concept? Solomon said: 'I have built thee an exalted house, a place for thee to dwell in for ever' (1 Kings 8: 13). He then proceeds to ask: 'But will God indeed dwell on the earth? Behold, heaven and the highest heaven cannot contain thee; How much less this house that I have built!' (1 Kings 8: 27). Solomon suggests a way out of this dilemma. The Lord has said of the Temple: 'My name shall be there' (1 Kings 8: 29). In other words, it was a special place of access to the Divine Presence; prayers made at the Temple, or even directed towards it from afar, would gain the ear of the Lord who was 'in heaven, thy dwelling place' (1 Kings 8: 30).

The Structure and Equipment

No archaeological remains of the First Temple have as yet been found. Its structure can however be visualized from the details given in three Old Testament sources: 1 Kings 6–8, 2 Chronicles 2–4 and Ezekiel 40–6. While there are discrepancies in these accounts, the general outline emerges with reasonable clearness.

The first point that strikes the present-day reader is that the dimensions of the Temple were small. The fame of the shrine would suggest a more imposing structure. Its lack of size and its proximity to the palace have prompted some scholars to suggest that the building may originally have been designed as a royal chapel, like those attached to the courts of other Near Eastern monarchs. Yet it did in fact serve as the central sanctuary and place of pilgrimage for the whole nation; and it held their most sacred object, the Ark of the Law. It must be borne in mind that the interior of the Temple was not a place of assembly for the congregation, as in a Jewish synagogue today, a Christian church or a Moslem mosque. The Temple was primarily God's house, a dwelling for the *Shechinah*, the Divine Presence, as the old desert Tabernacle had been.

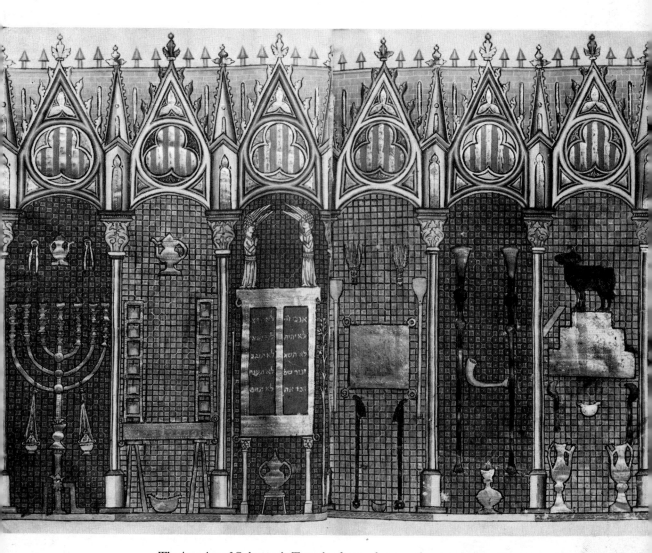

The interior of Solomon's Temple; from a fourteenth-century Spanish manuscript, *Historia Scholastica*, by Pedro Comesto.

The worshippers gathered in the great courtyard outside. Unlike lands in the northern hemisphere, Israel has an outdoor climate, except for periodic rainstorms in the winter months.

There is one engineering factor that had a bearing on the size of the Temple. Its design avoided the use of internal columns, and its chambers were the maximum width possible at that time without additional supports for the wooden roof span.

The building had three chambers of equal width – 10 metres or about 33 feet – one behind the other. The first was the *Ulam*, a porch or vestibule 16 feet deep. Through this one passed into the main hall, the *Hechal* or Holy Place, 66 feet deep. Beyond it was the Holy of Holies, the *Dvir*, 33 feet square and windowless. When Solomon said at the dedication: 'The Lord has set the sun in the heavens but has said that he would dwell in thick darkness . . .' (1 Kings 8: 12), he was referring to the fact that no light entered the Holy of Holies, except on the rare occasions when the door was opened from the *Hechal*. Including the small storage rooms round the two sides and the back, the outside dimensions of the building were about 166 feet (50 metres) long, 83 feet (25 metres) wide and 50 feet (15 metres) high.

The ground plan followed the common architectural pattern of the time in the region. Among the striking parallels uncovered by the archaeologist's spade are two small temples of the Canaanite city of Hazor in north-eastern Israel, destroyed by Joshua in the thirteenth century BC; and the small Syro-Hittite temple or royal chapel at Tel Tainet in northern Syria, dating from the eighth or ninth century BC. In each of these cases there was a porch, a main sanctuary chamber and an inner Holy of Holies. There are affinities in design also with the Late Bronze period Canaanite temples excavated at Lachish and Beit She'an in Israel, both several centuries older than Solomon's Temple.

The Temple was built of blocks of stone quarried in the hills. The inside was panelled with finely carved cedar wood overlaid with gold. The floor was made of cypress boards.

In the Holy of Holies the Ark was flanked by two cherubim (Hebrew: *heruvim*) 16 feet high, made of olive wood covered with gold. Each had two pairs of outstretched wings spanning the whole chamber from wall to wall. As with the smaller cherubim at each end of the Ark in the desert Tabernacle, those in the Temple were regarded as forming a kind of throne for the Divine Presence. Images of cherubim were prevalent in pagan Canaanite cults, and the Phoenician craftsmen lent to Solomon by Hiram would have been familiar with these winged creatures. According to the biblical account, they were liberally used as a decorative motif in the carvings and hangings of the Temple interior, together with palm trees, pomegranates and flower designs. The cherubim were later transmuted into Christian symbols as a minor species in the

This ivory 'cherub' found in Arslan Tash is thought to be similar to the winged figures that guarded the Ark in Solomon's Temple.

hierarchy of the angels. In Renaissance art they had become plump naked babies with tiny wings – a far cry from the guardians of the inner sanctuary in Solomon's Temple.

According to Talmudic tradition, there was a stone in the Holy of Holies called *Even Shetiyah* (The Foundation Stone) because it was said to be the central core from which the whole world had grown. In an anthology of biblical legends compiled by a fourth-century rabbi it is asserted that: 'The Land of Israel is the middle of the earth. Jerusalem is the middle of Israel. The Temple is the middle of Jerusalem. The Holy of Holies is the middle of the Temple. The Holy Ark is the middle of the Holy of Holies. And the Stone of Foundation is in front of the Holy of Holies.'

This legendary stone was also identified with Jacob's pillow, on the night when he had the dream of a ladder reaching up to heaven: 'And he came to a certain place, and stayed there that night, because the sun had set. Taking one of the stones of the place, he put it under his head and lay down in that place to sleep' (Genesis 28: 11). The next morning Jacob set the stone up as a sacred pillar and anointed it with oil, calling the place Bethel, God's house.

The name, Stone of Foundation, and the legends surrounding it became attached in due course to the great rock that was the site of the altar in the Temple courtyard and is now contained in the Dome of the Rock Mosque.

Other traditions placed in the Holy of Holies three objects connected with miracles performed at the time of the Exodus: a jar of manna, the staff of Moses and Aaron's flowering rod.

The manna was the 'bread that the Lord has given you to eat' (Exodus 16: 15) during the forty years the Children of Israel spent in the desert. It is described as 'a fine flake-like thing, fine as hoarfrost on the ground. . . . like coriander seed, white, and the taste of it was like wafers made with honey' (Exodus 16: 14, 31). The source of the manna remains uncertain. The prevailing theory is that it was the sweetish secretion dropping on the ground from tiny insects that feed on the tamarisk trees in the desert. The Bedouin still collect it for food. A golden jar of the manna was said to be kept in the Temple, as a reminder of the divine bounty in the wilderness. The jar is mentioned in the Epistle to the Hebrews in the New Testament, so this legend was still alive as late as the first century AD.

It was natural to assume that the rod of Moses was preserved in the sanctuary, as it figured so potently in his wonder-working. It was used, for instance, to part the waters of the Red Sea (actually the Reed Sea), to secure survival in battle against an Amalakite attack and to strike fresh water from a rock in the desert.

Aaron's flowering rod became a tangible symbol of his priestly authority. After the revolt led by Korah had been crushed in the desert, Moses ordered each tribe to place before the altar in the Tabernacle a rod bearing the name of the tribal leader. The rod of the priestly tribe of Levi carried Aaron's name. Next morning it was seen that Aaron's rod had burst into blossom and produced ripe almonds. This was accepted as a sign that the Lord had endorsed Aaron for his sacerdotal vocation. Moses then had the rod placed permanently before the Ark.

If these three sacred objects were at any time preserved in Solomon's Temple, they had disappeared before the destruction of 587 BC, as had the Ark itself. The Talmud expresses a belief that they were buried with the Ark for safe keeping, and will be restored by the prophet Elijah in the Messianic age.

The most valuable worker supplied to Solomon by King Hiram was a master-craftsman in bronze, also called Hiram. His father was a man from Tyre, and his mother an Israelite woman from the tribe of Naftali in the Galilee. Under his direction the courtyard before the Temple was furnished with a group of monumental bronze works.

The most conspicuous of these objects were two huge hollow bronze columns flanking the main entrance to the Temple vestibule. With their decorated capitals they were nearly 40 feet high and 6 feet in diameter. For reasons that are obscure, they were called Jachin and Boaz.

The 'molten sea' was a great bronze bowl over 16 feet in diameter, holding an estimated 16,000 gallons of water. It stood on the backs of twelve oxen in four groups of three, facing the cardinal points of the compass. The 'sea' weighed over 30 tons, so it is not surprising that during the fall of Jerusalem invaders broke it up and carried off the hunks of metal.

Near the 'sea' were ten smaller lavers or bowls of water used for the ceremonial ablutions of the priests. Each had an elaborate stand on wheels.

The main altar for sacrifices stood in the courtyard facing the entrance to the Temple. It was plated with bronze and was in the form of four stepped tiers, the lowest one being 33 square feet. The top tier, called *Har-el* (Mountain of God), had four horns at its corners. By ancient tradition a fugitive from justice could obtain sanctuary by grasping the horns. They were daubed with blood when the altar was consecrated.

Inside the main chamber of the sanctuary, in front of the steps leading to the Holy of Holies, was a small incense altar of cedar wood and gold.

It is surmised that Hiram used a process of sand-casting in making the large bronze objects, together with the numerous utensils required for the Temple service.

The exact origin and significance of some of the Temple equipment has been the subject of much learned speculation. The pillars, Jachin and Boaz, have been variously described as fire altars, incense altars, symbolic trees of life or a symbolic gateway for the sun. The 'molten sea' has been taken to represent the primal ocean of Mesopotamian mythology. The shape of the sacrificial altar has been compared to that of the Babylonian ziggurats, stepped pyramid temples, symbolizing the cosmic order. Much also has been read into the shape of the Temple, and its orientation eastward facing the rising sun. Whatever these esoteric meanings may have been, there is no doubt that the physical splendour of its materials and craftsmanship made the Temple one of the architectural wonders of the ancient Near East.

The Temple Services

The main religious events of the year were the three pilgrimage festivals: Passover (*Pesach*), the Feast of Weeks (*Shavuot*) and the Feast of Booths (*Succot*). These were agricultural festivals of pre-Israelite origin. Passover, in March–April, marked the end of the winter rains

The Temple furnishings were modelled on those of the Tabernacle but embellished, under the guidance of the Phoenician craftsmen, with a group of monumental bronze works.

OPPOSITE
above The main altar of sacrifice, plated with bronze and surmounted by four horns. An eighteenth-century English engraving.

below The 'molten sea', a vast bronze bowl weighing more than thirty tons, resting on the backs of twelve bronze oxen. A nineteenth-century engraving.

THIS PAGE
left A Phoenician colonette of gold and wood such as may have been the model for Jachin and Boaz, the huge bronze pillars that fronted the Temple. It was found at Biblos and dates from the twelfth century BC.

below left and right The golden lamp and table of shrewbread were placed in the new sanctuary as in the Tabernacle. Nineteenth-century engravings.

and the beginning of the spring planting season. *Shavuot*, in early summer, was also known as *Chag ha-Bikkurim*, the Feast of the First Fruits; and *Succot*, in October, was the autumn harvest festival. On this agricultural base the Israelites superimposed a historical dimension relating the festivals to the great Mosaic saga that dominated their faith. Thus Passover came to commemorate the Exodus from Egypt; *Shavuot* the giving of the Law at Mount Sinai; and *Succot* the nomad life of the Children of Israel in the desert.

At these festivals Jerusalem was crowded with out-of-town pilgrims. The Israelite farmers came with their wives and children from all over the kingdom to attend the services, bearing their offerings of animals and produce. The worshippers would march to the Temple area in procession, singing and chanting to the accompaniment of simple musical instruments – flutes, cymbals and lyres (small harps). The services took place in the main court, where the psalms of thanksgiving and praise to the Lord were sung by professional choirs of Levites. Some of the psalms of David that have survived still bear the names of individual choirmasters who may have composed them, such as Asaph, who is mentioned in the title of twelve of the Psalms.

The sacrifices were the central element of Temple worship. A regular order of prayers developed only centuries later. Animal sacrifices were a common feature of all Near Eastern religions, originally based on the belief that it was pleasing to a deity to be offered choice food and drink. He would then ensure the fertility of the fields and flocks, or respond to personal petitions and overlook transgressions. The more primitive custom of human (especially child) sacrifice still survived among some peoples in the region. The story of Abraham's near-sacrifice of Isaac, with the last-minute substitution of a ram for the youth, symbolized the rejection by the Hebrews of human sacrifice – though an echo of it may be detected in the episode of Jephtah's daughter, in the Book of Judges.

The Temple ritual included a very detailed code of regulations governing sacrifices. The animals had to be unblemished domestic livestock reared primarily for consumption – bulls, rams, sheep and pigeons – but not working beasts or wild animals. The kind of animal depended on the purpose of the offering and the status of the offerer. With burnt offerings, all of the carcase was consumed in the altar fire; in other cases only certain parts of the entrails or fatty tissue were burnt, the edible meat being left for the priests – or on specific occasions for the offerer and his family. Special attention was paid to the blood, since it was regarded as carrying the vital force – 'For the life of the flesh is in the blood' (Leviticus 17: 11) – therefore the people of Israel were forbidden to eat blood. It was always drained from the sacrificed animals, and some of it was sprinkled on the horns of the altar or round its base.

LEFT The mysterious *urim* and *thummim* carried beneath the high priest's breastplate is shown in this miniature from a thirteenth-century Hebrew manuscript.

RIGHT The high priest with the breastplate set with twelve precious stones inscribed with the names of the twelve tribes. A detail from 'David Playing the Harp' by Jan de Bray.

Generally animal sacrifices were accompanied by libation offerings of wine, and by meal offerings – cakes of fine wheat flour mixed with olive oil.

Sacrifices were offered for a large variety of purposes. Certain of them were made regularly by the priests themselves on behalf of the whole community, either daily or to mark the Sabbath, the new moon and the different festivals and fasts. Other than that, the sacrifices were made at the instance of individuals, and were classified as sin, guilt, fellowship, peace, votive, free will and ordination offerings.

The Priests and Attendants

The priests were a group of family dynasties of the sacred tribe of Levi, and by tradition descended from Aaron and his sons. They were called *cohanim* (singular, *cohen*). They conducted the Temple rituals, especially those concerning sacrifices. Only priests were permitted to enter the Temple, or to touch the main altar in front of it.

At the head of the priesthood stood the high priest, *ha-Cohen ha-Gadol*. He alone could enter the Holy of Holies where the Ark was kept, and that only once a year, on the Day of Atonement. Before the Temple period the leading priestly family had been that of Eli, the high priest, at the central sanctuary of Shiloh. After the destruction of the sanctuary by the Philistines the surviving priests from there settled at Nob, a centre outside Jerusalem, probably on the Mount Scopus ridge. In a fit of rage because the fleeing David was sheltered at Nob, King Saul had a number of the priests hauled before him and killed. One of them, Abiathar, escaped and joined David's fugitive band in the wilderness. Later David made him one of his two high priests, the other being Zadok. When Abiathar fell into disgrace and was sent back to Nob, the House of Eli was finally eclipsed. From then on the office of high priest was retained by the descendants of Zadok.

Apart from their role in the Temple cult the priests had other functions: they blessed the people; they carried out purification rites to drive out bodily diseases or halt plagues; they gave religious instruction; and they took part in prediction and decision-making by the ceremonial casting of lots. In matters of crucial national importance this last-named function could be exercised by the high priest, by invoking the mysterious *urim* and *thummim*. Worn over the high priest's ephod, an apron-like garment, was a breastplate set with twelve precious stones, the names of the twelve tribes being inscribed on them. It is believed that the *urim* and *thummim* were contained in a pouch attached to the breastplate; but what these objects were and how they were used to give oracular answers is unknown. It is improbable that they were used after the time of David and Solomon. In later centuries the divine will was usually ascertained through prophecy or dreams, and not by the casting of lots.

The Temple staff included a number of non-priestly Levites who served as singers, gatekeepers and treasury guards, and assisted the priests in their duties. The more menial tasks were performed by *nithunim* – members of the Gibeonite and other non-Israelite communities that had been conquered and absorbed into the kingdom.

The Temple Treasury

The king exercised some control over the Temple treasury and it does not seem to have been kept completely distinct from the royal coffers. For instance war booty would be deposited in the Temple, while Temple funds were used to pay tribute to foreign overlords or invaders. In the late First Temple period, when control was tightened over money donations, a special chest was placed next to the altar in the courtyard for their deposit. The proceeds were counted by one of the palace officials together with a representative of the high priest and then handed over directly to the contractors carrying out Temple repairs.

The revenues of the Temple came from various sources. The general treasury contained the funds used for current maintenance and expenses. In addition there was a special treasury of 'dedicated things' such as the war booty deposited in it by kings or military commanders, and voluntary donations to the Lord made by individual worshippers.

Solomon's Temple

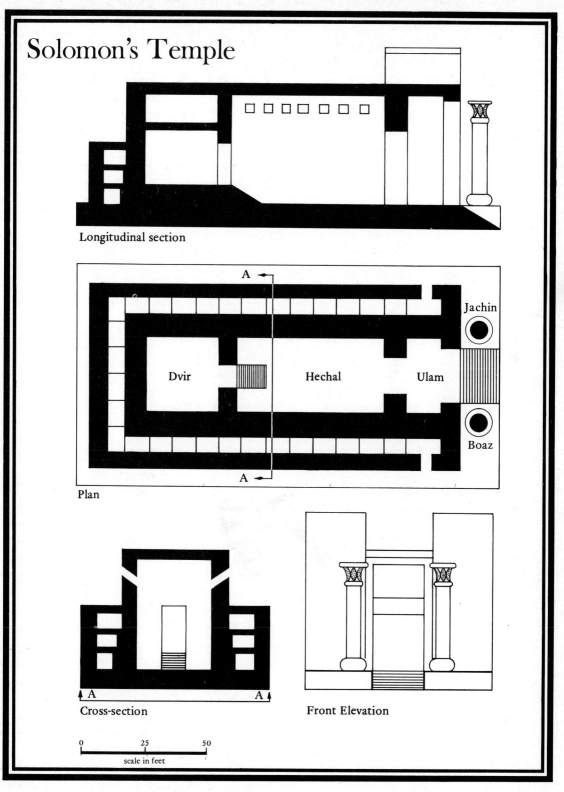

Longitudinal section

A

Jachin

Dvir

Hechal

Ulam

Boaz

A

Plan

Cross-section

Front Elevation

0   25   50

scale in feet

A reconstruction of the Temple of Solomon based on the description of the Old Testament and archaeological evidence.

The Temple compound included storehouses for the cattle, sheep and grain brought in as tithes and offerings.

The Second Book of Kings also refers to 'assessments', suggesting that a tax was levied for Temple upkeep. From the Book of Chronicles it appears that at some stage this tax was related to the half-shekel of silver each of the male Israelites over the age of twenty was required to pay in the wilderness for the Tabernacle. In the reign of Joash (835–796 BC) major renovations were undertaken for the Temple. To finance them, the Levites were sent out to collect 'the tax levied by Moses . . . on the congregation of Israel for the Tent of Testimony' (2 Chronicles 24: 6). When the Second Temple was being constructed after the return from Babylon, the annual Temple tax was reduced to one-third of a shekel (Nehemiah 10: 32). In the time of Jesus it was again a half-shekel, which the tax collector demanded of Jesus and Peter at Capernaum (Matthew 17: 24). By then the shekel had become a minted coin, but in the First Temple period it was still a unit of weight dating back to ancient Babylonia and comprising just over 11 grams of silver.

It is interesting to note that at the First Zionist Congress in Basle in 1897 the term 'shekel' was adopted for the membership dues of the Zionist Organization, carrying with it the right to vote for Congress delegates. The Zionist shekel was initially fixed at two shillings in English currency or fifty American cents, though it was greatly increased later.

The King and the Temple

It is not simple to define the position of the monarchy itself in relation to the Temple. Every regime in the ancient Near East was a theocracy and no clear distinction was drawn between political and religious power – between Church and State. A ruler represented the gods and governed with their sanction and support. The ruler might himself be vested with divine attributes and be a god-king, as with an Egyptian Pharaoh. In other cases he might be a priest-king, combining in his person the supreme political and religious offices. Melchizedek, the King of Salem (probably Jebusite Jerusalem), who extended hospitality and a blessing to Abraham, was such a ruler of a Canaanite city-state.

For the Israelites kingship was a new and dubious institution, alien to their traditions and faith. The appointment of Saul as a common leader for the tribes arose out of the sheer need for survival against external enemies. David fully understood that his throne had to rest on a religious platform and not just on military and political facts. Bringing the Ark to Jerusalem and building the Temple were steps taken by the throne to stress its divine mandate. A theological doctrine was evolved to fit the new political reality of kingship. God entered into a fresh covenant with David, promising his house perpetual rule, under the protection of the Divine Presence dwelling in the Temple. This concept was an extension of the Sinai covenant. The Temple symbolized the identification of the Lord not only with the people of Israel and the land of Israel, but also with the dynasty founded by David. The religious status of the king was made visual when David danced in an ephod on installing the Ark in Jerusalem, and when Solomon led the consecration ceremonies for the Temple. Solomon and his successors continued to play a leading part in Temple affairs.

The king could offer sacrifices at the altar, bestow the divine blessing on the people and participate in acts of worship, particularly in the New Year rituals. The Temple priests were in effect royal officials, and the Temple treasury was under royal control. At the same time no Hebrew king ever became a god-king, endowed with divine attributes. The sole source of authority was the Lord; an earthly king was his servant, subject to his laws and liable to be rebuked by his prophets. Nor were the Israelite monarchs priest-kings – they were not even allowed to enter the *Hechal*, the main chamber of the Temple, much less the Holy of Holies. It was not until the Hasmonean dynasty, in the second and first centuries BC, that the offices of temporal and religious leader were combined in a single person who was both high priest and king or ethnarch.

The shekel was originally a weight. This shekel weight of the ninth century BC was found at Ur.

6 The Divided Monarchy

Solomon died in 931 BC and was succeeded by his son Rehoboam. The new ruler was not a man capable of holding the disaffected realm together. He went to Shechem to accept the formal allegiance of the northern tribal leaders. When they presented him with a list of the reforms they demanded Rehoboam arrogantly spurned them, saying: '. . . my father chastised you with whips, but I will chastise you with scorpions' (1 Kings 12: 14). The assembly then turned on him and his party; the king managed to escape but the senior official in charge of the corvée was stoned to death. The northern tribes promptly seceded from the kingdom of Judah and proclaimed a separate kingdom of Israel. Jeroboam, who had fled from Solomon's wrath, was brought from Egypt to become their first king.

The Israelite empire had been torn asunder and replaced by two shrunken successor states. The neighbouring nations, made vassals in David's military campaigns, struck free of Jerusalem's domination: Aram-Damascus (Syria) in the north, Ammon and Moab across the river Jordan to the east, and to some extent Edom in the south.

Jeroboam understood that the Temple was a major buttress of the Davidic dynasty against which the northern kingdom had rebelled. A political break with Jerusalem required a religious break as well: '. . . if this people go up to offer sacrifices in the house of the Lord at Jerusalem, then the heart of this people will turn again to their lord, to Rehoboam, king of Judah, and they will kill me . . .' (1 Kings 12: 27). He therefore restored two ancient shrines in his territory and gave them the status of official sanctuaries for the kingdom of Israel. One was Bethel, 10 miles north of Jerusalem on the road through the hills to Shechem. The other was Dan, at the extreme north-eastern tip of the kingdom near Mount Hermon. He had a golden calf installed in these shrines and said to his people: 'You have gone up to Jerusalem long enough. Behold your gods, O Israel, who brought you up out of the land of Egypt' (1 Kings 12: 28).

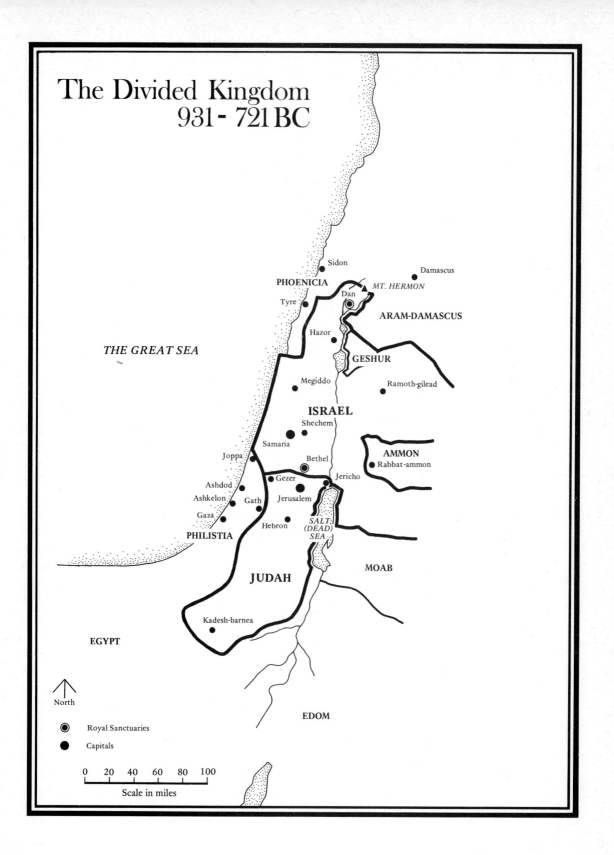

The Divided Kingdom
931 - 721 BC

Sidon

PHOENICIA

Damascus

MT. HERMON

Dan

Tyre

ARAM-DAMASCUS

Hazor

GESHUR

THE GREAT SEA

Megiddo

Ramoth-gilead

ISRAEL

Shechem

Samaria

AMMON

Joppa

Bethel

Rabbat-ammon

Ashdod

Gezer

Jericho

Ashkelon

Gath

Jerusalem

Gaza

Hebron

SALT (DEAD) SEA

PHILISTIA

MOAB

JUDAH

Kadesh-barnea

EGYPT

North

EDOM

◉ Royal Sanctuaries

● Capitals

0   20   40   60   80   100

Scale in miles

A Phoenician terracotta incense burner and offering dish of the second millennium BC.

In charging Jeroboam with a relapse into idolatry the Book of Kings reflects a Jerusalem bias against the break-away regime. Modern scholars presume that the golden calves were meant to be pedestals for the Divine Presence, and therefore a counterpart of the winged cherubim in the Temple.

Other actions taken by Jeroboam served to widen still further the breach with the Temple in Jerusalem. He set the annual feast of *Succot* in the northern kingdom for the eighth month of the Jewish calendar, instead of the seventh month, as in Judah. He also recruited the priests for the northern sanctuaries from the general population, and not from among the Levites. Presumably he did not trust the Levites, as the Temple priesthood and attendants in Jerusalem were drawn exclusively from their tribe.

Pressing the indictment against Jeroboam, the Book of Kings relates a long story to make the point that his regime had no religious legitimacy. While Jeroboam was offering sacrifices on the altar at Bethel, a 'man of God' appeared from Judah, denounced the proceedings and prophesied that one day the priests who officiated at that altar would themselves be sacrificed upon it. To placate him the king invited him home for refreshment, but he refused, claiming that he was forbidden to partake of food or drink in that place.

For two generations there was sporadic fighting between the two kingdoms, until they settled down to an uneasy coexistence. The general picture during the divided monarchy period is one of political and moral decline, though with interludes of revival and even expansion. For instance in the eighth century BC the reigns coincided of two able and successful kings, Jeroboam II of Israel (783–743 BC) and Uzziah of Judah (781–741 BC). The combined area they controlled corresponded to that of David and Solomon.

In Judah the dynasty founded by David remained intact to the end. But Israel failed to produce a stable dynasty and saw frequent and violent changes of regime, as a rule through coups by ambitious army commanders (all too common a happening in today's world).

The Struggle against Paganism

The Old Testament is not a work of history in the contemporary sense but a religious chronicle. In its account of events during the centuries of the divided monarchy the central theme is the struggle of the Mosaic faith to survive the inroads of the paganism that surrounded it. That is the criterion by which the performance of individual rulers is weighed, and the nation itself judged. The great prophetic utterances of the time lash out at the backsliding of the people and warn of its consequences; and external enemies are regarded as the divine instruments of punishment. In this general context the story of the Temple, too, is one of spiritual erosion, punctuated by intervals of reforming zeal, until its destruction four centuries after Solomon built it.

The northern kingdom was the larger and more populous of the two Hebrew states, but also the more vulnerable to pagan influences. It had a mixed population, nearly half of it Canaanite. Moreover it came more directly under the cultural impact of the Phoenicians, the clever and worldly seafaring race that inhabited the nearby Mediterranean coast, with Tyre and Sidon as its main centres. The chief Phoenician deities were the Baal (god), Melkart and the fertility goddess, Asherah.

The penetration of this pagan cult into the kingdom of Israel reached a climax under two outstanding ninth-century rulers: Omri, who founded the new capital of Samaria, and his son Ahab, who developed it. To ensure the Phoenician alliance Ahab was married to Jezebel, daughter of Ethbaal, King of Sidon. She was a woman of strong personality and religious convictions, determined to establish her own cult in her new home, which she did with little resistance from her royal husband. A temple of Melkart was erected in the palace at Samaria and hundreds of pagan priests were maintained there by Jezebel. Shrines to her native gods sprang up on the Samarian hilltops. The Israelite priests who opposed her were killed or driven out.

Suddenly there appeared a formidable champion of the Lord, Elijah the Tishbite, a fierce, ascetic reformer who became the scourge of the lax king and his pagan consort. The confrontation on Mount Carmel between the prophet Elijah and the 'false prophets of Baal' is the dramatic highlight in the struggle against paganism. This God-driven man was to become later a popular figure in Jewish folk legends.

The pagan infiltration in the northern kingdom ebbed again after Ahab's time, but was never wholly eradicated. It was projected into the southern kingdom of Judah as well, through the marriage of Athaliah, the daughter of Ahab and Jezebel, to Jehoram, heir to the Judean throne. During her husband's eight-year reign (848–841 BC) Athaliah followed her mother's example by promoting the Phoenician Baal-cult in and round Jerusalem, to the bitter dismay of the Temple priesthood. Jehoram was succeeded by his son Ahaziah, who was caught and killed a year later in the coup of Jehu in the northern kingdom. (The two kingdoms had at the time combined forces against the Syrian threat.) Athaliah seized the throne in Jerusalem and had the royal offspring slain to head off any challenge to her power. She reigned for six years, and was the only woman to occupy an Israelite throne.

Unknown to her, one royal grandchild, Joash, escaped murder at her hands. The infant was hidden in the Temple by the high priest Jehoiada, who reared him there up to the age of seven. Jehoiada then produced his secret weapon against the hated queen, by having the boy crowned king in the Temple under the protection of the royal guard. On hearing the ceremonial trumpet blasts and the shouts of acclamation Athaliah rushed to the Temple. The guards seized her and killed her at the palace gate. The crowd then destroyed the temple of Baal in the palace grounds and slew its head priest.

Joash remained under the influence of his spiritual mentor Jehoiada. He swept away the remnants of Baal-worship and took a practical interest in the administration of the Temple. On finding that the voluntary contributions made to the priests for Temple maintenance were going astray, he ordered that all donations should be deposited in a special chest near the Temple doorway and that one of his own officials should supervise the counting of the funds.

The External Threat

The adversary from within – religious and moral decay – weakened the two kingdoms in the face of the adversary from without. Canaan, a strip of land hemmed in between the sea and the desert, was from the beginning of history a corridor between the Nile valley to the south-west and the Euphrates–Tigris valley to the north-east. In these fertile river basins great empires rose and fell, with the small peoples of Canaan lying in their path.

The renewed threat now came first from the south. Before the end of Solomon's reign a tough Libyan officer called Shishak seized the

The black obelisk of Shalmaneser III records the tribute of silver and gold brought by Jehu, the tenth king of Israel, in 841 BC. In the only contemporary portrait extant of an Israelite king, Jehu is seen kneeling before the Assyrian king.

Tiglath-Pileser III, who defeated an alliance of Israel and Damascus and annexed part of the kingdom of Israel, rides in triumph in his war chariot. A stone relief from Nimrod of 740 BC.

Egyptian throne and swept away the weak twenty-first dynasty, to which Solomon was allied by marriage. Shishak sought to reassert Egyptian power over Canaan, and it was he who gave political asylum to Jeroboam, the fugitive from Solomon. Five years after the Israelite monarchy had split Shishak led an Egyptian expeditionary force that devasted a good part of Judean territory, threatened Jerusalem, marched across the kingdom of Israel and returned along the coast.

The Egyptian menace receded and for the next two or three generations the Israelite kingdoms were feuding with each other, or joining forces in local wars against Aram-Damascus (Syria). Then Israelites and Aramites alike, together with all the other peoples in the area, found themselves in the looming shadow of a far more powerful common enemy – Assyria. The Assyrians, a people from the northern Orontes valley, had subdued the old Babylonian empire and become the dominant power in Mesopotamia. In the ninth century BC they started to extend their sway westward across the Euphrates into northern Syria and down along the Mediterranean coastline towards Phoenicia, Aram-Damascus, the Hebrew kingdoms and the Egyptian border.

The Assyrians were the *Herrenvolk* of the ancient Near East. The massive buildings of their capital, 'towering Nineveh', and the famous bas-reliefs (now in the British Museum in London) with their arrogant bearded men, winged bulls and war chariots bespoke a master race that crushed without mercy all that stood in its way. At first the Assyrian

Hezekiah, seeking to restore the purity of the Temple cult, ordered the destruction of local shrines and pagan images. A nineteenth-century engraving.

forces striking into these western lands were not seeking territory, but were making forays in depth. They spread havoc and terror, brought home booty and exacted tribute.

The End of the Northern Kingdom

In the first half of the eighth century there was a respite while the Assyrians were absorbed in a Mesopotamian power struggle. During this short-lived interlude the two Israelite kingdoms were secure and prosperous, and expanded their borders under Jeroboam II in Israel and Uzziah in Judah.

Then the Assyrians reappeared on the horizon. Their greatest ruler, Tiglath-Pileser III, had consolidated their hegemony in Mesopotamia and made himself monarch of Babylonia as well. The westward thrust was resumed, but with a fateful difference. Tiglath-Pileser was an empire-builder: his armies came not just to despoil but to occupy and stay. His policy was to annex small conquered states, turn them into provinces under his governors and deport the bulk of the inhabitants elsewhere, filling their places with people from other territories in order to destroy local patriotism. This policy was to spell the doom of the kingdom of Israel within twenty-five years.

In a series of campaigns they pushed down the coast to the Egyptian border, taking Gaza and reaching El Arish. The kingdom of Israel was in no state to offer serious resistance, for its dying decades were marked by political and social disintegration. In 733 BC the kingdom was invaded; portions of it, including the Galilee, were annexed, and some of its people carried off. In 721 BC the new Assyrian ruler, Sargon II, captured the capital city of Samaria after three years of siege. Having lasted just two centuries, the kingdom of Israel was now wiped off the map and became an Assyrian province. Many of its inhabitants were exiled to distant and newly conquered localities in Mesopotamia. They were replaced by other settlers from Babylonia and Hamath, and a few years later from Arabia, where Sargon's troops had penetrated. The later Samaritans were the offspring of this mixture and those Israelites who had remained.

Religious Reforms

Judah survived for another century and a half, but without real strength or independence. For much of the time it was no more than a tribute-paying satellite state with a sense of impending calamity hanging over it. Prophetic sermons, notably those of Isaiah and Jeremiah, vehemently linked the misfortunes of the people to their religious laxity. Efforts to set Judah's spiritual house in order were made by two reformer kings of unusual calibre, Hezekiah (716–687 BC) and Josiah (640–609 BC). They tried to purge the Temple cult and infuse fresh meaning and spirit into it.

Hezekiah succeeded his father Ahaz to the throne of a kingdom shrunken in size, abjectly subject to Assyria and riddled with idolatrous practices. The first task he set himself was to restore the purity of the

Mosaic faith. The local shrines or 'high places' in the rural areas were closed down along with the street shrines his father had permitted in Jerusalem. The Temple was cleaned out, refurbished and consecrated again. From the rest of the kingdom people once more streamed to Jerusalem at Passover and other festivals, bringing their offerings to the Temple. Hezekiah also tried to revive national unity by sending messages to the conquered northern districts and inviting the surviving Israelite inhabitants to resume worship at the Temple.

Hezekiah's broad programme of reform was not limited to the spiritual health of the kingdom. The administrative and tax structures were overhauled, the border areas strengthened against external attack, the army was reorganized and given new weapons and the broken-down defence walls of Jerusalem were rebuilt. For the first time an adequate and protected water supply was ensured for the city, as the key to withstanding a siege. The water from the natural spring of Gihon was brought from its source in a cave outside the wall through a 600-foot rock tunnel to the Pool of Siloam inside the city. (The tunnel is still in use today.)

Hezekiah relied a great deal on the support and counsel of the most remarkable figure of his age, the prophet-statesman Isaiah, a resident of Jerusalem. However, in spite of Isaiah's misgivings, Hezekiah joined in a revolt of local rulers against Assyria. The revolt was encouraged by both Babylonia and Egypt. In 701 BC the Assyrian ruler, Sennacherib, having restored control over Babylonia, marched an army down the coastal plain, suppressed the Philistine rebels and routed an Egyptian force sent to help them. He then swung into the Judean foothills (Shefelah), occupied a number of towns and took the key fortress city of Lachish after a siege. In the palace at Nineveh the capture of Lachish was graphically detailed on four bas-relief panels that can be seen today in the British Museum in London.

Hezekiah sent a message of submission to Sennacherib at Lachish and emptied the Temple treasury and the royal coffers to pay the 300 talents of silver and 30 talents of gold exacted of him. The Assyrian ruler accepted the money, then sent envoys to Jerusalem demanding its surrender. The king and the court were in a panic, but Isaiah insisted that they should stand firm and rely on the Lord. He was proved right when a brief siege of the city was broken off and the Assyrian forces withdrew, apparently because of problems at home.

Under Hezekiah's son and successor, Manasseh, Judah slid back into pagan ways and the altars and images of heathen cults appeared in the very Temple itself. It is not surprising that the Bible deals harshly with this erring monarch. The Lord warned through his prophets: 'Behold, I am bringing upon Jerusalem and Judah such evil that the ears of every one who hears of it will tingle . . . and I will wipe Jerusalem as one wipes a dish, wiping it and turning it upside down' (2 Kings 21: 12–13). After his father's ill-fated revolt Manasseh was careful to be a docile vassal of the Assyrians and to pay his tribute as required.

Josiah became king at the age of eight. Ten years later the royal scribe read to him a 'book of the law' or 'book of the covenant' that the high priest Hilkiah said had been discovered in the Temple during renovations. Deeply moved, Josiah resolved to put into practice the precepts of this sacred work. He called a great assembly in the Temple, read the whole book in public and launched a programme of sweeping reforms. Again, as with his great-grandfather Hezekiah, the Temple was purged of pagan altars and cult objects, particularly those relating to the Assyrian worship of the sun, moon and stars. The profane articles were burnt in the valley of Kidron below the city wall. Pagan priests were put to death, as were the cult prostitutes, male and female. The rural shrines outside Jerusalem were destroyed, and defiled by burning human bones upon them. The Temple was made the exclusive place of worship – '. . . then to the place which the Lord your God will choose to make his name dwell there, thither shall you bring all that I command you . . .' (Deuteronomy 12: 11). Josiah also stopped child sacrifices to the god Moloch at Topheth, a spot in the valley of Hinnom under the Jerusalem city wall. This ancient and gruesome practice had allegedly been revived under Manesseh.

Having carried out this country-wide cleansing operation, Josiah once more reconsecrated the Temple and arranged a great Passover celebration, inviting worshippers to it from all over the kingdom; '. . . no such passover had been kept since the days of the judges . . .' (2 Kings 23: 22).

There is reason to suppose that the internal reforms ran parallel with revived political independence. Josiah seems to have gained control over parts of the Assyrian province that had been the northern kingdom of Israel, and to have extended to them his battle against paganism.

In the latter part of this reign a momentous shift began to take place in the Near Eastern power balance. Assyria was under attack by the Medes from the north, allied with a resurgent Babylonia – now also called Chaldea, since the Chaldeans, an Aramean people, were the dominant element in it. The colossus was toppled with startling speed. In 612 BC the Medes and Babylonians captured and sacked Nineveh and the vast Assyrian empire fell to bits. A shout of exultation rose from all the liberated peoples that had been under its sway:

Woe to the bloody city,
all full of lies and booty –
And all who look on you will shrink from you and say,
Wasted is Nineveh; who will bemoan her? [Nahum 3: 1,7].

OPPOSITE The army of Nebuchadnezzar before the Temple. A fifteenth-century miniature by Fouquet.

Q uant . Ezechie roy
de deux lignees . Anou
ia tenu quatorze ans
le royaume . le roy des
assyriens nomme sennacherub a
tresgrant main mist les tentes contre

li . et par fort bras prist toutes les ci
tes de iuda et de beniamin . Et ainsi
comme il aloit en iherusalem . Eze
chie enuoya legats au deuant de
li . En li promettant quil li obei
roit et quil paieroit les treus tels q

In 609 BC Pharaoh Neco belatedly rushed an Egyptian army north-ward to the help of Assyria, in the hope of curbing the renewed power of Babylonia. When Josiah led his forces into the pass of Megiddo to intercept the Egyptians, the Israelites were defeated and the king himself was killed.

The relief and joy at the fall of Nineveh had been premature. With the disintegration of the Assyrian empire the Babylonians filled the vacuum. Their armies too started marching west to the sea, then swinging south. In 605 BC the Babylonian general Nebuchadnezzar (who shortly after became king) defeated an Egyptian army in the battle of Carchemish in northern Syria. The whole of Syria and Canaan now lay open to the Babylonians. The little states in the area could survive only as docile vassals of the new overlords. The far-sighted prophet Jeremiah saw this clearly and urged prudence, but his counsel was unheeded. King Jehoiakim of Judah joined other local rulers in a revolt. The reaction was crushing. In 598 BC Nebuchadnezzar marched on Jerusalem. The eighteen-year-old King Jehoiachin, who had just succeeded his father to the throne, surrendered the city without a fight. He was carried off into captivity in Babylon, together with the royal household and thousands of leading citizens of Judah: nobles, army officers and craftsmen. None remained except the 'poorest people of the land' (2 Kings 24: 14). The palace and the Temple were plundered and their treasures removed, including the golden vessels Solomon had provided. Portions of Judean territory were stripped away. The king's uncle Zedekiah was installed as a puppet ruler.

The Fall of Judah

For the next decade revolt continued to simmer in Judah and some of the neighbouring states. The weak Zedekiah was under the influence of hawkish advisers, who believed that independence could be regained with Egyptian backing. In 589 BC Zedekiah hoisted the flag of rebellion, in alliance with Tyre and Ammon and with an undertaking of Egyptian help. A Babylonian army again marched in, cut off Jerusalem and proceeded to subdue the outlying towns and strongpoints in the countryside. The siege of the capital was temporarily lifted due to Egyptian pressure from the south, but was soon resumed.

In the summer of 587 BC the northern wall was breached and the city fell. This time the conquerors were merciless. Zedekiah slipped away and tried to escape with some of his troops towards the Jordan valley, but was captured and brought before the Babylonian king. His sons were killed in front of him, then he was blinded and taken in chains to Babylon, where he died soon after. The high priest and a number of other priests and notables were also put to death. Other men of position or skill were rounded up and taken in chains to Babylon. The palace and Temple compound were looted and put to the torch. The bronze works standing in the Temple courtyard were broken up and carted off for their metal, and all the Temple vessels and equipment were taken as booty. Much of the city was reduced to rubble. The sages afterwards said: 'A lion came, in the month of the lion, and destroyed the lion of God.' The lion that came was Nebuchadnezzar, the beast of prey. Av, the month of the destruction, had a lion as its symbol in the Hebrew zodiac calendar. Ariel, which means the 'lion of God', was a poetic name for Jerusalem and the Temple – maybe because the sanctuary reclining on its mount suggested the regal animal.

The Babylonians appointed Gedaliah, a member of a prominent Jerusalem family, as governor over the remaining Judean population. His father Ahikam had been a trusted counsellor of King Josiah. As Jerusalem was no longer habitable, Gedaliah stationed himself at Mizpah, 7 miles to the north, where he took care of the old people, women and children left as destitute refugees. He urged the commanders of the Judean forces still carrying on in the country districts to 'dwell in the land, and serve the king of Babylon, and it shall be well with you' (2 Kings 25: 24).

About five years later Gedaliah and his entourage were murdered by a band of Judean militants headed by Ishmael, a kinsman of the royal house. The attackers were pursued by a loyalist group led by one Johanan, and the Jewish refugees taken from Mizpah were released. Ishmael himself got away across the river Jordan. Afraid of Babylonian reprisals, Johanan consulted Jeremiah about taking refuge in Egypt. Jeremiah delivered an oracle forbidding this course, but Johanan's party left anyway, taking with them the venerable prophet and his scribe Baruch.

It would seem that even after the destruction of the Temple, pilgrimages continued to the sacred site. Jeremiah refers to one such pilgrimage from the northern part of the country: 'On the day after the murder of Gedaliah, before any one knew of it, eighty men arrived from Shechem and Shiloh and Samaria, with their beards shaved and their clothes torn, and their bodies gashed, bringing cereal offerings and incense to present at the temple of the Lord' (Jeremiah 41: 4–5).

7 The Bible, the Prophets and the Temple

At times of uncertainty and crumbling values, nations tend to reach back to a simpler past and to seek new strength in ancient verities. That was the case in the turbulent centuries of the First Temple period, when the two small Hebrew kingdoms were battling to survive against great powers, and their ancestral faith was on the defensive against the tide of paganism. The effort to preserve the Mosaic creed and make it relevant to the times was carried on along a broad front. There were the periodic reforms from the top carried out by pious kings like Joash, Hezekiah and Josiah – attempts by the establishment to purge itself from within, especially after the northern kingdom had been wiped out. At the same time two other developments were taking place that were to be of enduring importance in the spiritual history of mankind: the emergence of the Scriptures and the Hebrew prophetic movement.

The Emergence of the Bible

'The book of the law' or 'book of the covenant' that was found in the Temple and guided Josiah's reformation was probably the first edition of the Book of Deuteronomy. As such, it was one important stage in the evolution of the Old Testament over a period of more than a thousand years.

The work of collating the body of oral and written traditions started independently in each of the two kingdoms. The somewhat older compilation produced in Judah is known to Bible scholars as 'J', because it used the name Jehovah (*Yahweh*) for the Lord; while the 'E' version, compiled in the northern kingdom, used for the deity the word Elohim, derived from the Canaanite word *El*. (The 'J' and 'E' labels are used by some scholars with the alternative meanings of Judah and Ephraim, the regions where the respective versions were produced.) After the middle of the eighth century BC the two compilations were woven together into a single version, denoted by the symbol 'JE'.

The Book of Deuteronomy was an attempt to revise and develop the basic theology of JE, drawing also on additional material. Its author is

OPPOSITE The Shrine of the Book in the Israel Museum, Jerusalem. The central drum houses the Scroll of Isaiah, one of the Dead Sea Scrolls.

unknown and may have been a scholarly priest in the Temple, where the work came to light. It has also been suggested that he was a preacher from the northern part of the country, since much of the material seems to be derived from the northern traditions.

The main part of Deuteronomy as it exists today is in the form of three addresses delivered by Moses to the Children of Israel on the eve of their entry into the Promised Land. Through this vehicle the Mosaic laws – the Ten Commandments and the detailed statutes and ordinances – are restated in the light of the experience gained in the centuries the Israelites had lived as a nation in their own homeland. At the same time the book makes more explicit the basic theology of Hebrew monotheism, as outlined in the Sinai Covenant. The lofty ethical plane of the Deuteronomist was undoubtedly influenced by the classical prophets, particularly by Isaiah.

About the time of the Exile in the sixth century BC, a group of priestly scribes again edited the earlier books and added new matter from sources available to them. Their version is known as the Priestly Code, or simply by the symbol 'P'.

The process of biblical revision continued into the Second Temple period. In the fourth century BC Chronicles covered a good deal of the same ground again, painting an idealized picture of the Davidic era and elaborating the Temple rituals. Again the editor or editors are unknown.

The present-day Pentateuch (five books of Moses) and the historical books of Joshua, Samuel and Kings are an amalgam of the J, E and P strata. Bible scholars are able to relate each passage to its original version by studying the differences in language, style and thought.

It is not surprising that there should be repetitions and discrepancies in the extant text of the Old Testament. It is not a single work but a monumental anthology of Hebrew sacred literature, composed and edited by many hands over many centuries. The formative stage was in the period of the First Temple.

The Prophetic Movement

The great age of Hebrew prophecy accompanied the history of the divided monarchy. In the eighth century Amos was the first of the fifteen 'literary prophets' or 'classical prophets', whose discourses were written down in part and form separate books of the Old Testament. They were Isaiah, Jeremiah, Ezekiel and twelve minor prophets, so called because of their brevity: Hosea, Joel, Amos, Obadiah, Jonah, Micah, Naum, Habbakuk, Zephaniah, Haggai, Zechariah and Malachi.

In fact the role of the prophet goes back in the Bible to the most towering figure of all, Moses himself. The Hebrew term for prophet is *navi* (plural, *nevi'im*) which, from its Akkadian root, means 'one who is called'. After the moment of revelation, the 'call', the prophet is God's mouthpiece, and his vocation is to convey the Lord's will to his chosen people. The prophets served as the moral conscience of the community.

A section of the great Isaiah Scroll found in the caves at Qumran.

With no official status, they often defied kings and clashed with the established priesthood, because they were independent men of God, in the direct service of a higher master. The burden was a heavy one, and more often than not the prophets encountered persecution, scorn and loneliness. It is not surprising that they often felt inadequate and shrank from their mission. When God spoke to him from the burning bush, Moses stressed his speech defect. Isaiah cried out: 'Woe is me! For I am lost; for I am a man of unclean lips . . .' (Isaiah 6: 5). Jeremiah pleaded: 'Ah, Lord God! Behold, I do not know how to speak, for I am only a youth' (Jeremiah 1: 6). Told by the Lord to go on a prophetic journey to Nineveh, Jonah simply ran away and set out on the ill-fated voyage to Tarshish that landed him in the belly of a great fish.

The 'former' or pre-classical prophets in the books of Joshua, Judges, Samuel and Kings include charismatic leaders like Deborah and Samuel, court prophets like Nathan and Gad and guilds of religious ecstatics such as the band that the young Saul met coming down from the high places. In the ninth century BC the northern kingdom saw the terrifying figure of Elijah, followed by his gentler disciple Elisha.

The classical prophets, grouped together in the Bible as 'latter prophets', differed greatly in personal background and in style. They ranged from the rural simplicity and vigour of Amos the herdsman or Hosea the farmer to sophisticated urbanites and men of affairs like

Isaiah and Jeremiah. Yet certain themes are common to them – involvement in the political and religious struggles of the time; the fight against pagan seduction; the courage to preach the unpopular and the provocative; social concern for the poor and downtrodden and attacks on the privileged classes; blunt warnings of the calamities to come as a punishment for turning away from the true faith; and a gift of expression that produced some of the most sublime poetry the world has known.

It is often asserted that the prophets were opposed to the Temple cult with its professional priesthood and sacrificial rituals. They represented, it is said, right, not rites; devotion, not devotions. This antithesis is exaggerated. The prophets were not revolutionaries seeking to overthrow the established order. They were reformers trying to rid religion and society of abuses, and to restore the moral principles laid down in the *Torah*. Their approach was evident in the work of the two great prophets of the First Temple period, Isaiah and Jeremiah. They lived in Jerusalem a century apart, and were deeply involved in the life of the city and the Temple.

Isaiah

The most inspired of the prophets was born in Jerusalem in about 765 BC, in the reign of King Uzziah. At the age of twenty-five he had a vision in the Temple of God sitting upon a throne and saying: 'Whom shall I send, and who will go for us?' Isaiah replied: 'Here am I! Send me' (Isaiah 6:8). Henceforth he was bound to his prophetic vocation.

He rose to eminence in the capital and was consulted on affairs of state by King Ahaz and his son King Hezekiah. Four times in his lifetime the Assyrian cohorts rolled down from the north. He was in his middle forties when Samaria fell and the kingdom of Israel came to an end. Isaiah was scornful of the shifting political alliances on which Ahaz and later Hezekiah relied for the preservation of Judah. For the prophet, history was written by the finger of God, and only God's favour could save the state from mortal armies. He derided Hezekiah's preparations for the defence of Jerusalem and his attempt to gain support from Egypt against Assyria. '"Woe to the rebellious children", says the Lord, "who carry out a plan, but not mine . . ."' (Isaiah 30: 1). He pointed out: 'The Egyptians are men and not God; and their horses are flesh and not spirit' (Isaiah 31: 3). He loved Jerusalem, but castigated its people for the evils he saw round him: 'How the faithful city has become a harlot, she that was full of justice! Righteousness lodged in her but now murderers' (Isaiah 1: 21).

Isaiah utterly rejected the belief that cultic rituals could replace a religion of the heart. '"What to me is the multitude of your sacrifices?" says the Lord; "I have had enough of burnt offerings of rams and the fat of fed beasts . . ."' (Isaiah 1: 11). What the Lord wanted, he said, was not empty ceremonies but that each man should 'cease to do evil, learn to do good' (Isaiah 1: 16–17). Yet he had a mystic reverence for the Temple

Isaiah's vision of the Lord enthroned in the Temple. The seraphim places a burning coal from the altar in the prophet's mouth to cleanse him of sin. A nineteenth-century engraving.

הִלְכוֹתֵינוּ תָּטְעַה. (וְהֵן סְדוּרִין. הִלְכוֹת בֵּית הַבְּחִירָה. הִלְכוֹת כְּלֵי הַמִּקְדָּשׁ וְהָעוֹבְדִים בּוֹ. הִלְכוֹת בִּיאַת מִקְדָּשׁ. הִלְכוֹת אִסּוּרֵי מִזְבֵּחַ:
הִלְכוֹת וּמַעֲשֵׂה הַקָּרְבָּנוֹת. הִלְכוֹת תְּמִידִין וּמוּסָפִין. הִלְכוֹת פְּסוּלֵי הַמֻּקְדָּשִׁין. הִלְכוֹת עֲבוֹדַת יוֹם הַכִּפּוּרִים. הִלְכוֹת מְעִילָה:) וְכו'

הִלְכוֹת בֵּית הַבְּחִירָה

פֶּרֶק רִאשׁוֹן

יֵשׁ בִּכְלָל מִצְוֹת שָׁלשׁ מִצְוֹת עֲשֵׂה וּשְׁלשָׁה לֹא תַעֲשֶׂה וְזֶה הוּא
וּפְרָטָן לְרוּטָה:
לַעֲשׂוֹת בַּיִת לָעֲשׂוֹת כְּמוֹ תַבְנִית לָהֶם לְהִתְחַרְבְכֵן פָּנֵי קָרְמוֹת. וְנֶחֱזָן יְדֵי שֶׁלֹּט ק
מַעֲשֵׂה מֹשֶׁה שְׁכָּן וְשֶׁלֹּט מִקְדָּשׁ. וּבַד נֶחֱפָז סְתוּרָה תַּעֲשֶׂה מֶשֶׁךְ שֶׁעֲשָׂה מֹשֶׁה רַפְּע

and the mount on which it stood, and saw it as the source of light for all men in the Messianic kingdom of peace and brotherhood that he foretold. '. . . many peoples shall come, and say: "Come let us go up to the mountain of the Lord, to the house of the God of Jacob; that he may teach us his ways and that we may walk in his paths"' (Isaiah 2: 3).

Jeremiah

Jeremiah was the son of a priest in the small Levitical village of Anathoth, 3 miles north of Jerusalem. In his eighteenth year he felt the call to prophesy, at the time when King Josiah was carrying out his religious reforms. After Josiah was killed in battle against an Egyptian army in 609 BC Judah was for a few years a vassal of the Egyptians. They installed first one of Josiah's sons and then another as puppet rulers, while the kingdom slid back into religious and moral laxity. It was in these circumstances that Jeremiah emerged as an uncompromising preacher and reformer. By the authorities he was regarded as nothing but a trouble-maker.

The book that bears his name reveals Jeremiah's inner conflict. He was a solitary and sensitive figure, full of self-doubt and spiritual anguish, feeling alienated from his fellow-men and hurt by their hostility towards him. The outward impression he made on his fellow-citizens must have been quite different. His conduct of the Lord's work was fearless and defiant, especially in relation to the Temple priesthood.

Even more than Isaiah, Jeremiah believed that faith was an intensely personal matter, and God would judge each man by what was in his heart. Appearing before a crowd in the courtyard of the Temple, he denounced the hypocrisy of their worship, and shocked them by declaring that if they did not mend their ways God would destroy the sanctuary itself. On the Lord's behalf he thundered at them: 'Will you steal, murder, commit adultery, swear falsely, burn incense to Baal, and go after other gods that you have not known, and then come and stand before me in this house, which is called by my name, and say, "We are delivered!" — only to go on doing all these abominations?' (Jeremiah 7: 9,10). The angry crowd swarmed round him, and some of the priests and worshippers seized him and threatened to kill him. A group of the king's officials arrived from the nearby palace and conducted an impromptu inquiry at the Temple gate. Arguments swayed back and forth over whether the prophet should be put to death for his predictions of doom. Jeremiah pleaded in his defence that he was only calling for repentance. He was saved by being taken under the protection of one Ahikam, an important official at the palace.

Undeterred by this experience, Jeremiah came before a gathering in the valley of Hinnom and dramatically smashed an earthenware jar, crying out: 'Thus says the Lord of hosts: "So will I break this people and this city, as one breaks a potter's vessel, so that it can never be mended"' (Jeremiah 19: 11).

OPPOSITE Isaiah spoke out against what he saw as the empty ceremonies and rituals that were replacing a religion of the heart. The offering of sacrifices in the Temple forecourt is depicted in this illustration from a fifteenth-century Italian *Mishnah Torah* of Maimonides.

The prophet
Jeremiah; this
statue by Claus
Sluter, a Flemish
sculptor of the
fourteenth century,
was commissioned
for the Charter-
house at Champnol
near Dijon.

The prophet returned to the Temple courtyard and once more harangued the worshippers there in the same strain. This was more than the priesthood would tolerate. The indignant chief priest, Pashhur, had Jeremiah beaten and placed in the stocks that stood at the upper gate of the Temple. The next day, when Pashhur released him, the unrepentant Jeremiah predicted that the city would be destroyed and its inhabitants carried off to Babylon as captives – including Pashhur and all his friends!

Banned from the Temple area, Jeremiah dictated his prophecies to his faithful scribe Baruch, who was then sent to read this scroll publicly in the Temple courtyard. Palace officials brought it to King Jehoiakim, who had it read out to him. Enraged by its contents, the king cut the scroll to pieces, threw them on the fire and ordered the prophet and his scribe to be arrested forthwith. On the advice of sympathetic friends at court the two of them had already gone into hiding. Jeremiah promptly dictated the scroll again.

After the first Babylonian capture of Jerusalem, in 598 BC, Jeremiah tried desperately to head off further acts of resistance, convinced that they would spell disaster. He preached a policy of submission, until God would in his good time free the country and bring back the exiles. He wrote a remarkable letter to the captives, urging them to ignore false prophecies of a quick return and settle down in Babylon.

In Jerusalem patriotic sentiment ran high and the prophet was assailed as a pessimist and an appeaser. Given to dramatic symbols, the obdurate Jeremiah walked round with a yoke on his neck, to signify acceptance of foreign domination. A leading priest, Hananiah, smashed the yoke and predicted liberation within two years. Jeremiah retorted that the priest would be dead within that time – and he died soon after.

When Jerusalem and the Temple were destroyed in 587 BC Jeremiah was among the captives led off in chains. On the orders of the Babylonian ruler, he was released as a holy man who had also been a leading pacifist. The commanding general gave him the option of going voluntarily to Babylon or remaining in Judah. He chose the latter, and was put in the care of Gedaliah, the governor at Mizpah. When Gedaliah was assassinated some years later the aged prophet was taken to Egypt. The date of his death is unknown.

PART III

THE SECOND TEMPLE

8 The Babylonian Exile

The end of the Judean kingdom and the destruction of the Temple meant a spiritual shock as well as a physical and political disaster. For four centuries the official religion of the State had rested on the Mosaic code and the doctrine of the covenant of David. If David's dynasty was to occupy the throne for ever, surely the kingdom could not go under? If God dwelt in the Temple, surely the Temple was indestructible?

The liquidation of the northern kingdom had not produced a serious religious problem for Judah. Twenty years later, when Sennacherib invaded Judah and demanded the surrender of Jerusalem, Isaiah himself had urged them to have faith in the Lord, and the Assyrians had withdrawn as if by a miracle. Even the first Babylonian occupation and deportations in 598 BC had not given a fatal blow to belief. After all the kingdom and the Temple remained intact, and Zedekiah, the newly installed ruler, was of David's line. There was room for hope that the Lord's displeasure would soon pass, and with it the foreign occupation.

In this atmosphere it was little wonder that Jeremiah's doom-laden prophecies provoked such fury. He was committing a double offence: blasphemy against God and sedition against the State. The final calamity shattered the belief that the kingdom, the dynasty and the Temple were secured by divine providence. It appeared as if God had turned against his own people. Lamentations, a series of mourning poems dubiously attributed to Jeremiah, is filled with a sense of bitter betrayal:

> The Lord has become like an enemy,
> he has destroyed Israel . . .
> the Lord has brought to an end in Zion
> appointed feast and sabbath,
> and in his fierce indignation has spurned
> king and priest.
> The Lord has scorned his altar,
> disowned his sanctuary [Lamentations 2: 5, 6].

It is remarkable that the small Hebrew people – defeated, partially uprooted and with its faith in God's protection shaken – did not at this point fade out of history, as the other nations round them were to do. Yet their religion withstood the test and held them together as a community in exile, without state or sanctuary.

The prophets had refused to accept the official credo that God had given David's kingdom and the Temple a certificate of perpetual immunity. They reached back to the spirit of the earlier Sinai covenant and insisted that it had been a two-way pact: God's favour could not be taken for granted; it had to be earned by right conduct. In their discourses, not just pagan practices but all corruption, injustice and evil were offences against God, and they therefore endangered the people's survival. Unless the nation cleansed itself, it would be brought to judgement in an awesome 'Day of the Lord'.

But the prophets also held out a promise. The divine retribution, when it came, would not end the national destiny. There would be restoration; the Temple would rise again; and a new and purer kingdom would be established. The book of the earlier prophet Amos concludes with this theme of rebirth: 'I will restore the fortunes of my people Israel, and they shall rebuild the ruined cities and inhabit them . . . and they shall never again be plucked up out of the land which I have given them . . .' (Amos 9: 14,15).

Isaiah speaks eloquently of the remnant that will return and of Zion restored, in the Messianic kingdom to come. Jeremiah predicts that the return will take place after seventy years of exile, and that the Lord will then make a new covenant that will be inscribed in the hearts of men.

The prophets thus played an important part in explaining events in terms of God's will and holding out hope for the future. In this way they helped in advance to condition the national mind for the change.

The Babylonian exile was the beginning of minority life in the diaspora. Already after the first deportation, in 598 BC, Jeremiah's letter to the exiles had offered them a recipe for survival during the interval of their dispersion (which he set at seventy years): 'Build houses and live in them; plant gardens and eat their produce. Take wives and have sons and daughters . . . multiply there, and do not decrease. But seek the welfare of the city where I have sent you into exile, and pray to the Lord on its behalf, for in its welfare you will find your welfare' (Jeremiah 29: 5–7). This was sensible advice, but hard to accept in the first cruel transition. The pain and longing of the homeless found immortal expression in Psalm 137:

By the waters of Babylon,
there we sat down and wept,
when we remembered Zion.

How shall we sing the Lord's song
in a foreign land?
If I forget you, O Jerusalem,
let my right hand wither!

Let my tongue cleave to the roof of my mouth,
if I do not remember you,
if I do not set Jerusalem
above my highest joy! [Psalms 137: 1–6].

But in time they settled down to their exile. They were sustained by a fresh and resounding message of comfort and hope from the two great prophets of the exile. One was Ezekiel. The other was the unknown preacher of a universal god, who has become known as the 'Second Isaiah'.

Ezekiel Ezekiel is the strangest and most complex of the prophets. At times he is a priest absorbed in legal and ritual technicalities; then again he is a mystic pouring out bizarre and baffling images. His disturbing visions

ABOVE 'By the waters of Babylon there we sat down and wept. . . .' An interpretation of Psalm 137 by John Martin, the nineteenth-century English engraver.

were later echoed in the Books of Daniel and Revelations, and they had a strong effect on painters two thousand years later, such as Hieronymus Bosch, William Blake and the Surrealist school.

Ezekiel probably served in the Temple priesthood in Jerusalem before being carried off to Babylonia in Nebuchadnezzar's first deportation. Five years later he had a blinding revelation in which the Lord appeared to him on a wheeled throne borne aloft by four winged creatures. From that moment he was bound to the prophetic vocation.

The first half of the Book of Ezekiel contains prophecies of doom that parallel those of his older contemporary Jeremiah. The second half turns to consolation, and was no doubt written in the period after the final fall of Jerusalem in 587 BC. At that stage Ezekiel's chief concern was to maintain the morale of his fellow-exiles by depicting the future restoration. The Hebrew people would then live in a reunited and peaceful kingdom, under a Davidic ruler, with the Temple standing again on Mount Zion and the divine covenant renewed. Ezekiel's powerful symbol for this resurrection was the valley of dry bones that were brought to life again.

In the twenty-fifth year of his exile – that is, fourteen years after the destruction of Jerusalem – Ezekiel was transported in a vision to Mount Zion and shown the reconstructed Temple. His guide was 'a man, whose appearance was like bronze, with a line of flax and a measuring reed in his hand . . .' (Ezekiel 40: 3). The two of them proceeded to tour the entire Temple area and Ezekiel noted the measurements as his guide took them. (He probably drew on his intimate knowledge of the Temple as a young man in Jerusalem.) In this way a detailed record was set down of the dimensions of the Temple, the altar of burnt offering, the auxiliary buildings for storerooms, robing rooms, kitchens and other services, the courtyards, gateways, flights of steps, windows, and even the decorative motifs of alternate cherubim and palm trees. At the end of this section of the book, one half expects architect's plans and working drawings to appear as appendices.

The design of Ezekiel's Temple corresponds generally to the description of Solomon's Temple, with an entrance hall, a main sanctuary chamber and an inner Holy of Holies, into which Ezekiel had never been taken. His description of the imposing gateways into the Temple enclosure corresponds closely in plan to those found in the excavations of Solomon's chariot cities at Gezer, Megiddo and Hatzor.

In his vision Ezekiel witnesses the glory of the Lord returning to the Temple from the east: '. . . and the sound of his coming was like the sound of many waters; and the earth shone with his glory' (Ezekiel 43: 2). The Lord speaks to him, and commands him to describe to the House of Israel 'the temple, its arrangement, its exits and its entrances, and its whole form; and make known to them all its ordinances and all

OPPOSITE The disturbing visions of Ezekiel have inspired many artists, among them Raphael. His 'Vision of Ezekiel' depicts the prophet's revelation of the Lord borne aloft by winged creatures.

its laws . . .' (Ezekiel 43 : 11). The Lord insists that the palace should no longer be adjoining the Temple, as the royal court has been a source of contamination and idolatrous practices.

In addition to the physical description of the Temple area, Ezekiel sets down rules concerning the priesthood, the Levitical attendants and the nature and order of the sacrifices. In the Talmud many centuries later the rabbis had a reserved attitude towards Ezekiel, because his requirements differed in some respects from those laid down in the Pentateuch, particularly in Leviticus.

Ezekiel was recording this vision in exile, at a time when the Temple was a heap of rubble, Jerusalem devastated and the Judean kingdom a neglected colony of the great Babylonian empire. It was Ezekiel's faith in the future that drove him to bequeath to a succeeding generation a precise blueprint for the rebuilding of the Temple, together with a manual of instructions for its priesthood and its rituals.

After these prosaic and meticulous directions, the book ends with a burst of fantasy. A little stream of water comes out from underneath the threshold of the Temple's eastern gateway. As it flows down the mountainside it broadens and deepens into a great river that enters the Dead Sea and turns it into fresh water. The river and the Dead Sea abound with fish, and the banks and shores are lined with green trees. Thus Ezekiel indicated the fresh life and vitality that would emanate from the Lord's house when the nation was reborn in its homeland. It was a striking simile of hope for his fellow-exiles who still remembered the barren wilderness of Judea that dropped down east of Jerusalem, and the bitter-tasting brine of the Dead Sea, devoid of living creatures.

In its present form the Book of Isaiah contains sixty-six chapters. From chapter 40 onwards it undergoes a perplexing transition. The great prophet of the kingdom of Judah in the eighth century BC seems to have leapt forward in time to the sixth century, and to be consoling the exiles after the final fall of Jerusalem. The famous opening words of chapter 40 are:

> Comfort, comfort my people,
> says your God.
> Speak tenderly to Jerusalem,
> and cry to her
> that her welfare is ended,
> that her iniquity is pardoned,
> that she has received from the
> Lord's hand
> double for all her sins.

It is now accepted that these chapters are the work of a prophet of the Babylonian exile whose identity has been completely lost. The biblical

Ezekiel receives a scroll from the hand of the Lord. An illuminated letter from the twelfth-century Lambeth Bible.

The Second Isaiah

A model reconstruction of Megiddo, one of Solomon's chariot cities. Excavations at Megiddo have revealed huge double gateways corresponding closely to the description of the Temple gateways given by Ezekiel.

editors of a later age identified the loftiness of thought and style with Isaiah, and added the work to the book of that name – consequently the unknown prophet is today simply known as the Second Isaiah (or Deutero-Isaiah).

The historical context for his utterances was another shift in the Near Eastern power equation. In the middle of the sixth century BC the Persian King Cyrus successfully revolted against his Medean overlord. In 550 BC Ecbatana, the capital of Medea, fell to him. A series of brilliant campaigns soon gained him a vast new domain that covered Asia Minor and extended eastward to Afghanistan. The Persian shadow now lay across the Mesopotamian basin, with Babylonia isolated and threatened. When Cyrus took Babylon in 539 BC and his son and successor, Cambyses II, went on to conquer Egypt, the Persian empire was the greatest the world had yet seen, and included the whole Near East as far as India.

The spectacular rise of Cyrus sent a surge of hope through all the subject peoples of Babylon, including the Hebrew exiles. The Second Isaiah gave sublime expression to their dream of return. He did so not in parochial terms, but against the giant background of contemporary events. Cyrus himself, the prophet foretold, would be the instrument of redemption: '[The Lord] says of Cyrus, "He is my shepherd, and he shall fulfil all my purpose"; saying of Jerusalem, "She shall be built", and of the Temple, "Your foundations shall be laid"' (Isaiah 44: 28).

The prophet describes the Children of Israel being led through the desert on another exodus to a shining New Jerusalem, with God once more present in his Temple. But a return to Zion does not mean simply restoring the Davidic kingdom to its former state. The ancient covenant is given a broader dimension. God is no mere Hebrew tribal deity; he is the Lord of all creation. On the return of the Jews to their homeland the rest of mankind will abandon their pagan gods and embrace the pure monotheistic faith, with the Temple of Jerusalem as its centre. God had elected his people to be a prophet-nation. In this context, the metaphor of the suffering servant is repeatedly used; it was later to have a profound impact on Christian doctrine. The Second Isaiah is the most universal in outlook of all the Hebrew prophets.

'The Fall of Babylon' by John Martin. In 539 BC the Persian king Cyrus captured Babylon and the Babylonian exile was effectively over.

9 *The Return*

When the return to Zion did come about it was a small and struggling venture, bearing no resemblance to the soaring vision of the Second Isaiah or the new commonwealth projected by Ezekiel.

In 538 BC, a year after he became master in Babylon, Cyrus the Great issued a decree favouring the return of his newly acquired Jewish subjects to their country and the rebuilding of their Temple there. It may seem odd that he should have paid such special attention to a community of no importance in the affairs of his vast realm. Six centuries later the Jewish historian Josephus suggested that Cyrus had been given the prophecies of the Second Isaiah to read, and had been deeply moved by the special role they assigned to him. No such fanciful reason need be sought; the decree concerning the Jews was in line with Cyrus' general policy. He was a remarkably enlightened and tolerant ruler. Unlike the repressive Assyrians and Babylonians, he fostered the distinctive national identities and religious cults of the non-Persian peoples in his realm. On gaining control of the Babylonians he had won them over by treating them mildly, respecting their institutions and even attending the worship of their chief god, Marduk. The Hebrew God was one of innumerable deities tolerated in the Persian empire.

There may also have been an element of strategic self-interest in restoring a grateful group of Judeans to a sensitive locality close to the border of the Persian empire with Egypt. Five centuries later imperial Rome would support Herod's kingdom for similar reasons. Nearly twenty-five centuries later the strategic importance of Palestine would weigh with imperial Britain in sponsoring a Jewish national home there.

Cyrus' decree occurs in two versions in the Book of Ezra. The text given at the beginning of the book is the basic charter for the return:

> Thus says Cyrus king of Persia: The Lord, the God of heaven, has given me all the kingdoms of the earth, and he has charged me to

build him a house in Jerusalem, which is in Judah. Whoever is
among you of all his people, may his God be with him, and let him
go up to Jerusalem, which is in Judah, and rebuild the house of the
Lord, the God of Israel – he is the God who is in Jerusalem; and let
each survivor, in whatever place he sojourns, be assisted by the men
of his place with silver and gold, with goods and with beasts, besides
freewill offerings for the house of God which is in Jerusalem [Ezra
1 : 2–4].

A generation later, in the reign of the Persian King Darius, the
regional governor in Damascus sent a report to the king about trouble in
Jerusalem over the construction of the Temple. He asked for confirmation of the claim by the Hebrew settlers that the work had been authorized by a special decree of Cyrus himself. Darius ordered a search to be
made in the royal archives at the summer palace of Ecbatana, and a
document was found which the Book of Ezra quotes in Aramaic and
calls a *dikrona* – an *aide-mémoire* putting on record a verbal order by the
king. This version stipulates that the cost of rebuilding the Temple was
to be borne by the royal treasury; and that the gold and silver vessels
which Nebuchadnezzar had removed and taken to Babylon should be
sent back to the Temple. The *aide-mémoire* lays down the measurements
for constructing a new altar for the sacrifices – which was understand-
able seeing that Cyrus was footing the bill.

It is likely that the first group of returnees was small, the majority
of the community preferring fund-raising to *aliyah* (immigration). A
half-century had gone by since the fall of Jerusalem. The exiles had
settled down, as Jeremiah had urged them to do, and a new generation
had been born and grown up in the diaspora. For many it was easier to
stay where they were than to undertake the arduous and risky 600-mile
trek across the desert in order to live as pioneers in Zion.

Sheshbazzar, a 'prince of Judah', was made leader of the party and the
Temple vessels were handed over to him. It is thought that he was a
son of King Jehoiachin, who had been taken as a captive to Babylonia
in the first deportation. Sheshbazzar's name soon fades out of the
narrative and it is unclear whether he actually started work on the
Temple, or when he died. His name is replaced as governor by that of
his nephew Zerubbabel, who may have arrived at a later date with a
second and larger contingent of settlers. There is some confusion between the two persons in the Books of Ezra and Nehemiah, compiled
nearly two centuries after the event by the editors of the Book of
Chronicles. According to the Book of Ezra, Zerubbabel shared authority
with the high priest Jeshua. They set up an altar on the Temple site and
began the regular daily sacrifices. The feast of *Succot* was duly celebrated, as had been done in the time of the First Temple.

Work proceeded on the foundations of the new sanctuary, where Solomon's Temple had stood on Mount Moriah. Like Solomon before him, Zerubbabel ordered cedar logs from Phoenicia and had them floated down the coast to the port of Joppa (Jaffa), from where they were hauled up to Jerusalem. He also hired skilled Phoenician masons and carpenters. The kings of Tyre and Sidon in Phoenicia were again paid in kind with foodstuffs and olive oil. The Levites were made over-seers of the work. When the foundations were completed, a celebration took place. The priests wore ceremonial robes and the songs of praise, the shouts of joy and the sounds of trumpets and cymbals mingled with the sobbing of old men who still remembered the First Temple.

The rejoicing was short-lived. The hill country to the north of Jerusalem was inhabited by the Samaritans, the mixed offspring of the Israelites who had survived the destruction of the northern kingdom of Israel in 721 BC, and the colonists brought in at that time from other parts of the Assyrian empire. These Samaritans had maintained a form of Hebrew religion, blended with Canaanite practices. At first their notables demanded that they should share in the work on the new Temple. But Zerubbabel bluntly refused: 'You have nothing to do with us in building a house to our God ...' (Ezra 4: 3). From then on the Samaritans stirred up constant trouble for the returnees, and tried to stop the Temple project. The local Persian governor, Rehum, was induced to write home an adverse despatch, asserting that Jerusalem had a bad record in the past as 'a rebellious city, hurtful to kings and provinces ...' (Ezra 4: 15). As a result the work was suspended by royal decree.

For a number of years afterwards the small settler community struggled to survive against hardship and hostile neighbours. The primitive conditions of their lives, and the fading of the Zionist dream that had brought them back, left them with little impulse to carry on with Temple building, even if they had wanted to ignore the order.

Cyrus died in 529 BC and was succeeded by his son Cambysis. In 522 BC, on coming back from an Egyptian campaign, Cambysis was told that the eastern provinces of the empire had revolted under his own brother and he committed suicide. One of his officers and kinsmen, Darius, proclaimed himself king and marched against the rebels. Two years of confusion and civil war ensued, until Darius consolidated his power. Against this background of upheaval and uncertainty in the empire the Jerusalem prophets Haggai and Zechariah preached a revival of religious zeal and urged faith in the liberation of Judea, with Zerubbabel, a descendant of David, as its king. The key to these hopes lay in the erection of the Temple without delay, so that God's presence would once more reside in their midst.

Under the moral pressure of these prophets the work was resumed in 520 BC. Apparently fresh complaints and difficulties were made from Samaria. They came to the attention of Tattenai, the governor of the region known as 'Beyond the River', that is, west of the Euphrates, that included Syria, Canaan, Phoenicia and Cyprus. The governor came to Jerusalem himself to investigate the matter. It was in response to his report that King Darius sent him a copy of the Aramaic document found in the royal archives, confirming the edict of Cyrus. Darius added instructions to the governor that the building should be financed from provincial revenues, and that the animals and provisions needed for the sacrifices were to be provided by the government. In return the Temple service was to include prayers for the well-being of the king and the royal family.

With this official sanction and practical support the work went ahead without further obstruction and the Second Temple was completed by 515 BC. The consecration took place in March of that year, with public rejoicing led by the priests and the sacrifice of a great number of animals, including twelve he-goats as a sin offering for the twelve tribes of Israel.

The building corresponded in size and design to the First Temple, though it must have been simpler and more austere, with none of the sumptuous adornment Solomon had lavished on the original one. The difference was not just material. The new Temple was no longer the central shrine of an independent kingdom, but the house of worship of a struggling religious sect in a neglected corner of the Persian empire. It was, however, of profound importance for the survival of the Jewish people that they should once more have acquired a focus of faith and identity in their ancestral homeland and its holy city.

The next seventy years are a blank in the Jewish saga. The Messianic expectations aroused by the major prophets, and revived by Haggai and Zechariah, failed to materialize. The kingdom was not restored; Jerusalem and its environs rated merely as a sub-district of the local province of Samaria, forming part of the Fifth Satrapy. (Darius had organized the sprawling empire into twenty autonomous regions or satrapies.) Zerubbabel is not mentioned again after the building of the Temple, nor is anyone else referred to as a governor in Jerusalem until Nehemiah. Presumably the communal leader during this period was the high priest. It can be learnt from Nehemiah's memoirs, and from the prophetic books of Obadiah and Malachi in the first half of the fifth century BC, that there was a good deal of religious laxity and inter-marriage with other local peoples.

The community grew in numbers, partly by absorbing elements of the Judean population that had remained behind after the fall of Jerusalem. The archaeological evidence suggests that while Jerusalem and the

OPPOSITE The celebrations at the founding of Zerubbabel's Temple are recorded in this late nineteenth-century stained-glass window in Wells Cathedral.

PONTIFEX MAXIMVS

SALOMO

EDSECHIEL

DSERVBABEL

JACOBI JEHVDÆ LEONIS
DE
TEMPLO HIEROSOLYMI-
TANO
Libri   IV.
Jussu et auspiciis
SERENISSIMI PRINCIPIS
DN. AVGVSTI,
Ducis Brunsuic. et Lunæb. etc.
ex Ebræo
Latinè recensiti
à
JOHANNE SAVBERTO.
CIƆ.IƆ.C.LXV.

Solomon, Zerubbabel and Ezekiel, all of whom were associated with the building of the Temple, are portrayed, together with the high priest, on the frontispiece of this seventeenth-century edition of *The Temple of Jerusalem* by Jacob Judah Leon.

Judean hill terrain around it had been virtually depopulated by the Babylonian deportations, a number of Israelite towns and villages had remained intact in the Shefelah (lowlands), the Negev and the Benjaminite territory north of Jerusalem. There may also have been further parties of returnees from Babylonia, though on a small scale. No mass influx took place from the diaspora communities in Babylon, Egypt and Asia Minor, which were growing in prosperity and status.

In the Book of Ezra, and repeated in the Book of Nehemiah, is what purports to be a tally of returnees from Babylonia by family clans, totalling 40,360 souls. It is assumed that this statistic reflects a census of the whole resident Judean population carried out about Nehemiah's time—that is, roughly a century after the beginnings of the return.

The return might have fizzled out, and the remnant replanted in Zion slowly withered away, but for the regeneration brought about by two outstanding men, Nehemiah and Ezra. One shaped it as an entity capable of governing and defending itself; the other reformed its faith and gave it new impetus.

Nehemiah Nehemiah held the high office of cupbearer to King Artaxerxes I (465–423 BC) in the Persian capital of Susa (Shushan). A kinsman visiting him from Jerusalem gave an unhappy report on conditions there, and stressed how vulnerable the city was to marauders because its walls were still heaps of debris. A devout Jew, Nehemiah was disturbed by this account, and made up his mind to visit Jerusalem himself. The king must have liked him, for he was given permission to leave, together with an armed escort and royal letters ordering provincial authorities to provide him with timber and other requirements.

Nehemiah arrived in Jerusalem in 445 BC. After an inspection by moonlight of the derelict gates and walls, he called together the leading citizens and produced the letters from the king, on the strength of which they accepted his authority over them as governor. He then outlined his plans for the urgent task of restoring the shattered fortifications and making the city secure. This was done on a voluntary basis, with specific sectors allocated to the guilds of craftsmen, to the priests and merchants who lived next to the walls and to labour gangs supplied by other Judean towns.

The able and energetic Jewish palace official who had arrived so unexpectedly had infused fresh spirit into the community. At the same time his presence drew a hostile reaction from several external sources: Sanballat, the local governor in Samaria; Geshem, leader of the Edomites who had occupied the Hebron hill country south of Jerusalem; and Tobiah, a wealthy Jew who owned estates in Trans-Jordan. At first they derided the construction project; but when the walls were halfway up they took it more seriously and tried to disrupt the work by force. Nehemiah countered with vigorous security measures, including

a full-time system of armed patrols and a weapon provided to each worker for self-defence – 'And each of the builders had his sword girded at his side while he built' (Nehemiah 4: 18).

Stoutly ignoring further intrigues by his enemies, and even charges of sedition, Nehemiah pressed on with the work at full speed. When the walls and gates were completed the dedication ceremonies took place. Two processions, headed by the priests and leading citizens, went round the ramparts in opposite directions and met at the Temple, where a special service was held, followed by a feast.

With the city secured by its reconstructed walls, and gates that were shut at night, Nehemiah turned his attention to organizing the community. The capital was still largely derelict – 'The city was wide and large, but the people within it were few and no houses had been built' (Nehemiah 7: 4). A census was taken. Nehemiah moved into Jerusalem 10 per cent, chosen by lot, of the residents of the outlying towns. The border areas that remained intact after the Babylonian deportations were again integrated into the Jerusalem district.

After twelve years of firm administration Nehemiah returned to Persia and rejoined the service of the king. Some time later he obtained permission to go back to Jerusalem, and was horrified to find how much slackness had crept in during his absence. The high priest had allowed Tobiah, the Trans-Jordanian landowner, to use a room in the Temple compound in which sacrificial foods and incense had been stored. Nehemiah flung out Tobiah's possessions and returned the room to its proper purpose. He stopped the selling of produce on the Sabbath, shut the city gates before the Sabbath started and on that day chased away the Phoenician traders squatting outside the walls waiting to sell their fish. The delivery of the tithes of corn, wine and oil to the Temple had become lax. The Levites and Temple servants, left without support, had returned to their villages to till their fields. Nehemiah rounded them up and put them back to work, while ensuring that all tithes were fully and promptly brought in. He also banned mixed marriages, and by way of example expelled from Jerusalem the son of the high priest, who had married the daughter of his old Samaritan enemy, Sanballat.

Nehemiah's mission ended in 425 BC, twenty years after it began. He wrote a first-person account of his governorship in Jerusalem that was later included in the Book of Nehemiah. The account ends with the devout claim that he had provided for strict religious observance in Jerusalem, so 'Remember me, O God, for good' (Nehemiah 13: 31).

Ezra

Ezra was a priest and scribe in the Babylonian community of exiles living under Persian rule. A scholarly and zealous man, he seems to have held a position at the Persian court as a commissioner for the affairs of the Jewish minority. He resolved to carry out a mission to Jerusalem, and to reorganize the religious life of the community there.

OPPOSITE Nehemiah and his companions inspect the ruins of Jerusalem. An engraving by Gustave Doré.

The Book of Ezra states that he set out 'in the seventh year of Artaxerxes the king' (Ezra 7: 7). The dating remains an unresolved problem of biblical scholarship. If the king referred to was Artaxerxes I (465–423 BC), then the date of Ezra's mission would be 358 BC, that is, before Nehemiah. If the king was Artaxerxes II (404–359 BC), the year would be 398 BC, long after Nehemiah. Professor Albright suggests an ingenious third possibility: that 'seventh year' should read 'thirty-seventh year', which would place the beginning of Ezra's mission in 528 BC, that is, near the end of the reign of Artaxerxes I, and while Nehemiah was still in Jerusalem. That date would fit into the general context, but is textually improbable. (For one thing, the part of the Book of Nehemiah that is Nehemiah's personal memoir makes no mention of Ezra.)

Like Nehemiah, Ezra obtained royal approval and material support for his journey. The book quotes the Aramaic document that was Ezra's commission from the king. The official purpose of the trip was defined as 'to make inquiries about Judah and Jerusalem according to the law of your God, which is in your hand' (Ezra 7: 14). The document provided that Ezra should take with him any other members of the community who might be willing to accompany him, including priests and Levites. He would receive a money grant from the palace and could add to it voluntary donations from his fellow Jews. These funds were to be used for buying animals to sacrifice in the Jerusalem Temple on behalf of the king. Any balance could be spent by Ezra at his discretion. The treasury of the 'Beyond the River' satrapy was to provide him with the money, wheat, wine, oil and salt that he might require for the Temple within specified limits, and its priests and attendants were to be tax-exempt. Ezra was authorized to appoint scribes to teach the Jewish law, and judges to administer it. Severe penalties would be imposed for disobeying these instructions.

It is recorded in Ezra's diary that the party that assembled to accompany him numbered fifteen hundred men and their families, some five thousand souls in all. Ezra notes down with charming candour that he was ashamed to ask the king for an armed escort, as this would have seemed a lack of trust in the protection of the Hebrew deity. Instead they fasted and prayed to God 'and he listened to our entreaty' (Ezra 8: 23). The gold, silver and sacred vessels they were bringing for the Temple were entrusted to the care of twelve priests in the party, after Ezra had prudently drawn up an inventory.

On their safe arrival in Jerusalem Ezra presented his royal commission. The valuables were delivered to the Temple authorities and sacrifices were made as the king had ordered. Ezra then took the first drastic step to implement his mission. Like Nehemiah, he saw that widespread intermarriage with local pagan women eroded adherence to the Mosaic faith. He convened an assembly in the Temple courtyard of

Ezra the scribe; from an eighth-century Northumbrian manuscript.

the men of Jerusalem and the outlying Judean towns. Shivering in the
rain and cold of an early winter day, they were dismayed when he proclaimed to them: 'You have trespassed and married foreign women. . . .
Now then make confession . . . separate yourselves from the peoples
of the land and from the foreign wives' (Ezra 10: 10–11). They had
little option but to obey, since this important newcomer was armed with
official powers in matters of religion and had already threatened expul-
sion from the community and loss of their property for those who failed
to attend the meeting. Ezra appointed a committee of two priests and
two Levites to supervise the enforced mass divorces.

At the beginning of the seventh month, at the time of the Feast of
Booths (*Succot*), the community gathered together in the square in
front of the Water Gate. Ezra mounted a wooden pulpit, bearing the
'Book of the Law of Moses' he had brought from Babylon. When he
opened it the assembly rose to their feet and bowed their heads in worship. All morning Ezra read aloud passages from the book, and a group
of Levites translated from Hebrew into Aramaic, the colloquial tongue,
so that everyone could understand. Many in the audience were so deeply
moved that they wept. Ezra called out to them: '. . . do not be grieved,
for the joy of the Lord is your strength' (Nehemiah 8: 10). Instructions
were no doubt included on the traditional manner of celebrating the
Feast of *Succot*, for the inhabitants gathered branches and constructed
outdoor booths in which they lived for the next seven days. Each day the
scripture lesson continued.

Part of Ezra's reforms were designed to place Temple worship on a
sound footing. He laid down precise regulations for providing the
sacrificial offerings and for the payment of annual tithes, fixed at a
third of a shekel. In this respect he revived what Nehemiah had done
in his second term as governor. However the importance of Ezra's work
went far beyond strengthening the Temple cult. He brought the Mosaic
code directly to the people and established it as the basis for their way of
life. Thus Ezra founded a Judaism that could be practised anywhere
without a fixed territory, a temple or a priesthood.

Ezra's measures in Jerusalem must be understood against the background of the Babylonian community from which he came. In the sixth
and fifth centuries BC the Jews were already a dispersed people, a
nation of scattered minorities struggling against assimilation. If they
were not to disappear, they had to stress whatever common concepts
could hold them together and keep them distinct from their neighbours.

The first of these concepts was the clinging to a centre in Zion. The
prophets and sages had kept alive from afar a deep attachment to the
holy land, the holy city and the holy sanctuary. Even after the return,
the majority of Jews continued to live outside Judea, without access to
the rebuilt Temple. Their faith now had to be a portable one, resting on

the Scriptures rather than on the rituals and sacrifices of the Temple cult. Scribes and teachers of the Law like Ezra were the prototypes of the rabbis in later ages. Small gatherings for prayer and study were the germ of the synagogue. The objection to mixed marriages arose from the urge of a minority group to maintain its distinctive culture and faith.

From the beginning of the exile these trends must have been developing among the Babylonian Jews. Ezra's genius lay in bringing them into focus. He organized the Judean community on a pattern that would ensure the survival of Jewish community life everywhere and so is regarded as a pivotal figure in the history of the Jewish people and of its faith.

The traditional celebration of the Feast of *Succot*; the worshippers built booths of branches in which they lived for the period of the festival. A nineteenth-century engraving.

10 *The Hellenist Period*

From the events in the Books of Ezra and Nehemiah to the events in the Books of the Maccabees, there is a gap of some two centuries in the recorded history of Judea. While empires rose and fell, it remained a quiet backwater. The Judeans were mainly occupied as hill farmers and shepherds. They lived by the laws Ezra had once more taught them, and faithfully brought their tithes and offerings to the Temple at the appointed seasons. They were left by distant rulers to enjoy local autonomy, with the high priest as both spiritual and civil leader.

In the meantime there was another change of imperial masters. The Persian empire came to an end in 331 BC, with the meteoric advent of that boy-wonder of ancient times, Alexander the Great of Macedonia. He was a provincial governor at sixteen, an army general at eighteen and master of the known world while still in his twenties. The vast empire he carved out did not survive his death in 323 BC, but was split up between his leading generals. Ptolemy seized Egypt, with his capital at Alexandria. Seleucus gained control of Persia, Babylonia and Syria and set up a capital at Antioch in northern Syria. Palestine lay, as usual, in the disputed border-land between the two. For a century it was held by the Ptolemaic dynasty in Egypt. In 198 BC the Seleucid ruler, Antiochus III (the Great), defeated an Egyptian army at Panias (the present Banias at the foot of Mount Hermon) and established dominion over Palestine.

(The name 'Palestine', from the Hebrew *Pleshet*, meant originally the coastal territory occupied by the Philistines. However, as early as the fifth century BC, the Greek historian Herodotus referred to the whole of southern Syria, including Judea, as 'Palestine Syria'. In due course 'Palestine' by itself came to denote the area roughly corresponding to ancient Canaan or the biblical 'Land of Israel'. The first official use of the name by the Romans was in the second century AD.)

In Judea the change from Ptolemaic to Seleucid masters was at first

OPPOSITE Modern *Succot* pilgrims at the Western Wall.

Ptolemy II Philadelphus of Egypt dictating the decree in which he authorized a Greek translation of the Bible (the Septuagint); from an eleventh-century manuscript of the *Letter of Aristeas*.

welcome, and the Jews of Jerusalem helped to oust the Egyptian garrison from their city. Antiochus III went out of his way to gain the allegiance of his new subjects. By a series of measures he helped Judea recover quickly from the ravages of war. Captives were released; refugees were allowed to return home; tax relief was granted; and freedom of worship was guaranteed. Special consideration was given to the Temple in Jerusalem – repairs were subsidized from public funds, priests and Temple staff were made exempt from taxation and even the wood for the sacrifices was tax free.

The Seleucid empire reached its zenith under Antiochus the Great. But he over-reached himself when he pushed westward across Asia Minor towards Greece and Macedonia. At Magnesia, on the eastern shore of the Aegean Sea, he was defeated and turned back by the well-trained legions of a new power rising in the west – Rome. Among the twenty high-born hostages handed over to the Roman victors was his younger son, later to be Antiochus IV.

Antiochus III was succeeded by his elder son Seleucus IV (187–175 BC). He continued his father's policy of religious tolerance. But the Seleucid rulers were chronically short of money and on occasion found a pretext for laying hands on the treasures of a temple in their domain. Towards the end of his reign Seleucus received a report from intriguers in Jerusalem that fabulous wealth was hidden in the Temple, and that the devout high priest, Onias III, had pro-Egyptian sentiments. The king's chief minister, Heliodorus, was sent to Jerusalem to check the story and to confiscate the treasure for the king. The minister was refused entry into the sanctuary and returned angry and empty-handed. According to a legend recorded in the Second Book of Macca-bees, the Temple was protected against this foreign intrusion by super-natural means. Heliodorus was driven out by a figure in golden armour and a white horse and was then soundly flogged by two angel-youths.

In 175 BC Seleucus IV was assassinated, probably in an attempted coup by the same chief minister, Heliodorus. The king's younger brother returned from Rome and mounted the throne as Antiochus IV (175–163 BC). The new ruler possessed his father's vigour and ambition and was vain enough to copy Alexander by taking the second name of Epiphanes, meaning 'the god manifest', thereby identifying himself with Zeus, chief god of the Greek pantheon. His critics were later to suggest that he should have called himself Epimanes, 'the mad one'. He was an ardent devotee of everything connected with the Hellenist (Greek) way of life; his determination to force it on his subjects brought him into savage collision with the orthodox in Judea, and provoked the Maccabean revolt.

Alexander had not been a barbarian leader driven by mere lust for conquest. He regarded his campaigns as a civilizing mission, bringing in their wake the benefits of Greek culture – somewhat like the 'white man's burden' in the British empire of Queen Victoria's reign. He encouraged his soldiers to marry local women and settle in occupied areas and brought in groups of colonists from Greece and Macedonia.

Long before Alexander the small city-states of Hellas (the ancient name for Greece), especially Athens, had attained levels of excellence hitherto unknown in philosophy, science, athletics, drama, architecture, art and the principles of democratic government. In the centuries after Alexander's death Hellenism became the dominant culture throughout the eastern Mediterranean and western Asia. Greek cut across national boundaries as the common language of administration, the wealthy and the educated. Everywhere it was the upper-class fashion to adopt Greek names, manners, costumes, arts and sports. The two main centres of Hellenist influence in the Near Eastern region were the Ptolemaic and Seleucid capitals: Alexandria and Antioch. In the pro-vincial areas new cities developed on the Greek model; in Palestine they included Philadelphia (Amman), Scythopolis (Beit She'an), Ptolemais (Acre) and Sebaste (Samaria).

The Jews could not remain immune to the pervading Hellenist influence. Obviously the diaspora communities were more susceptible than the Judean homeland. By far the largest and most affluent of these

The tomb of Jason in Jerusalem; a fine example of a Hellenistic tomb of the second century BC.

communities was that of Alexandria, where approximately a million Jews, merchants and artisans, inhabited two of the city's five quarters, and had a place in its life similar to that of New York Jewry today. During the third century BC the Hebrew Scriptures were translated into Greek (the Septuagint version) for the use of congregations in Alexandria. The writings of the great Alexandrian Jewish philosopher Philo Judeus (*c.* 20 BC–AD 50) reveal the intellectual struggle to reconcile the ancestral beliefs with the rationalism of Greek systems of thought.

There were areas in the Near Eastern world where the native culture, language and religion were too firmly entrenched to be submerged by the Hellenist tide, even though affected by it. Persia was one; Judea was another. The orthodox elements of Judean society, and the common people of Jerusalem and the Judean countryside, continued to live and worship as their fathers and grandfathers had done. The Temple remained the centre of their faith. There was a growing schism between them and the pro-Hellenist groups. The latter were able to gain the favour of Antiochus IV by appealing both to his passion for promoting Hellenism and to his greed for larger revenues. At the beginning of his reign Antiochus was persuaded to depose the respected high priest, Onias III, and appoint his more pliant brother Jason in his place. (The name Jason was the Hellenized form of the Hebrew Joshua.) It was at this time that a gymnasium was constructed in Jerusalem, where young Jews exercised and conducted athletic sports in the nude, in the Greek manner. It was said that some of them submitted themselves to the painful operation of stretching the foreskin forward to conceal their circumcision. Since the gymnasia were dedicated to Greek gods, these activities were regarded by older Jews as both ungodly and unseemly.

After three years further intrigues led to Jason's being ousted in favour of the obsequious and unprincipled Menelaus, who was not of the high priest's dynasty and perhaps not even a priest. The highest religious office in the country had thus been captured by the Hellenists. Menelaus soon betrayed his stewardship by selling some of the Temple vessels to pay the monies he had promised to raise for the king.

This violation of the Temple treasury touched off fresh trouble in Jerusalem. The orthodox Jews rose in anger against the Hellenistic group and rioted in the street, killing a number of them, including Menelaus' brother, and demanding the removal of Menelaus. Antiochus responded by crushing them, confirming Menelaus in office and giving him military protection.

In 168 BC Antiochus invaded Egypt (for the second time), occupied most of it and marched on Alexandria. With success almost in his grasp he was stopped in his tracks by the arrival of a legate with an ultimatum from the Roman Senate, demanding immediate and complete withdrawal. Antiochus did not dare proceed on a collision course with

Rome. Swallowing his humiliation and rage, he turned round and marched back again through Palestine to Antioch. On the way reports reached him of a grave uprising in Jerusalem. Jason, who had been dismissed four years earlier and had taken refuge in Trans-Jordan, had now returned to drive out Menelaus. The report added that Jason was welcomed by the Jews of Jerusalem, who were now in open revolt. Antiochus was in no mood to act with restraint. One of his top commanders, Apollonius, was sent with an army to occupy the city. It was given savage treatment. A number of inhabitants were butchered; some quarters were destroyed and the rest looted; the defence walls were pulled down. A citadel called the Acra was constructed and a Seleucid garrison stationed in it. It soon became clear these measures had horrified the Jewish population but not cowed it. A spirit of rebellion simmered under the surface. It erupted when Antiochus launched a frontal assault on the Jewish religion as such.

There were general causes for this policy of repression. The Seleucid empire was on the defensive. It was under pressure from Parthia in the east and Egypt in the south, while Roman power was beginning to move into the Near East. Antiochus had always wanted to Hellenize his subject peoples – an aim now reinforced by the need for cohesion against external foes. In this frame of mind he regarded cultural and religious separatism as internal weakness that could no longer be tolerated. The political unrest in Judea and the obstinate resistance to Hellenism by most of its people were obviously rooted in their strange faith. The time had come to stamp heavily on that faith. He was no doubt advised by leading pro-Hellenists in Jerusalem that opposition would quickly yield to a show of firmness. He underrated the strength of Jewish convictions, as other persecutors would do in centuries to come.

A series of royal decrees in 167 BC wiped out the guarantee of religious tolerance given by the king's father, Antiochus III. The Temple sacrifices, the observance of the Sabbath and the feast days and the practice of circumcision were all forbidden on pain of death. Copies of the sacred books were destroyed. Altars were erected throughout the country, where Jews were forced to take part in pagan rites and eat pig's flesh. The Second Book of Maccabees, written a hundred years later, compiles a list of official atrocities against offending Jews, designed to intimidate the general population.

The most shattering blow came in December of that year, when the Temple itself was defiled. An altar to Zeus was put up in the sanctuary and swine were sacrificed upon it. It is likely that an image of Zeus was

RIGHT The Ark of the Covenant was brought into Jerusalem amid scenes of great rejoicing. David danced before it with his harp and the Ark was placed in the Tabernacle. The king then offered sacrifices and blessed the crowd in the name of the Lord. An illustration from *A Book of Old Testament Miniatures of the Thirteenth Century* which originated in Paris about 1250, was once in the possession of the Shah of Persia and is now in the Pierpont Morgan Library in New York.

OVERLEAF An eighteenth-century idea of the Temple of Solomon during the ceremonies of the eighth day of the Feast of *Succot*. An engraving from an English edition of Josephus' *Works*, published in 1754.

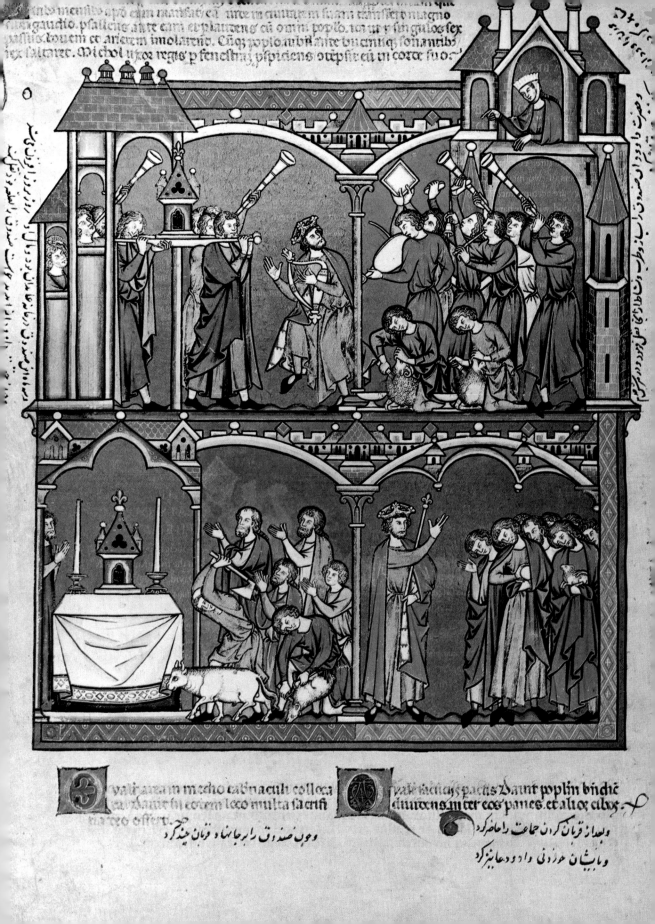

nbs mentis apo can marasec ca urce m cuntan in sua chiisec pmagno
gaudio. psallente auc cam eplaudens cu omni poplo. tot ur r singulos sex
passit iouem co ariccm molarent. Cuq poplo urbs ante huentucs sonantibs
ex saltauc. Michol uxor regis p fenesti pspiciens ocpsit eu in corte suo.

yalt aram in mecho tabnaculi collea
 cauauit su cocem loco multa sacri
fi arco offer.

yalt sactias pactis baunt poplin buche
dinuxens mi ter cos panes. et alios cibos.

also set up. The feast of the Greek nature-god Dionysus (the Roman god Bacchus) was celebrated in the Temple with Jews forced to participate in the licentious rites. These acts were indeed 'the abomination that makes desolate' as they were called in the Book of Daniel and the First Book of Maccabees.

The Maccabean Revolt

Officials were sent through the countryside to supervise the Hellenizing programme, with platoons of armed soldiers as escort. One of them came to the village of Modi'in on the coastal plain, near the present town of Lod. The villagers were lined up round three sides of the market square and a rough altar was erected on the fourth side. A pig stood tethered next to it, waiting to be sacrificed to Zeus. The officer briefly addressed the crowd, referring to the king's orders and demanding their compliance. When they remained rooted to the spot he turned to the priest Mattathias, who stood a little aside with his five stalwart sons: John, Simon, Judah, Eleazar and Jonathan. Knowing that if the priest would set the lead the rest would follow, the officer promised him money and favours if he would co-operate in the ceremony. The old man stared defiantly at the king's representative and flung back his declaration of faith: 'Even if all the nations that live under the rule of the king obey him . . . departing each from the religion of his fathers, yet I and my sons and my brothers . . . will not obey the king's words by turning aside from our religion to the right hand or the left' (1 Maccabees 2: 19–22). In the tense silence one of the villagers shuffled shamefacedly forward to the altar. Mattathias sprang at him and knifed him to death on the spot, then turned and slew the officer. Before the lolling soldiers could gather their wits, the excited crowd overwhelmed and killed them too. With his own hand Mattathias tore down the altar. The standard of revolt against Seleucid rule had been hoisted in this sleepy peasant village.

Mattathias and his sons, with the bolder men of the village, fled to the nearby Gophna hills in the Judean range north of Jerusalem, where they took refuge in the rocky bush-covered ravines. Joined by other rebels and religious diehards, they lived the tough and dangerous existence of a partisan group, receiving supplies and support from friendly villages and farmsteads. They harried military patrols, knocked down pagan altars, had male Jewish infants circumcised and spread their message of sedition in the name of the Lord. A short while later Mattathias died, after naming his third son, Judah, as commander. He had become known as Judah the Maccabee – Hebrew for Judah the Hammerer (in the Greek form, Judas Maccabeus) – and the adjective Maccabean came to be applied to all the brothers and the uprising.

At first the authorities regarded Judah and his men as no more than a local nuisance. A detachment sent from Samaria to mop them up was ambushed and routed and its commanding officer killed. A much

LEFT The Second Temple was the most magnificent of all Herod's building projects. Its size and splendour, towering above the surrounding city, is evident from this model, built to scale by Professor Michael Avi-Yonah, in the gardens of the Holyland Hotel, Jerusalem.

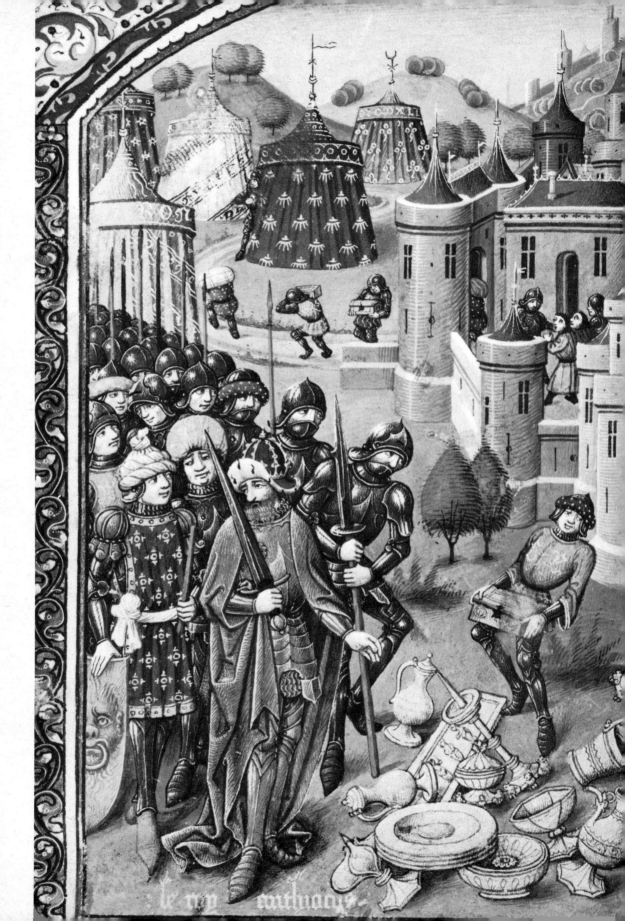

le roy carthage

Jherusalem

The site of ancient Modi'in.

larger force advanced into the hills from the coastal plain, but its leading column was attacked and thrown back before it could get to the head of the pass. After these successes the revolt spread across the Judean hills, and Jerusalem was virtually cut off.

The Seleucid military command now faced the classic problem of using regular troops to subdue guerillas in rough and hostile terrain. (Two thousand years later a British army would cope with the same problem in the same hill country.) In the third year of the rebellion Antioch launched a major campaign to reassert control over Judea. An army marched down the coast, personally led by Lysias, a royal kinsman appointed as regent while the king was engaged in a war against the Parthians in the east. Lysias skirted the hills and advanced towards Jerusalem from the south, through the area occupied by the friendly Idumeans (Edomites). Judah by now had at his disposal a substantial force of seasoned guerilla fighters. They intercepted and drove back the Seleucid vanguard at the defile of Beth-zur, on the Hebron–Jerusalem road, and this led to a complete rout of Lysias' troops.

Lysias did not stage a counter-attack, apparently deciding that he had underrated the fighting capacity of the Maccabees. He accordingly withdrew. Judah seized the respite – and the opportunity – to go into Jerusalem.

PREVIOUS PAGES The pillage of Jerusalem and the Temple by the troops of Antiochus IV. An illustration from a fifteenth-century illuminated manuscript of *The Jewish Wars* by Josephus.

Mattathias slays a man about to sacrifice a pig in the market place at Modi'in;
from a tenth-century illuminated manuscript of the Books of the Maccabees.

The Maccabees and their followers entered the city in an exalted mood. They left the Acra citadel severely alone, with the Seleucid garrison marooned in it. They had no means of taking a heavily fortified building by assault and would have incurred heavy casualties in the attempt. In any case it was another nearby objective that had drawn them like a powerful magnet to Jerusalem – the Temple Mount. There a harrowing scene met their eyes. 'And they saw the sanctuary desolate, the altar profaned and the gates burned. In the courts they saw bushes sprung up as in a thicket, or as on one of the mountains. They saw also the chambers of the priests in ruins' (1 Maccabees 4: 38).

After a brief display of grief Judah set to work. Some of his bowmen were detailed to shoot back at the Seleucid soldiers raining down arrows from the ramparts of the Acra, only a few hundred yards away across a narrow valley. This Jewish counter-fire damped down harassment of the work in the Temple area and prevented sorties from the fortress. The rest of his men, under the supervision of priests, set about clearing the sacred site. They removed and stored the defiled stones of the altar, erected a new one of unhewn stones (as prescribed in the holy books), and restored the damaged buildings and courts. On the twenty-fifth day of the ninth month (December 164 BC) – exactly three years to the day after the Temple had been profaned – it was solemnly reconsecrated with fervent prayers and songs, and with sacrifices offered on the new altar. The ceremonies went on for eight days.

These events gave rise to the annual festival that became known centuries later as the Feast of *Hanukkah* (Dedication). The Jewish historian Josephus, writing at the end of the first century AD, refers to it as the Feast of Lights, though he is vague about the reason for this name. In the course of time the historical facts became mixed with legends. The best known of them related that when the Maccabees entered the Temple they found only one cruse of pure oil with which to light the Temple candelabrum. The rest of the oil had been defiled. But this cruse, which still bore the seal of the high priest, held only enough oil for one night. However, by a miracle, it lasted for eight nights. Ever after the Feast of *Hanukkah* was celebrated for eight days, and the custom grew up of having in each synagogue and Jewish home an eight-branched candelabrum (a *Hanukkiah*) during the feast, and lighting one more candle each evening.

After the purification of the Temple and the resumption of regular worship in it Judah consolidated his military gains. The Temple Mount was fortified and a stronghold was constructed at Beth-zur to block the southern approach to Jerusalem. The Maccabees were now in virtual control of Judea. They carried out a series of swift campaigns into adjacent territories: round the Dead Sea in the south; across the Jordan into Gilead; through Galilee in the north; and along the coast.

A *Hanukkiah*. One more candle on the eight-branched candelabrum is lit each evening during the Feast of *Hanukkah*.

Jewish communities in these areas were evacuated to the capital.

But the hard-won independence proved to be precarious. In 163 BC Antiochus IV died in his eastern campaign. The new king installed in Antioch, Antiochus V, was his nine-year-old son, and responsibility for managing the affairs of the western and southern portion of the Seleucid empire still rested on Lysias as regent. Lysias now gathered a formidable army and in 162 BC moved southward once more against Judea. This time he included in his force a unit of Indian war elephants. In the battle of Beth-Zechariah, between Hebron and Jerusalem, the Maccabees were heavily defeated and one of the brothers, Eleazar, was killed. Judah had no choice but to order a withdrawal from the battlefield. It is believed that he then rushed back to Jerusalem to organize in haste the defences of the Temple Mount, leave a Maccabee unit there and take to the Gophna hills again with the rest of his men. When Lysias reached Jerusalem shortly afterwards he was dismayed by the struggle put up by the Temple defenders, for he could not afford to spend time on a long siege. Disturbing reports from Antioch made his presence there essential. He therefore sent a message to the besieged Maccabees on the Temple Mount with a truce offer: annulment of the anti-Jewish decrees imposed by Antiochus IV and the guarantee of religious toler-ance. This was confirmed by a letter on behalf of the king, granting permission 'for the Jews to enjoy their own food and laws, just as formerly . . .' (2 Maccabees 11: 31). In the covering letter to Lysias the king states: 'We have heard that the Jews do not consent to our father's change to Greek customs but prefer their own way of living . . . our decision is that their Temple be restored to them and that they live according to the customs of their ancestors' (2 Maccabees 11: 24–25). The Seleucid dynasty did not again attempt the disastrous policy of religious coercion.

However Antioch was not prepared to countenance political inde-pendence for Judea, which was the goal the Maccabees now set for themselves, and in the next two years Seleucid troops struggled to wipe out Jewish resistance. At the beginning of 161 BC, after a Seleucid military setback in Judea, the Maccabees won a brief breathing spell, and Judah sent two envoys to Rome, seeking outside intervention. The Roman Senate ratified a treaty of friendship with the Jewish rebels, as it was not averse to fomenting trouble for the Seleucid regime. But no practical support was forthcoming. In 160 BC, at the battle of Elasa, the Maccabean guerillas were crushed by the Seleucid general Bacchides, and Judah was killed. His brothers recovered his body and buried it in the family tomb at Modi'in, next to their father Mattathias.

Though their cause now seemed hopeless, the three remaining brothers continued to act in the dauntless and tenacious spirit of Judah, who was to remain a Jewish national hero for all time. It was agreed that the youngest brother Jonathan should take over the command of the remnant that was left, less than a thousand in all. The aim of political independence still seemed illusory, but the rebellion had achieved its initial purpose – the fight for religious freedom.

The survivors took refuge in the desolate wilderness of Judea, between the Hebron hills and the Dead Sea, where the fugitive David had held out against King Saul nine centuries earlier. For about four years Jonathan and his group eluded the attempts of General Bacchides to stamp out the last embers of the revolt. During this period the eldest brother, John, was killed in a tribal skirmish in the desert east of the Dead Sea.

In 156 BC Bacchides, after suffering a reverse at the hands of the Maccabees, had to return to Antioch, and he made a kind of truce with Jonathan, as Lysias had done with Judah in similar circumstances. The Maccabees were not given access to Jerusalem, but Jonathan established himself north of the city of Michmash and steadily gained control of the rest of Judea. At that time the Seleucid kingdom was torn by a dynastic struggle between the reigning monarch, Demetrius I, and the young pretender, Alexander Balas, supported by Rome. With great political finesse Jonathan played one faction off against another and obtained concessions from both.

In 152 BC Demetrius tried to gain his support by allowing him to enter Jerusalem. The Jewish hostages held in the Acra fortress were released and Jonathan was authorized to maintain his own armed forces for Judean defence. The Seleucid troops in the country were withdrawn, except for small garrisons remaining in the Acra and at Beth-zur, commanding the southward road through the hills. These detachments, and an annual tribute paid by Jonathan, were the only remaining signs of Seleucid suzerainty.

Not to be outdone, Alexander Balas bestowed on Jonathan the official status of ethnarch and high priest. Ethnarch (a Greek word meaning 'leader of the people') was a title used by the Romans for a local ruler of a semi-independent area. The office of high priest has been vacant for six years since the death of Alcimus, a member of the priestly dynasty installed by the Seleucids. When Jonathan officiated for the first time in the Temple he broke the line of succession of the Jerusalem high priests that extended back eight centuries to Zadok, in the time of King David. For over a century the office was to be held by the Hasmonean dynasty, so called because Mattathias, who started the Maccabean revolt, had been of the House of Hasmon.

In 142 BC Jonathan was treacherously captured and killed by the invading Seleucid general Trypho, who had seized the throne in Antioch. The torch of leadership was immediately picked up by Simon, the last survivor of the five brothers. He too was recognized as ethnarch and high priest, and served as the Judean leader for the next eight years. He consolidated the political autonomy gained by Jonathan and symbolized this status by minting and issuing Judean coins. The payment of tribute and taxes to Antioch was suspended. When Simon laid siege to the Acra fortress in Jerusalem its Seleucid garrison surrendered to him. He built up a reputation as a wise and successful ruler, and the First Book of Maccabees lauds his peaceful achievements. Among other benefits, 'He made the sanctuary glorious and added to the vessels of the sanctuary' (1 Maccabees 14: 15). Simon was murdered by his own son-in-law, who had been plotting to seize power. All five of the Maccabean 'glorious brothers' had died violent deaths in battle or by murder.

The thirty-year rule of Simon's eldest son John Hyrcanus I (134–104 BC) started badly. The Seleucid monarch, Antiochus VII, made a bid to reassert authority over Judea. He led an army southward and occupied Jerusalem, but withdrew again under Roman pressure. Not long after he was killed in the chronic war against the Parthians and the Seleucid empire began to disintegrate. For a long time there would be no external pressure on the Jewish state. It now entered a period of prosperity and military expansion.

John Hyrcanus incorporated Samaria, part of the coastal plain, Perea across the Jordan and Idumea in the south. Galilee was added by Hyrcanus' son Judah Aristobolus (104–103 BC) and there were further additions by the latter's brother Alexander Jannai (103–76 BC). By then Judea once again spread over an area on both sides of the Jordan roughly corresponding to that of the united kingdom under David and Solomon. The monarchy was revived after the death of John Hyrcanus, and the Hasmonean rulers combined the functions of king and high priest for over forty years until the Roman annexation, when the royal title was again downgraded to ethnarch.

As a rule non-Jewish groups in the occupied territories were converted to Judaism, and in due course absorbed. The conspicuous example was that of the Idumeans, who had settled in the southern hills of Judea after the destruction of Jerusalem by the Babylonians.

John Hyrcanus settled one religious account by destroying the Samaritan temple on Mount Gerizim at Shechem. It had originally been erected as a competitor to the Jerusalem Temple, and in the time of Antiochus Epiphanes had blended the worship of Jehovah with that of the Greek god Zeus.

Religious Trends

The reign of John Hyrcanus saw the emergence of two conflicting trends or parties in the state: the Sadducees and the Pharisees. The differences between them were primarily doctrinal, but had political and class overtones. One difference related to the role of the Temple cult in the national life.

Cy commence lystoire iehan hyrcan. Et pre
mierement. comment iehan hyrcan assist
tholomee a dobi

pres la mort symon frere
iudas le machabee. qui fu
le daurenier des filz matha
thie duc et souuerain pre
stre en iudee. iehan son filz
qui par surnom fut appe
lez hyrcan pour ceulx de hyrcanie quil veinq
et conquist. fu fait souuerain mestre. Il e

The Sadducees (Hebrew: *Zadukim*) derived their name from Zadok, the high priest in the time of David and Solomon. The establishment they represented, with the Temple and the palace at its centre, included the priesthood and an upper class of nobles and wealthy merchants. It was natural for this privileged group to be conservative in outlook. The Sadducees staunchly adhered to the rituals of Temple worship and the literal acceptance of the Mosaic code as set out in the Pentateuch. Paradoxically, it was these elements of Judean society that were most susceptible to Hellenist influence in their social and personal lives.

While not rejecting Temple worship, the Pharisees stressed expounding the law directly to the people as the basis for their daily conduct. Interpretation of the law had in the past been the function only of ordained priests. With the Pharisees it was done informally by scribes and learned men, addressed by their pupils as *rabbi*, the Hebrew for 'my teacher'. This was in the tradition of the reforms introduced by Ezra the scribe. The Pharisees were a populist party that appealed to ordinary men lower down the social and economic ladder: artisans, small traders and peasant farmers. Since their teachings were regarded as non-conformist, undermining the regime and the official cult, they were called Pharisees, from the Hebrew word *perushim*, meaning separatists or deserters. They themselves welcomed this name as it also carried the meaning of expounders.

In the religious domain the fundamental difference between Sadducees and Pharisees lay in their attitude to the *Torah*, the Mosaic code. The Pharisees accepted the Scriptures as sacred, but interpreted them in a flexible manner, so that they could be adjusted to the changing needs and concepts of the times. In this way a body of precedents and rulings was built up, known as the Oral Law. For example the doctrine of 'an eye for an eye' was taken out of the primitive context of physical revenge for injury, and given the civilized modern interpretation of monetary damages. By the Pharisaic belief the Oral Law had been handed down to Moses at Mount Sinai at the same time as the Written Law, and had equal validity with it. Such a concept was rejected as heresy by the Sadducees.

The Pharisees evolved other concepts that may have had parallels in certain Near Eastern pagan religions, but could find only slender authority in the Pentateuch. They came to believe in the resurrection of the dead; in an after-life where reward or punishment would balance the accounts of earthly conduct; and in the existence of angelic or demonaic beings that were the agents of good and evil. These ideas too were unacceptable to the Sadducees, but they became grafted on to the main stem of Judaism.

By the reign of Herod the Great the Pharisaic movement had produced two rival schools headed by and named after the sages Hillel and

John Hyrcanus at the siege of Dagon. Horrified at seeing his mother and brothers being whipped on the battlements, he withdrew his troops from the siege. The episode is recorded by Josephus in *The Jewish War*. This illustration is from a fourteenth-century French manuscript.

The differences between the Sadducees and the Pharisees had political and class overtones. The Sadducees (*left*) were wealthy landowners, merchants and priests. The Pharisees were men of the people and stressed the importance of expounding the law directly to the people. Eighteenth-century German engravings.

Shammai, co-presidents of the Sanhedrin. The celebrated debates between them on some three hundred disputed questions gave great impetus to the development of the Oral Law. In general Bet (the house of) Shammai took a conservative position, while Bet Hillel was more flexible in adapting the laws. In opposition to Shammai, Hillel was in favour of accepting gentile converts. When a would-be convert, bewildered by the intricacies of Judaism, challenged Hillel to expound his faith while standing on one leg, the gentle sage replied: 'What is hateful to you, do not unto your neighbour; this is the entire *Torah*, all the rest is commentary.'

Some of Hillel's teaching was to be reflected in the sayings attributed to Jesus. In general the New Testament was strongly influenced by the Pharisaic beliefs about resurrection and an after-life, and by the revived emphasis on Messianism. The founder of a separate Christian church, St Paul, was a Jew from a Pharisee family in Tarsus in Asia Minor, and studied the *Torah* with a renowned Pharisee sage in Jerusalem, Rabbi Gamaliel. In spite of the debt of Christianity to the earlier Jewish sages, the Gospels are hostile to Sadducees and Pharisees alike.

The Pharisaic movement was important not only to the common people of Judea, but also to the large diaspora communities in Alexandria, Babylonia, Cyrene and elsewhere. By the beginning of the Christian era there were at least as many Jews living outside Judea as in it. Physically distant from Jerusalem, the diaspora took readily to a Jewish way of life based not on participation in the Temple cult but on the Written and Oral Law, on prayer meetings in their synagogues, and on rabbis who expounded ethical principles and individual responsibility before God. These developments went back through Ezra to the Babylonian exile. They now served as advance training for the survival of Judaism after the destruction of the Second Temple in AD 70. In the Hasmonean-Herodian state a portable faith was being prepared for a people who would again be left without state or temple. The work of the Pharisees would lead straight to the *Mishna* and the Talmud.

Two smaller sects require mention. One was the Zealots, whose origin went back to the Hassidim (pious ones) who joined in the Maccabean revolt. The Pharisees were accused by their enemies of lack of patriotism, of indifference to political independence as long as they were left free to pursue their spiritual concerns. That could not be said of the Zealots. They combined the religious fervour of the Pharisees with the nationalist spirit of the Sadducees. In the final act they were to go down fighting to the bitter end against the Roman conquerors.

The Essenes represented a different strain of Judaism. They tended to withdraw from the main stream and set up ascetic and monastic communes of their own, isolated in the wilderness. Here they devoted themselves to the study of the *Torah*, unconnected with the Temple and its sacrificial cult. The excavated monastery at Qumran, near which the Dead Sea Scrolls were discovered, probably housed such a group. A study of these scrolls shows the impact of the Essenes on early Christian doctrine, maybe through John the Baptist, who could have been one of their adherents.

The scrolls are suffused with the Messianic spirit of the time. They relate to the Jewish apocalyptic literature that appeared between the second century BC and the second century AD – the period that witnessed both the birth of Christianity and the end of the Jewish state. The Greek word *apokalupsis* means revelation. Works of this kind expressed the belief that the 'End of Days' was coming, and would be preceded by wars and natural upheavals. They are filled with visions, strange symbols and superhuman beings, and purport to disclose secrets regarding the nature of God, creation and the heavens. A number foretell the coming of the Messiah. The only apocalyptic work later included in the Bible was the Book of Daniel. Other well-known ones that have survived as pseudepigrapha are the Apocalypse of Baruch, the Book of Enoch, the Book of Jubilees and the Testaments of the Twelve Patriarchs.

LEFT The sandstone cliffs overlooking Qumran on the Dead Sea where it is thought the Essenes took refuge.

RIGHT The excavated monastery at Qumran.

11 *Under Roman Sway*

By the first century BC Rome had become the leading power of the ancient world. It dominated the Mediterranean basin and its legions moved into the Near East, led by the popular Roman triumvir, Pompey. At the time, a struggle for the succession was taking place in Judah between two sons of Alexander Jannai, Hyrcanus II, the high priest, and Aristobulus II, who had been put in charge of the armed forces and had proclaimed himself king. Both of them appealed for support to Pompey when he arrived in Damascus. He marched to Jerusalem and occupied it, after the gates had been opened to him by the Hyrcanus party. Aristobulus was taken into captivity, but a number of his followers dug themselves in on the Temple Mount, after burning the bridge connecting it with the Upper City.

Pompey's troops laid siege to the Temple area from the northern side, where it was defended by a deep moat and towers. The moat was laboriously filled in, taking advantage of the reluctance of the Jewish defenders to attack on the Sabbath. The siege engines and battering rams were then rolled forward and made a breach in the wall. The final assault was launched on a fast day. Josephus notes that the priests bravely went on with their ceremonial duties during the attack. The mount was captured and thousands of its defenders put to death. Pompey did not destroy or despoil the Temple, though he profaned it in Jewish eyes by walking into the Holy of Holies. He found it empty; since a god without a tangible image was inexplicable to the Romans, a rumour spread that the Temple contained an ass's head worshipped by the Jews. At the beginning of the second century AD, the Roman historian Tacitus recorded:

> Pompey was the first Roman that subdued the Jews. By right of conquest he entered their temple. It is a fact well known, that he found no image, no statue, no symbolical representation of the Deity: the whole presented a naked dome; the sanctuary was unadorned and simple. By Pompey's orders the walls of the city were levelled to the ground, but the temple was left entire.

Pompey's force besieged the Temple area and breached the northern wall with battering rams. An engraving from a seventeenth-century edition of Josephus' *Works*.

Another Roman writer, Dio Cassius, tried to describe in his history (about AD 230) the peculiar ways of the Jews:

> They are distinguished from the rest of mankind in practically every detail of life, and especially by the fact that they do not honour any of the usual gods, but show extreme reverence for one particular divinity. They never had any statue of him even in Jerusalem itself, but believing him to be unnameable and invisible, they worship him in the most extravagant fashion on earth.

In the same passage Dio Cassius showed that the Temple remained a legend 160 years after Titus had destroyed it. The Jews, he wrote, built a shrine to their deity 'that was extremely large and beautiful, except in so far as it was open and roofless, and likewise dedicated to him the day of Saturn on which, among many other most peculiar observances, they undertake no serious occupation'. In calling the Temple 'open and roofless' Dio Cassius was confusing the building with the surrounding courts. The 'day of Saturn' was Saturday, the day of the Jewish Sabbath.

The Holy of Holies would not have been found empty in the First Temple period. The Ark of the Covenant installed in it by King Solomon had apparently disappeared before the destruction of the Temple in 587 BC. It is surmised that the Ark may have been removed and hidden; there was no mention of it among the sacred vessels carried off by the Babylonian conquerors and restored by King Cyrus at the time of the return. In this mysterious fashion the most sacred cult object of the Hebrew faith and nation vanished from history, never to reappear. In the Second Temple period nothing is heard either about the large images of cherubim that flanked and guarded the Ark in Solomon's Temple. But the Holy of Holies retained its sacred character as the abode of the Shechinah, the Divine Presence, and was still entered only by the high priest, once a year on the Day of Atonement, as had been the case when the Ark rested in it.

Pompey confirmed Hyrcanus II as high priest, handed over command to one of his generals and returned to Rome, taking with him Aristobulus II and his two sons in chains. Judea was stripped of some territories – the coastal plain, Samaria, the plain of Esdraelon and the area east of the Dead Sea – leaving the Galilee cut off from the rest. Most of the Hellenist cities were freed of Jewish rule, and ten of them across the Jordan were grouped together in the Decapolis, the League of Ten Cities.

The Roman occupation marked the end of Jewish independence for two thousand years, except for three brief intervals – the three-year reign of Mattathias Antigonus from 40 to 37 BC, the five-year period of the Jewish Revolt from AD 66 to 70, and the Bar-Kochba uprising from AD 132 to 135.

The Rise of Herod

Hyrcanus was a feeble character and the affairs of Judea were in the hands of his chief minister, Antipater, a wily and energetic Idumean chieftain. He entrenched his position by appointing his elder son Phasael as governor of Jerusalem and his younger son Herod (then twenty-five years old) as governor of the Galilee. Antipater fully grasped that the survival of Judea, even as a shrunken vassal state, depended on the favour of whatever Roman leader was in a position to exercise power in the area. In the civil war that rent the Roman empire Antipater remained loyal to Pompey while he appeared to be in control, but shifted support to Julius Caesar when the latter landed in Egypt. As a reward for backing the right Roman, Judea regained the port of Joppa and some other lost possessions, while the secular position of ethnarch was restored to Antipater's master, the high priest Hyrcanus.

In 44 BC the internal Roman struggle erupted again with the assassination of Julius Caesar by the rival faction headed by Brutus and Cassius. In the following year Antipater was poisoned by enemies. Herod promoted his own fortunes by continuing his father's timely shifts of allegiance. At first he switched to Cassius, who had taken charge in the east; but when his patron was defeated and killed at Philippi in 42 BC Herod quickly gained the ear of the new leader, Mark Antony.

Taking advantage of the conflict, a Parthian army moved westward and occupied Judea, in support of Mattathias Antigonus, the Hasmonean heir, son of Aristobulus II, who became king. Herod's brother Phasael was jailed and committed suicide. The aged Hyrcanus was mutilated by having his ears chopped off, thus disqualifying him to serve as high priest. Herod fled to Rome, where Mark Antony brought him to the favourable notice of Julius Caesar's nephew Octavian. With this powerful backing Herod audaciously sought and obtained the endorsement of the Roman Senate for his aspiration to be made King of Judea. The Romans rightly saw in him a suitable instrument for regaining control of Judea, and for then keeping that troublesome but strategic territory within the Roman orbit.

In 39 BC Herod landed on the Palestine coast with a mercenary force and established a base in the Galilee. It took two years before Mark Antony ousted the Parthians from Syria and could free troops for a campaign in Judea. The Roman general Sosius was sent with his legions and a large force of cavalry to join Herod, who had already moved southward and laid siege to Jerusalem. At this point Herod bolstered his claims to the throne by taking as his second wife Mariamne (Miriam), the niece of Antigonus and the great-granddaughter of Alexander Jannai, the former Hasmonean king of Judea.

To the chagrin of Herod and Sosius, Jerusalem did not surrender to the overwhelming force they had deployed round it. The city remained loyal to Antigonus, and held out for five weary months. Although there was friction between different factions of the defenders – a pattern that would be disastrous a century later – all of them feared that Jerusalem would be sacked and the Temple destroyed if these foreign troops and mercenaries broke in. Moreover they did not recognize the legitimacy of the Idumean upstart, appointed as their king by an outside power.

When the city walls were breached the hard core of the resistance concentrated on the Temple Mount. Herod prepared to take it from the northern side, as Pompey had done twenty-six years earlier. It was essential for his own future that he should protect the Temple from the Roman legionaries, who were already on the rampage in other quarters, massacring the inhabitants and pillaging their homes. When Herod appealed to Sosius to impose discipline the general replied with a shrug that it was only fair to let his men gain plunder after the hardships of the siege. Herod had to use all his available funds to buy off the troops and their commanders and restore order. He acceeded to a message from the Temple authorities asking for animals required for the sacrifices to be allowed through the lines. Once he had succeeded in occupying the Temple area he was able to ensure that it was kept safe.

Antigonus was carried off by Sosius and was later executed. Herod was installed as king, and promptly had a number of Antigonus' followers put to death. He confiscated the property of wealthy Sadducee families to pay tribute to Antony and replenish his own coffers.

On the factual record of his thirty-three-year reign Herod was one of the ablest and most successful rulers in Jewish history. The key to his policy was the client–state relationship that provided the Roman overlord with a reliable and effective vassal in a sensitive area near the Parthian border. For that reason Herod survived Octavian's defeat of his friend Mark Antony, together with Queen Cleopatra of Egypt, at the battle of Actium in 31 BC. Octavian, who proclaimed himself the Emperor Augustus, found it convenient to maintain Herod on the Judean throne.

In exchange for his usefulness to Rome Herod enjoyed a free hand in Judea. He was able to expand its territory and give it a long period of peace and prosperity. In a broad sense he also became accepted as King of the Jews by the diaspora communities in other parts of the Roman empire, who regularly sent funds to Jerusalem for the upkeep of the Temple. His building programme probably earned him the title of Herod the Great.

Yet the image he left behind was besmirched by his acts of cruelty and despotism, and by the improbable legend in the Gospel of St Matthew about the 'slaughter of the innocents' in Bethlehem after the birth of Jesus. In the later years of his life Herod became obsessively jealous and suspicious of his Hasmonean family connections. At various times, and on various pretexts, he put to death his wife Mariamne, the two sons he had by her, her mother and her younger brother. This brutal conduct further antagonized the Sadducean priests and nobles, who had been identified with the Hasmonean dynasty and resented Herod as its supplanter. On the other hand, until late in his reign Herod enjoyed support from the Pharisee party, whose influence was growing. The breach between the king and the Judean aristocracy widened through his handling of two major religious institutions in which the Sadducees had a vested interest: the office of the high priest and the Sanhedrin.

During the Hasmonean period the holder of the dual position of high priest and ethnarch had been the source of both spiritual and political authority. Herod may well have toyed with the idea of assuming the clerical office as well, but that would have outraged all religious opinion in the country. He could hardly fabricate a claim to priestly descent, being of the Idumean stock that had been forcibly converted to Judaism only two or three generations earlier. Nor did he pretend to be a pious Jew; on the contrary, he was known as an ardent admirer of all Hellenist-Roman culture. His interference with religious affairs was prompted by political, not doctrinal motives. As an autocratic ruler he would not brook any institution in the State that was independent of himself. If he could not be high priest, he saw to it that the high priest should be his docile nominee, and that the Temple should remain under his control. He discarded the principle that the office was hereditary; it became not even a life appointment, but one held at the king's pleasure.

At the beginning of Herod's rule the high priest's office should by right of descent have gone to Mariamne's brother Aristobulus III, on the death of her uncle, Antigonus. But Herod passed him over in favour of one Hananel, an obscure Babylonian Jew of priestly lineage. Yielding to the outcry of his family-in-law, Herod dismissed Hananel and appointed Aristobulus. When the handsome seventeen-year-old Hasmonean prince appeared in the Temple in the high priest's vestments and was greeted with joy by the congregation, it was too much for Herod. He had the youth 'accidentally' drowned while taking the waters in Jericho. Hananel was then restored to office.

Later high priests tended to be drawn from a few select families favoured by Herod, notably the House of Boethus from Alexandria. The position was still an honour, but in practice had been reduced to that of an official in charge of Temple ritual and administration. The subordinate status of the high priest was marked by the fact that his ceremonial vestments were kept by the king in the Antonia fortress and released only when required for special feast days. When Judea was annexed as a Roman province soon after Herod's death the Roman procurator appointed the high priest and kept custody of his vestments—although these prerogatives were later handed back to King Agrippa.

Herod's treatment of the Sanhedrin was even rougher. It was a central council of seventy-one members with jurisdiction on religious and legal questions. Its origins, composition and powers before the end of the Second Temple are unclear.

While still governor of the Galilee, Herod had had a confrontation with the Sanhedrin that nearly put an end to his career. He had rounded up and executed without trial a group of Jewish guerilla fighters led by one Hezekiah, a man of good family. Josephus later referred to them as 'bandits', but they were probably a small underground resistance movement against Antipater and Herod and the Roman power they served. The Sanhedrin, dominated by Sadducee supporters of the Hasmonean dynasty, summoned Herod to appear before it in Jerusalem. The charge was that he had broken the law by imposing the death penalty, which could properly be done only by the Sanhedrin itself. Popular feeling ran high over the case, and the mothers of the executed men publicly mourned each day in the Temple, demanding that justice be done. As high priest, Hyrcanus II presided over the Sanhedrin; and though a weak and irresolute man he felt forced by public pressure to endorse the summons issued to Herod.

Antipater felt it would be imprudent to let his son defy the Sanhedrin in this tense atmosphere. He told Herod to appear at the hearing with an armed bodyguard large enough to pull him out of trouble if necessary, but not so large that it would seem to be a provocative show of strength. The Sanhedrin was at first taken aback by Herod's truculent manner and the presence of his soldiers. They were stiffened by a firm protest from one of the leading Pharisee members. Herod was in danger of being condemned, and was saved only by the intervention of the Roman governor of Syria, who supported the strong measures Herod had taken to suppress trouble in the Galilee. The governor wrote to Hyrcanus demanding an acquittal. This Hyrcanus could not obtain, but on his private advice Herod fled from Jerusalem and returned to the protection of the Roman authorities in the north. Furious at his humiliating experience, Herod talked about raising a force to invade Judea, but was dissuaded by his sagacious father.

Years later, when Herod became king in Jerusalem, one of his first and most vindictive actions was to cripple the Sanhedrin, and bring it under his control. Forty-five members of the august tribunal were arrested and executed and their places filled by Herod's supporters. The council was stripped of its judicial function and its task confined to clarifying points of religious doctrine.

With his high-handed conduct towards the religious authorities and his own lack of religious conviction, why should Herod have gone to enormous trouble and expense to rebuild the Temple, and seen in this project the crowning achievement of his reign? In fact he was driven not by piety but by a potent blend of two other motives: the pride of a

One of Herod's first actions on becoming king was to bring the Sanhedrin under his control. The great council in session, from an eighteenth-century English Bible.

Hellenistic towers at Samaria, the Herodian city of Sebaste.

great builder and the political instincts of an unpopular ruler seeking the esteem of his subjects.

Not since King Solomon, a thousand years earlier, had a Judean monarch launched such a monumental construction programme as did Herod. In this respect the conditions in the two reigns had much in common – an able and ambitious ruler, political stability and a level of affluence capable of providing the necessary resources.

Herod's building operations were not confined to the capital. They extended throughout Judea, and beyond it to other parts of the Roman empire. A number of purposes were served: prestige; internal and external security; economic and commercial development; provision of Greek-style amenities, especially for athletics; flattery of his Roman masters; the allegiance of the diaspora communities; and his personal relaxation from the burdens of office.

He reconstructed and fortified Samaria, which had been the hill capital of Omri and Ahab in the northern kingdom eight centuries before. The city was renamed Sebaste, from the Greek name for the Emperor Augustus, and a temple was built there in the emperor's honour. Another small temple of Egyptian granite, erected at Panias (Banias), was also dedicated to Augustus.

A number of fortresses were built or rebuilt: Antonia at the north-western corner of the Temple Mount, formerly the Hasmonean fortress of Baris and now named after Mark Antony; Herodium, on the verge of the desert south-east of Bethlehem; Masada, on the great flat-topped rock on the western shore of the Dead Sea; the Hasmonean stronghold of Machaerus, on the opposite side of the Dead Sea in Trans-Jordan; and Cypros (named after his mother), in the Jordan valley near Jericho. These and other strong-points made it possible to control the roads, to stamp out brigandage and to guard the borders.

On the Mediterranean coast Herod constructed the city of Caesarea (named after Caesar Augustus) and made it the main port of the country. In Jerusalem he erected a new palace and citadel at the highest point of the Upper City, next to the present Jaffa Gate. The lower courses still remain of one of its three massive towers, the one named after his brother Phasael. (The other two were named for his wife Mariamne and his close friend Hippicus.)

His winter palace was established at Jericho in the Jordan valley, with groves of date palms and balsam trees planted round it. On the Masada rock Herod had another winter palace, and a small villa cut out of the northern rock-face with a dizzy view across the Dead Sea. Still another Herodian palace had a spectacular location inside the rim of the Herodium fortress. At this spot there had been twin conical hills, which Josephus describes as resembling a woman's breasts. Herod demolished the upper part of one and used the earth and rock to construct great retaining walls and ramparts on top of the other in a complete circle.

Herod also used his passion for building to foster the development of the Graeco-Roman way of life in Judea. He endowed Jerusalem, Caesarea, Jericho and the Greek cities in his domain with theatres, gymnasia, stadia, hippodromes (racecourses), public baths and temples. He was willing to make financial grants to public buildings in Greece and Asia Minor; this enhanced his reputation in the Roman world, and pleased the local Jewish communities. A substantial contribution to the cost of the Olympic Games in Greece earned him the title of honorary life-president of the games.

The Temple Project

Nothing in all these building operations was comparable in scale and splendour to the Temple project. On the Temple Mount there stood the simple and by now shabby building erected five centuries earlier in the time of Zerubbabel, based on the plan of Solomon's Temple. In 22 BC Herod convened a national assembly and announced his plans for its reconstruction. His presentation revealed how much Herod hoped the project would redeem him with his Jewish subjects. In the *Antiquities of the Jews* Josephus writes that Herod esteemed this work to be 'the most glorious of all his actions ... and that this would be sufficient for an

everlasting memorial of him; but as he knew the multitude were not ready nor willing to assist him in so vast a design, he thought to prepare them first by making a speech to them, and then to set about the work itself . . .' (Book xv, Chapter 11). Josephus proceeds to quote this speech in full. In it Herod referred to all the other buildings he had erected in the kingdom till then, and maintained (rather defensively) that they were not for his own glory or protection but for the security and dignity of the nation as a whole. The task he was now about to begin they would find 'of the greatest piety and excellence that can possibly be undertaken by us'. The existing Temple, as built by Zerubbabel after the return from Babylon, was considerably lower than that of Solomon:

> . . . but since I am now by God's will your governor, and I have had peace a long time, and have gained great riches and large revenues, and what is the principal thing of all, I am in amity with, and well regarded by the Romans who, if I may so say, are the rulers of the whole world, I will do my endeavour to correct that imperfection . . . and to make a thankful return after the most pious manner, to God, for what blessings I have received from him, by giving me this kingdom, and that by rendering his temple as complete as I am able.

Unfortunately his audience remained sceptical and suspicious. They were fearful that Herod would pull down the existing Temple and then fail to carry out the grandiose plan he had in mind. To reassure them he gave a public undertaking that no demolition would start until all the preparations had been made for the rebuilding.

These preparations occupied the next two years. A labour force of some ten thousand workmen was assembled, including a thousand priests trained as masons and carpenters to do the work inside the sanctuary where laymen were forbidden. A thousand carts and waggons were acquired to transport the huge quantities of stone and other building materials. The actual building was started in 20 BC and the Temple structure itself was erected in eighteen months. But the completion of the great complex of buildings and courtyards, and their adornment, took forty-six years in all – in fact a generation beyond Herod's death in 4 BC. It was to be destroyed a few decades after it was finished.

Herod had deluded himself – the magnificent new Temple did not win for him the hearts of the Jewish people. In the last decade of his life he became increasingly morose and vengeful, and alienated even the Pharisees who had supported him against the old nobility and clergy. The incident of the golden eagle, when Herod was already dying, demonstrated how much he was still distrusted by orthodox Jews.

The eagle had been fashioned out of solid gold and affixed over the front entrance to the Temple. Presumably it was meant to represent the imperial Roman eagle and was a political gesture to Augustus, whose

OPPOSITE The site of Herod's citadel in Jerusalem, strategically placed at the highest point of the Upper City.

friendship had cooled during the ugly feuds Herod was having with his own sons. An agitation started among the more extreme Pharisees that the Temple was being desecrated by the eagle, an image of a living creature. The validity of this charge was dubious. Solomon's Temple had been decorated with figures of bulls, lions and eagles, and similar representations have been found on the remains of synagogues built long after Herod's time. It could be argued that the second commandment forbade graven images only if they were the objects of worship. But with a ruler as disliked as Herod, offence was easily taken.

Believing a rumour that the ailing king had already passed away, two Pharisee teachers of the Law incited their pupils to climb on to the Temple roof in the middle of the day, lower themselves with ropes and remove the eagle. It was hacked to pieces in front of an approving crowd. The students involved in this escapade were arrested and jailed with their two teachers. Herod summoned an assembly of notables, was carried before them on his sickbed and bitterly berated them for ingratitude after all he had done – far more, he pointed out, than had been done by the whole Hasmonean dynasty. The act of the students, he said, was sacrilege against God. The notables pleaded that they were not to blame, and that only the culprits should be punished. This Herod did – by having them burnt alive! He dismissed the high priest and appointed someone else to replace him.

A few days later Herod died in great agony, after the physicians had failed to help him. He was buried in state on the top of the Herodium mount he had constructed.

The Herodian Dynasty

On Herod's death in 4 BC the Judean kingdom was partitioned between his three surviving sons, in accordance with his last will. Archelaus was to be king over a truncated Judea. Herod Antipas was appointed Tetrarch of the Galilee and of Perea, the Jewish territory across the Jordan river. The third son, Herod Philip, was also given a tetrarchy – Gaulinitis (the Golan Heights) and the newly settled Syrian territory to the east of it. Herod's sister Salome received the two coastal towns of Jamnia and Azotus (south of Joppa) and the town of Phasaelis in the Jordan valley. The Gaza district and another district south-east of the Sea of Galilee were incorporated directly into the Roman province of Syria.

Archelaus succeeded in alienating both the Judeans and the Samaritans, his mother's people, and his rule was a decade of discord. Before he was confirmed by the Roman emperor he appeared in the Temple seated on a golden throne, and listened to the grievances of the crowd without yielding to them. An ugly mood developed in Jerusalem, its population swelled by the thousands of pilgrims camping round the Temple Mount for the forthcoming Passover festival. A squad of soldiers sent by Archelaus to arrest agitators was driven back under a hail of stones. Archelaus then ordered his troops to clear the Temple area, which was done with much loss of life.

He hurried off to Rome to press for his confirmation as king. The emperor was faced with a family counter-claim by Herod's sister Salome on behalf of her young son; by an adverse report from his own representatives in Judea; and by a Jewish deputation urging that the monarchy be abolished and direct Roman rule be established. In the end the imperial decision was a compromise. Archelaus was confirmed as the successor in Judea, but with the reduced rank of ethnarch, while the tetrarchies of his half-brothers Antipas and Philip were made independent of him.

Before Archelaus returned there was fresh trouble in Jerusalem, provoked by Sabinus, the tough Roman commander on the spot. Jewish rioters occupied the Temple compound and the Roman soldiers who tried to dislodge them were attacked with arrows and stones from the roofs of the colonnade round the Temple square. Unable to reach the men on the top, the soldiers set fire to the colonnade and the wooden roof caught fire. Many of the Jews were caught in the blaze or killed trying to escape. The whole city was now in uproar and disorder spread through the country. It was suppressed only when Varus, the Roman legate of Syria, marched south with all the troops he could muster.

In the end the Judeans and the Samaritans made joint representations against Archelaus to the emperor, who banished him in AD 6. Judea and Samaria then came under direct Roman rule as a sub-province of Syria governed by procurators, with the administrative capital at Caesarea.

Herod's grandson Agrippa grew up in Rome and gained the favour of the Emperor Caligula, who granted him first the tetrarchy of his uncle Herod Philip and then that of his uncle Herod Antipas in AD 39. Two years later Caligula was assassinated. Agrippa rendered services to the new emperor, Claudius, and was rewarded by being made King of Judea as well. For a brief while the unity and status of Herod the Great's kingdom had been restored.

On Agrippa's sudden death in AD 44, while he was attending a performance at the Roman theatre in Caesarea, Judea reverted to being a sub-province under a procurator. Agrippa's young son was left with territories further north, including the Galilee, and ruled them under Roman protection as Agrippa II (AD 44–66).

The damage caused to the Temple during Archelaus' disturbed reign was repaired only in the procuratorship of Pontius Pilate (AD 26–37). He proposed that the surplus funds in the Temple treasury should be used for an aqueduct from the Hebron district twenty-four miles away, to improve the inadequate water supply of Jerusalem. But this interference with the Temple administration caused a furore, and again there were disorders suppressed with bloodshed. Pontius Pilate inflamed feelings even more by having his troops march into Jerusalem carrying their standards with animal and bird emblems, thereby offending the religious sentiments of orthodox Jews. The protests reached the emperor, who intervened. A harsh and tactless governor, Pontius Pilate was eventually recalled to Rome to stand trial for the severity with which he had crushed the restive Samaritans.

One of the many executions Pilate had ordered was that of a young Jewish preacher called Jesus of Nazareth. The procurator's responsibility in this matter was subsequently blurred in the Gospels, at a time when the new Christian sect was trying to make its way in the Roman world and was hostile to the parent Jewish faith.

In spite of the periodic unrest in Jerusalem during this period, Herod's magnificent Temple continued to be the focus of pilgrimage throughout the Jewish world, and of sightseeing for great numbers of non-Jews. During the three pilgrimage festivals of the year – Passover, the Feast of Weeks and the Feast of Booths – Jerusalem was crammed with thousands of visitors. Organized 'group tours' arrived on foot or on donkeys from the towns and villages of Judea and gathered in dense and colourful crowds in the Temple Square, or in the open plaza leading to the southern gates of the Temple Mount. They were joined by parties of pilgrims who made the long journey from the Jewish communities of Alexandria, Babylon, Antioch and elsewhere in the eastern Mediterranean region. The pilgrims found room in overflowing hostels or camped in the open. Wealthy families from outside the country maintained their own villas in Jerusalem. The strangest and most distinguished of these were members of the royal house of Adiabene, a small but prosperous kingdom in Parthia. The Queen Mother Helena and her son had become converted to Judaism, and came on visits to the Holy City. She built a lavish family tomb which became known as 'The Tomb of Kings'. The courtyard, the staircase and the catacomb area can still be visited today.

Jesus and the Temple

Jesus is the Greek form of the Hebrew name Joshua. Christ is a Greek word meaning the Messiah, i.e. the anointed one. Jesus was born about 4 or 5 BC into the family of a humble carpenter in the Galilean village of Nazareth. The events of his life are difficult to reconstruct, as there is no contemporary record of him. The chief sources of information are the Gospels of Mark, Matthew, Luke and John, written between forty and seventy years after the death of Jesus by evangelists of the early Christian Church, who had not themselves known him. The first Gospel, that of Mark, appears to have been composed in Rome between AD 67 and 70, after the deaths of Peter and Paul and during the Judean War. The Gospels of Matthew and Luke were apparently written in Palestine after the destruction of Jerusalem and the Temple in AD 70. They drew on the Gospel of Mark with considerable divergencies. These three are known as the 'synoptic Gospels', because they have enough in common

OPPOSITE 'The Circumcision' by Mantegna from the Uffizi triptych. The sacrifice of Isaac and Moses presenting the Tablets of the Law to the Israelites are depicted in the lunettes at the top.

to be written in parallel columns for comparison. The fourth Gospel, that of John, was produced about AD 100. It is markedly different in content and style from the earlier three, and is designed to present a coherent theology for the new church.

Jesus himself lived and died a Jew, and the followers he drew to him were all Jews. It was some time after his death that the sect started to admit gentile converts, and it eventually broke away altogether from Judaism. This was largely due to the influence of Paul – a Jew, originally called Saul, from Tarsus in Asia Minor.

Only Matthew and Luke refer to the birth of Jesus. They trace his descent to King David, and place his birth in David's native town of Bethlehem, thereby bringing the story of Jesus into line with the Jewish traditions about the coming of the Messiah. Luke alone adds that Joseph and Mary had the infant circumcised on the eighth day and presented him to the Lord in the Temple on the fortieth day, offering a sacrifice of two pigeons. John of Würzburg, a German priest who came on pilgrimage to Crusader Jerusalem some time between AD 1160 and 1170, records the legend that the foreskin of the infant Jesus was presented by an angel to the Emperor Charlemagne, and subsequently came into the possession of the Emperor Charles the Bald, who placed it in the church he had built in Charroux in France: '. . . which relic has been from that time to the present day solemnly kept and worshipped there' (Palestine Pilgrims' Text Society 1896).

Luke further relates that when the boy was twelve years old and had come with his family on the annual Passover pilgrimage to Jerusalem he stayed behind when his parents set out on the return journey. Three days later they found him in the Temple 'sitting among the teachers, listening to them, and asking them questions; and all who heard him were amazed at his understanding and his answers' (Luke 2: 46–47). When his parents rebuked him for the anxiety he had caused them, he replied: 'How is it that you sought me? Did you not know that I must be in my Father's house?' (Luke 2: 49). This incident does not appear in the other three Gospels, and is the only one in the New Testament relating to the childhood of Jesus.

The ministry of Jesus started in the Galilee when he was about thirty, and is usually estimated to have lasted a year until his death, though some conjecture that the period was up to three years. The synoptic Gospels do not mention Jesus coming to Jerusalem until the last week of his life. However John places a good deal of his ministry in and round the capital. He relates that at the Feast of Tabernacles (*Succot*), Jesus appeared and taught at the Temple, entering into a lengthy debate with his opponents, particularly over his claim to be the Son of God. In the excitement he provoked he was threatened with arrest by the authorities and with stoning by the mob. John also depicts Jesus attending the Feast

'The Purification of the Temple' by Bassano; Jesus drives the money-changers and merchants from the sanctuary.

of *Hanukkah* (Dedication) in Jerusalem: '. . . it was winter, and Jesus was walking in the temple, in the portico of Solomon. So the Jews gathered round him and said to him, "How long will you keep us in suspense? If you are the Christ, tell us plainly"' (John 10: 22–4). He was accused of blasphemy for saying that 'I and the Father are one' (John 10: 30), and once more was nearly stoned.

A week before Passover Jesus travelled with his disciples from Jericho up the mountain to Jerusalem, in the stream of pilgrims coming to celebrate the festival in the Temple. As usual at this time, the city was crowded. He found lodging outside the walls at Bethany, a village on the eastern slope of the Mount of Olives. On the Sunday he entered Jerusalem riding on a young donkey, while the crowd strewed branches and palm leaves before him and shouted 'Hosanna'. He visited the Temple and returned to Bethany. The next day he was back at the Temple Square, and caused a commotion by trying to drive out the traders and overturning the tables of the money-changers. He cried out that his Father's house was meant to be a place of prayer and not a den of robbers. According to the Gospels, all the following day was taken up in heated controversy with the priests, scribes, Pharisees and Sadducees who attacked his doctrines, asked him pointed questions and then rejected

The sound of the *shofar* greets the Passover pilgrims making their way up to Jerusalem in 1968.

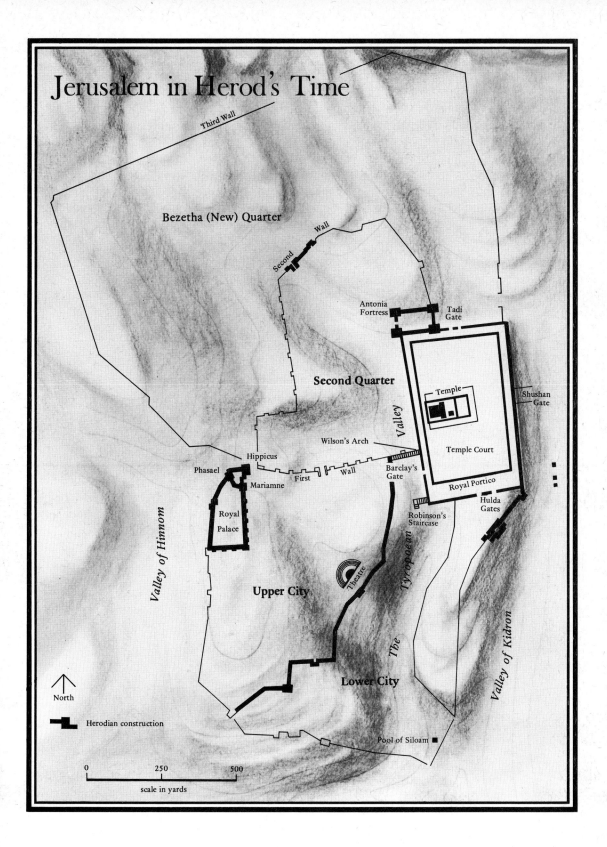

Jerusalem in Herod's Time

Third Wall

Bezetha (New) Quarter

Wall

Second

Antonia
Fortress

Tadi
Gate

Second Quarter

Temple

Shushan
Gate

Wilson's Arch

Valley

Temple Court

Hippicus

Phasael

First   Wall

Barclay's
Gate

Mariamne

Royal Portico

Royal
Palace

Robinson's
Staircase

Hulda
Gates

Valley of Hinnom

Upper City

Theatre

Tyropoeon

The

Valley of Kidron

Lower City

North

Herodian construction

Pool of Siloam

0   250   500

scale in yards

him. By this time there is attributed to Jesus foreknowledge of his imminent end.

Preparations were made for the Passover meal, which was to be the 'Last Supper' of Jesus with his twelve disciples. At dawn next morning he was arrested, after having been betrayed by Judas Iscariot.

The trial of Jesus went through a preliminary stage involving the high priest Caiaphas and, according to the three synoptic Gospels, also the Sanhedrin. He was brought before the Roman procurator Pontius Pilate, who sentenced him to death for sedition and had him crucified – the standard Roman form of execution. It is improbable that there was a Jewish trial at all. As modern authorities have pointed out, the account in the Gospels does not accord with the Jewish law and judicial procedures of the time. In any case, it is hard to imagine that the Sanhedrin, the highest Jewish tribunal of the country, would have been convened at a few hours' notice at the beginning of the Passover festival in order to try an obscure preacher from the Galilee. If such a session did take place, the venue would presumably have been the Chamber of Hewn Stone in the Temple court, the usual meeting-place for the Sanhedrin.

The other events connected with the death of Jesus were all close to the Temple Mount – the Garden of Gethsemane just across the Kidron valley; the house of Caiaphas, by tradition on the slope of Mount Zion; the Antonia fortress, where the Roman procurator is presumed to have sat in judgement; and Golgotha, where the Crucifixion took place, located, according to legend, where the Church of the Holy Sepulchre now stands in the Old City.

One of the New Testament books, The Epistle to the Hebrews, is interesting in that it vindicates Christianity in terms relating to the Temple cult. It is a sustained argument by an unknown author, some time before the destruction of the Temple in AD 70, addressed to a group of wavering Christians who thought of reverting to the ancestral Jewish faith. Christ is referred to as the high priest of a heavenly temple, of which the earthly Temple is but a poor copy. The death of Christ is described as a single, eternal sin-offering that has superseded the Temple sacrifices.

RIGHT 'In the time of King Josiah the land was purified. . . .' Josiah (640–609 BC) purged the Mosaic code of pagan influences and purified the Temple with the sacrifice of three thousand bulls. In this miniature from an eighteenth-century Ethiopian hymn book, Josiah, having left his kingly raiment in the Temple, oversees the sacrificial ritual.

OVERLEAF The events of the life of Jesus in Jerusalem, culminating in the Crucifixion, painted by an anonymous Flemish artist of the late fifteenth century.

ተወከፍኩ፡ለኢዮስያስ፡በፃ   ንዘ፡ትቂድሳ፡ወአጕኍይይ፡ጸሳኅ

እመ፡ሥዓ፡ለከ፡መሥዋዕተ፡   ትየ፡እምገጸ፡አሐዱ፡እንበሳ፞

ተድ፡ወጎሠዄ፡እግዚአብሔ   ከመ፡ይጐይዮ፡አኔሳፍ፡እንከ፞

ተወከፍ፡ተኃርባነ፡ጸሎትየ፡እ

12 Herod's Temple

Herod's structure continued to be called the Second Temple, though it was really a third one. There are three sources of information about it. The most important is Josephus, who was on the whole a careful reporter of matters he observed personally and was himself trained as a priest. His detailed account is substantially corroborated, though with some differences, by the oral traditions recorded in certain tractates of the Talmud. Lastly there is the evidence of archaeology, though that relates mainly to the external walls of the Temple Mount and its vicinity.

To understand Herod's plan one must grasp the topography of the city and the manner of its growth. The Jerusalem of Herod's time, like the walled Old City of today, occupied a low, irregular plateau. On the eastern side it was bounded by the valley or *nahal* (dry water-course) of the Kidron; to the west and south, by the valley of Hinnom that curves round to join the Kidron below the south-eastern corner of the Old City. From here a single wadi descends through the wilderness of Judea down to the Dead Sea.

The plateau within the fork of these two valleys is not on one level. It has a western ridge and an eastern ridge, separated by a third wadi, also coming down to the junction of the Hinnom and Kidron valleys. This central wadi is not named in the Bible, but Josephus refers to it as the Tyropean valley, 'the valley of the cheesemakers'. In the course of time it has filled up with debris, and remains today as a shallow depression. In Herod's time it was between 70 and 80 feet deeper than it is now.

David's city, like the Jebusite Jerusalem he had captured, occupied only the lower and narrower half of the eastern ridge, known as the Ophel. Solomon expanded it upward along the ridge. The broadest part was Mount Moriah at the top, where he built the Temple. A little below that, between the Temple and the beginning of David's city, Solomon put the palace complex. The city walls were then extended northward to include the Temple and the palace.

In about the eighth century, in the period of the divided monarchy, the first habitations were built on the slope of the western ridge across the Tyropean valley. The westward expansion continued, and it is probable that at the end of the First Temple period, when Jerusalem was destroyed by the Babylonians in 587 BC, it included what is now the Jewish Quarter of the Old City up to Mount Zion.

In the period of the return and the beginning of the Second Temple, the shrunken city once again occupied only the eastern ridge. The defence walls rebuilt by Nehemiah more or less followed those of Solomon's time. During the Hasmonean dynasty, in the second and first centuries BC, rapid expansion took place again over the western ridge, especially its higher part that became known as the Upper City. The late Hasmonean wall extended as far as the present Jaffa Gate, where Herod constructed his palace and citadel. The citadel guarded the western ridge of the city, as the Antonia fortress did the eastern ridge.

The ground sloped down steeply from the Temple site on three sides – on the east into the Kidron valley, on the west into the Tyropean valley and southward down the Ophel ridge. Only on the northern side was the Temple vulnerable to attack across ground that was more or less level. That side was secured by man-made defences: a wide moat or fosse protected by a wall and towers.

Solomon had done some levelling and filling in of Mount Moriah for his Temple and palace. Herod's bold plan called for turning the mount into a rectangular platform, thereby doubling the site. This enlarged Temple area was then linked with the Upper City and the palace by a bridge across the Tyropean valley. In creating the platform, the first phase was the construction of enormous retaining walls on the steep sides of the mount. Many of the blocks of limestone used for this purpose were quarried a few hundred yards away in the cavern still known as Solomon's Quarries or the Cave of Zedekiah. Others were hauled longer distances. These stones were not of uniform size, but all of them were far more massive than anything previously known in Judean building. One of them visible today is 40 feet long; another, 24 feet by 6 feet, has an estimated weight of over 100 tons. The outside face of these stones is dressed, and round the edges they have a chiselled margin 2 to 5 inches wide and about half-an-inch deep. No mortar was used, but the blocks were fitted together so precisely that two thousand years later one can hardly insert the blade of a penknife between them.

The cavity between Solomon's original wall and Herod's new one was filled with thousands of tons of earth. In the south-eastern corner, where the platform was 154 feet above the ground, about two-thirds of the space behind the retaining wall was filled. The uppermost third was taken up with a vaulted underground chamber 300 feet long, supporting the Temple platform. In the Crusader kingdom of Jerusalem this

OPPOSITE A section of the Western Wall; the huge blocks of Herodian masonry are distinguished by the marginal draft, cut around the edge of the face.

vaulted space was called Solomon's Stables, the name it still bears.

On the north-western edge of the Temple area the rock had to be cut away in order to bring it down to the level of the platform.

By these large-scale engineering operations Herod formed a flat rectangular site 35 acres in area, and almost a mile in circumference.

As far as is known there were six gates through the external walls to the Temple area. In the middle of the northern wall was the Tadi Gate. In the eastern wall, opposite the entrance to the Temple, was the Shushan Gate, with a picture engraved on it of Persepolis in Persia. It was a little to the south of the present walled-up Golden Gate, the Jewish name of which is the Mercy Gate. From the Shushan Gate arches carried a narrow bridge across the Kidron valley, called in the Talmud 'the heifer's gangway'. In the southern wall were the two Hulda Gates – the Double Gate and the Triple Gate. In the Western Wall Josephus refers to four gates and the *Mishna* to only one. In fact two have been found. One of them, the Priest's Gate, opened on to the bridge across the Tyropean valley, of which Wilson's Arch is a remnant. The other, Barclay's Gate (named after its American missionary discoverer), is low down near the south-western corner, just below the stairway leading up to the present Moors' Gate, through which one enters the *Haram esh-Sharif*.

The Porticoes and Courts

Round three sides of the Temple platform ran a covered portico with two rows of Corinthian columns spanned by cedar beams carrying a flat roof. The colonnade along the eastern side was known as Solomon's Portico. The one on the southern side of the square was larger and more elaborate, and was called the Royal Portico (or Stoa Basilica). Its central aisle was 100 feet high, with a richly decorated vaulted roof, and may have been used for assemblies. At its western end one could descend into the valley below by a monumental staircase of which Robinson's Arch (see page 162) is a relic.

The area of the Temple Square adjacent to the porticoes on all sides was known as the Court of the Gentiles, because it was open to the general public, whether Jewish or not. This public area was usually thronged with people. Under the porticoes were the stalls of traders, selling doves and other requirements for the sacrifices, and money-changers converting Roman coins into the shekels used for offerings.

The inner part of the Temple Square, round the sanctuary itself, was the consecrated area. It was enclosed by the *soreg*, a stone-latticed fence 5 feet high. On the fence were plaques written in Greek and Latin, forbidding Gentiles to pass through on pain of death. Two of these notices have been discovered.

This restricted area consisted of a series of courts on ascending levels, connected by staircases, with the Temple building at the highest point. First came the Court of the Women, beyond which females were

OPPOSITE The vaulted underground chamber in the south-eastern corner of the Temple Mount known as Solomon's Stables. Its name derives from Crusader times when it was used to stable the knights' horses.

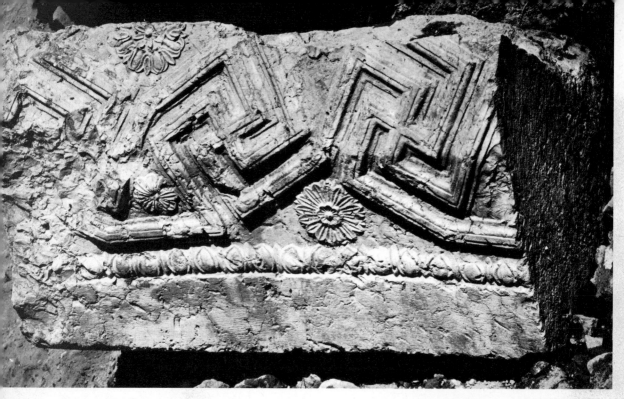

ABOVE A fragment of a frieze tablet
from the southern portico of the
Temple Mount.

RIGHT Inscriptions in Greek and
Latin warned strangers from entering
the sacred enclosure. A fragment of
one such tablet found in 1935.

not allowed. The square chambers in the four corners of this court were used respectively by Nazirites, by lepers and for the storage of wood and oil. A semicircular flight of steps led up from the Court of the Women through the magnificent Nicanor Gate into the narrow Court of the Israelites (the term used for Jews who were not priests or Levites). Here stood the Chamber of Hewn Stone used for meetings of the Sanhedrin.

Immediately beyond that lay the Court of the Priests, from which another flight of steps led up to the entrance of the Temple itself. In this court, in front of the Temple, was the great altar of burnt offerings, 48 feet square at its base and 24 feet high, with four horns projecting from the corners at the top. The priests mounted the altar by means of a ramp from the south. To one side of the altar were the slaughtering arrangements for the animals used in the sacrifices. (There was no slaughtering on the altar itself, except for pigeons.) To the other side was the large laver basin with twelve spigots for ritual washing. The Court of the Priests was entered by five gates, named for the purposes they served: flame, offerings, kindling, firstlings and water. In the north-eastern corner of the court an underground staircase led to the cistern used by the priests for ritual baths.

The Sanctuary   In planning the sanctuary building itself Herod's architects faced a problem. He was keen to have a more imposing structure than the one he was replacing. But the Second Temple erected after the return had followed the dimensions of Solomon's Temple, as set out in the First Book of Kings. Herod too was bound by the recorded internal length and breadth of the main hall (*Hechal*) and the inner sanctum (*Dvir*). However he seized on a passage in the Book of Chronicles (2 Chronicles 3: 4), which gave the vestibule or porch the fantastic height of 120 cubits (200 feet) instead of the 30 cubits (45 feet) given in Kings. That was what Herod meant when he told the assembly, in announcing his plans, that the existing Temple building was too low, and that he intended to rectify the defect.

At the eastern end of the Temple as reconstructed the vestibule (*Ulam*) was 150 feet high and 150 feet broad. Since it projected beyond the Holy Place on either side the ground plan of the whole Temple was T-shaped. Coming up the steps from the court inside, one entered the vestibule through a huge opening flanked by columns. A double door-way covered in gold opened into the *Hechal*, the main chamber. Above the doorway was suspended a spreading vine made of gold, its grape clusters and leaves representing individual donations. Inside the *Hechal* were the table of shewbread, the small incense altar and a golden seven-branched *menorah* (candelabrum). Only priests could enter this chamber. An embroidered curtain hanging on its far (western) wall concealed the entrance to the Holy of Holies, which remained the size it was in Solomon's Temple – 33 feet in length, breadth and height.

A number of small rooms used for storage, robing of priests and such purposes were ranged in three tiers round the sides and back of the Holy Place and the Holy of Holies. When a second storey was added the height of the whole building was brought to that of the front vestibule – that is, 150 feet – and it was covered by a flat roof.

Sir Charles Wilson, who carried out a survey of Jerusalem a century ago, gazed at the portions still visible of Herod's great wall around the Temple Mount, and wrote:

> Partly concealed as the walls are by rubbish, they still fill the traveller with admiration and they must, when fresh from the builders' hands, have been the finest specimens of mural masonry in the world. . . . Above all this stood the Temple, of pure white glittering stone covered, in part, with plates of gold, and surrounded by its courts and cloisters – a tout ensemble unsurpassed in magnificence by any temple of ancient times.

Archaeological Evidence

The pioneer of modern biblical research in Palestine was the American Dr Edward Robinson, a professor of theology in Boston and New York. He carried out extensive explorations in Egypt and Palestine in 1837 and 1852. In Jerusalem he made topographical studies and threw fresh light on the ancient city walls. At the southern end of the western wall of the Temple Mount he discovered a projection which he correctly identified as the beginning of a great stone arch stretching out in the direction of the Upper City, across the Tyropean valley. Later, the opposite pier of the arch, and the stones that had fallen from it, were excavated 40 feet below present ground level. This find was called Robinson's Arch. He assumed that it was a fragment of an arched bridge that in Herodian times had connected the Royal Portico on the Temple platform with the Upper City across the valley. This view was accepted until recently. The excavations carried on since 1968, under the direction of Professor Mazar of the Hebrew University, have established that Robinson's Arch was the beginning not of a bridge but of a great staircase that led from the Temple area down to the street along the bottom of the Tyropean valley.

In Victorian England there was a great surge of interest in biblical research, and in the scientific exploration of the Holy Land. The efforts were channelled through the Palestine Exploration Fund, founded in 1865 with Queen Victoria as its patron and the Archbishop of York as its president. The first project of the Fund was a methodical ordnance survey of old Jerusalem, with special attention to the Temple Mount. The survey was carried out by two remarkable captains in the Royal Engineers – Wilson (later Major-General Sir Charles Wilson) and Warren (later General Sir Charles Warren). As early as 1864 Wilson published the first exact map of Jerusalem. He also excavated the remains of an archway thrusting out from the Western Wall of the Temple Mount, about halfway along it. As with Robinson's Arch, it was assumed that Wilson's Arch marked the location of a bridge connecting the Temple area with the Upper City across the Tyropean valley. In this case the bridge theory has not been questioned.

From 1867 to 1870, under the auspices of the Palestine Exploration Fund, Warren conducted excavations round the outer walls of the Temple area, digging a number of shafts and underground tunnels with extreme difficulty. Warren's precise notes were a model for later archaeologists. To the body of information he provided about the Temple Mount and its walls little of importance was added for a century, until the current Mazar dig.

In Volume 1 of *Picturesque Palestine* (1880), Sir Charles Wilson states that 'Captain Warren's excavations for the Palestine Excavation Fund are, for their extent, for the boldness with which they were conceived, and for the skill with which they were carried out, without a parallel in the history of archaeological exploration'. Wilson then

Members of the 1868 expedition. From left to right: Captain Warren, Dr Joseph Barclay, Dr Chaplin, the British consul in Jerusalem at that time, and in the foreground, Corporal Philips, the official photographer to the expedition.

Extensive excavations of the Temple Mount since the mid-nineteenth century have revealed a wealth of information about the structure and functions of Herod's Temple. The research was pioneered by Dr Edward Robinson, after whom Robinson's Arch is named. A major contribution was made by the intrepid Captain Charles Warren in the 1860s but little more was done until the recent excavations by Professor Mazar.

The excavation of Wilson's Arch, illustrated for a book by Captain Wilson and Captain Warren, *The Recovery of Jerusalem*, published in 1871.

OPPOSITE PAGE
above left Robinson's Arch before excavation. Professor Mazar's work has established that it was the beginning, not of a bridge as first thought, but of a great staircase.
above right A member of the Royal Engineers' expedition exploring the fallen masonry of Robinson's Arch. A watercolour by William Simpson.
below Professor Mazar's excavations around the south-western corner of the Temple Mount.

quotes Warren's own account of one of the shafts by means of which he penetrated to the foundations of the Temple platform, in October 1867. The shaft was near the south-western angle of the wall, among a thicket of prickly pears. The soil was brought up by a rope running over an iron wheel, and the men went down on rope ladders. At a depth of 79 feet the ground suddenly gave way, and the men digging just saved themselves from dropping down into the darkness below. Beneath that point they found an overflow aqueduct from the Temple, along which Warren crawled for 400 feet through mud until he got stuck. He had to wriggle out backwards on his stomach, with the air supply diminishing rapidly.

Warren was one of the outstanding group of Gentile Zionists produced by nineteenth-century England. His book, *The Land of Promise* (1875), advocated a large-scale resettlement of Jews in Palestine, and predicted that with intensive development the country could eventually support a population of fifteen million. That was an astonishing display of optimism in a sober British engineer, as the Ottoman Palestine of his time was backward and much of it was barren.

The Mazar excavations round the south-western corner of the Temple Mount were begun in 1968, the year after the Old City had come under Israel control. The dig has revealed the approaches to Herod's Temple from the southern side, where the main access lay.

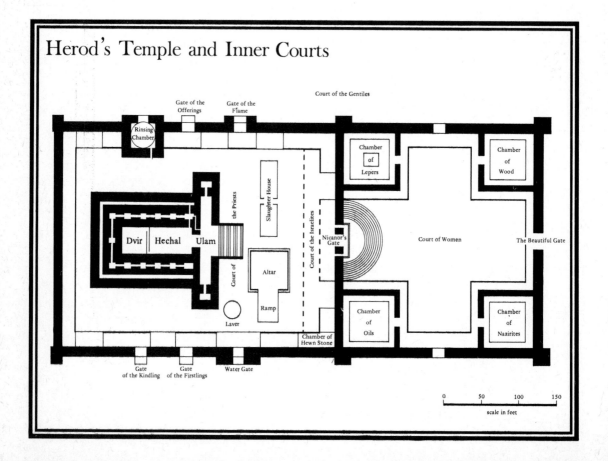

Herod's Temple and Inner Courts

And the Lord called Moses...

The public entered through two gates in the southern wall, now blocked up, called the Double Gate and the Triple Gate from the number of arches framing them. They are also known as Hulda's Gates after the seventh-century BC prophetess in the time of King Josiah, who was said to have conducted a teaching academy below the Temple Mount. These gates are 250 feet apart. From them underground galleries run into the Temple Mount and emerge up flights of steps on to the Temple platform. The Mazar expedition has uncovered a wide street paved with slabs of Jerusalem stone, and running all along the foot of the wall beneath the gates. A flight of stone steps 350 feet wide led down from the street to a spacious plaza that was almost as long as the Temple enclosure. In the centre of the plaza are the remains of a structure that housed ritual baths. Underneath the street, on the level of the plaza, were rows of shops serving the needs of the thousands of worshippers and pilgrims who thronged the area on feast days.

Near the south-western corner of the Temple Mount the street lies 40 feet below the present surface of the ground. When it was uncovered there were found on it blocks of stone and other fragments of masonry thought to have dropped or been flung down during the savage fighting before the destruction of AD 70. In places the paving stones of the street had been cracked by the impact.

OPPOSITE A reconstruction of the Second Temple according to Josephus.

The excavation has brought to light thousands of coins and pottery sherds. One of the most interesting finds is a piece of a stone Temple vessel, inscribed in Hebrew with the word *korban* (sacrifice), flanked by two birds.

These excavations near the south-western corner have exposed another nineteen courses of the great stone blocks of the retaining wall. They have also thrown more light on the water system of the Temple Mount, including underground cisterns, aqueducts and channels. An abundant supply of fresh water was required all the year round on the Temple Mount for the services and the crowds of worshippers. The turbulent history of Jerusalem also stressed the need for adequate reserves of water in case of siege. Yet Israel is rainless throughout the hotter part of the year, normally from May to November. Moreover there was no natural water source in the Temple area itself, the nearest one being the Gihon spring that flowed into the Pool of Siloam through Hezekiah's tunnel at the lower end of the Ophel ridge. The Temple Mount therefore had to rely on cisterns for water storage.

Underneath the platform of Herod's Temple is an elaborate system of thirty-four cisterns cut out of the rock. They were used for storing the run-off of the winter rainfall in the Temple area. The supply was augmented by water brought by an aqueduct from the Pools of Solomon, huge reservoirs just off the Bethlehem road. This water was brought on to the Temple Mount over the bridge of Wilson's Arch, and distributed among the cisterns by conduits. An overflow passage led under the southern wall to the Pool of Siloam lower down.

The cisterns are from 25 to 50 feet high and vary in size. The largest one was known as the Great Sea, and can hold over 2 million gallons. The total capacity of all the cisterns is estimated to be over 12 million gallons. Some of them were excavated out of the soft limestone, through a hole in the surface of the platform, leaving sections of the rock to support the roof. Others, in the northern part of the Temple area, were cut out of the rock as open tanks, and then given a vaulted roof, supported in some cases by arches.

Part of the underground excavations are relatively narrow and are reached by flights of steps, suggesting that they may have been internal passageways underneath the platform.

How the Temple Functioned

A wealth of material about the Temple services was afterwards available to the compilers of the Talmud from the accounts of the priests and rabbis who survived the destruction. The rituals and staff followed the pattern of the First Temple, but there were some important differences.

At the head of the Temple hierarchy was the high priest, who officiated on special occasions, resplendent in his golden vestments. His deputy, the *segan*, was in charge of the day-to-day administration. In the last period before the destruction the Pharisees were sufficiently strong

OPPOSITE The fountain of the Gate of the Chain in Jerusalem was supplied by water from the Pools of Solomon near Bethlehem. A wood engraving from *Jerusalem* by Sir Charles Wilson, published in 1889.

to impose their opinions on disputed questions of ritual, and the *segan* was their representative in the Temple establishment. Other hereditary officials, usually related to the high priest, were the treasurers (*gizbarim*), the trustees (*amarkalim*) and the controller (*catholicos*). The high priest, the deputy and these officials formed the governing body of the Temple.

For purposes of rotation the priests were divided into twenty-four watches (*mishmarot*). Priests who came to the Temple from other Judean towns and villages, or from the diaspora communities, were attached to specific *mishmarot* and participated in their work and meals. The priests were responsible for making the sacrifices, offering the incense, lighting the *menorah* and the Temple lamps, blessing the congregation and sounding trumpets for religious signals.

The Levites were also divided into twenty-four shifts. Their functions were twofold: they were the choir singers and musicians, and the gatekeepers, also responsible for cleanliness and other routine services.

The ordinary worshippers, simply called Israelites, were not allowed into the sanctuary building at all. They entered the courtyard before the Temple to join in the prayers, witness the sacrifices, receive the priestly blessing and undergo purification rites. They would remove their shoes and most of them would wear white robes on festivals and Sabbaths. After the return and Ezra's reforms, reciting prayers and reading portions of the Pentateuch became a feature of the services.

The first of the two regular daily sacrifices (*olat ha-tamid*), each of two lambs, started the service just after dawn, and the second ended them towards sunset. During this period the doors to the sanctuary were kept open. Thirteen priests chosen by lot took part in the rituals connected with the sacrifice. One such ceremony was the burning of incense by a single priest on the small incense altar inside the sanctuary, just before the entrance to the Holy of Holies. Each service ended with the pouring of wine libations and the singing of the Levite choir, usually reinforced with young boys. The songs were psalms and certain poetic passages from the Scriptures. The *hallel*, the hymn of praise still used in synagogues today, was sung in the Temple on festivals.

Music played an important part in the Temple services, especially in the Second Temple period. The choral singing of the Levites was accompanied by an orchestra. The main instrument used was the *kinnor*, a lyre of ten strings in general use in Canaan. This was the harp on which David played so sweetly. In modern Hebrew the term is used for a violin – thus the Hebrew name for the musical *Fiddler on the Roof* is *Kannar al ha-Gag*. The *nevel* was a somewhat larger lyre or harp with twelve strings, and a deeper tone than the *kinnor*. Other orchestral instruments were the *chalil*, a double-pipe wind instrument like a simple type of clarinet, and bronze cymbals. The *chotzotzerah* or silver trumpet was used only by priests for important ritual occasions – coronations, proclamations of war, sacrifice ceremonies, and for marking the beginning and the end of the Sabbath. Two long trumpets are prominent in the Temple booty carried by Judean captives, as depicted on Titus' Arch of Triumph in Rome. In the recent excavations at the south-western corner of the Temple Mount a stone was found that had apparently fallen from the top of the wall when the Temple was destroyed. Incised on it are the words *beit ha-tekiah* – 'the place of blowing'. It is presumed to have marked the position from which a priest would blow the trumpet to signal the Sabbath and its cessation.

The *shofar*, a ram's horn, is an instrument of ancient origin. It was originally used in war; in the taking of Jericho by Joshua the *shofar* figures as a military rather than a religious implement. Its use in modern synagogues on High Holy Days is connected with the loud blast that announced the Lord's presence on Mount Sinai. (English Bibles render this as a 'trumpet blast', but the Hebrew refers to 'the voice of the shofar'.)

In between the morning and afternoon *tamid* the various other types of sacrificial offerings were made on the altar. On the Sabbath, feast days and the days of the new moon there were additional sacrifices known as the *mussaf*. The fire on the altar was never allowed to go out and the wood was replenished even at night by the priests on duty. One of the lights on the *menorah* inside the Temple was also kept alive at all times and acted as an eternal flame. The priests were allowed to keep the hides of sacrificed animals – a valuable fringe benefit.

The shewbread consisted of twelve loaves placed in two rows on a golden table in the sanctuary, and changed every Sabbath. This custom was of primitive origin, when the bread was no doubt part of the food set out for the gods. The meat from the sacrifices, together with the shewbread and the first fruits, provided the ceremonial evening meal for the priests.

Sacrifices were acceptable from Gentiles as well. It was not uncommon for sacrifices to be offered and gifts to be made by foreign leaders who ruled over Judea, or who wished to make a gesture to it. During the periods when Judea was under external domination it was customary for the Temple itself to make special sacrifices in honour of the foreign ruler. This practice survives in the form of the special prayers Jewish communities make in synagogues today in honour of the royal families or the heads of state of their countries.

Two unusual kinds of sacrifice merit special mention. One is connected with the 'scapegoat'. A passage in Leviticus (16: 8–10) states that Aaron the high priest should on the Day of Atonement take two he-goats, and by drawing lots determine which of them would be sacrificed as a sin-offering to the Lord, and which would be sent away 'into the wilderness to Azazel' to carry away the sins of the people of Israel. It

OVERLEAF An impressive but imaginary representation of Herod's Temple.

has been disputed whether the name Azazel here refers to a place, or to some demoniac force or to the goat itself. In the Second Temple period the practice was to bind a thread of crimson wool on the head of the scapegoat, after the high priest had drawn the lots. A priest would then take the beast through the Temple gate and into the wilderness of Judea east of Jerusalem, where it was pushed over a high cliff, at a place that has not definitely been located. The Hebrew expression *sa'ir le-azazel* literally means 'the hairy one to azazel', and in modern Hebrew is used for a scapegoat in the general sense. Most ancient Near Eastern religions had some parallel sacrifice, animal or human.

The ritual of the red cow or heifer also dated back in the Old Testament to the desert period of Exodus, and was retained throughout the Temple period. For purification of someone defiled by contact with a corpse, the ashes of an unblemished red heifer were used. They were mixed with spring water and other ingredients and used for sprinkling. The origin of this rite is obscure; one theory connects it with the belief that red, the colour of blood, is symbolic of the source of life.

The burning of incense was an important feature of the sacrificial rites in the Temple, as it was in all ancient religions of the Near East. The idea was that what was pleasing to human beings would please their deities as well, and that included not only food and wine but also sweet odours. There was no doubt a functional side as well. In a hot climate, the Temple precincts crowded with worshippers, the carcasses of the slaughtered animals and the lack of sanitation together produced smells that were uncomfortable and regarded as injurious to health.

The Hebrew use of incense was probably absorbed from surrounding pagan religions, and in the prophetic books there are strong reservations about it, as being associated with idolatry in the Canaanite high places. In Hosea the Lord complains about his chosen people that 'they kept sacrificing to the Ba'als and burning incense to idols' (Hosea 11: 2). Jeremiah criticizes the Israelite women for offering incense to the queen of heaven, a reference to the Egyptian moon-goddess.

According to Leviticus, the original recipe for the incense (Hebrew: *ketoret*) used in the desert Tabernacle contained equal parts of four ingredients: stacte, onycha, galbanum and frankincense.

Stacte was for long identified with resin from the balsam tree, but it is now thought to have been balm – drops of gum from a certain desert bush, with a vanilla smell when burnt. These bushes grew plentifully in the land of Gilead across the Jordan, from where the gum was exported to neighbouring countries. It was regarded as possessing medicinal properties, hence Jeremiah's despairing cry: 'Is there no balm in Gilead? Is there no physician there?' (Jeremiah 8: 22). Onycha was the upper part of the shell of a mollusc found in the Red Sea area. Galbanum was a gum-resin obtained from the Syrian fennel, a plant with carrot-like feathery leaves. Frankincense was also a gum-resin, from a type of terebinth tree in south-western Arabia. It came in by the spice route along the Red Sea. Called *lavan* because of its whitish colour it was used not only in the incense but also with burnt-offerings and shewbread.

During the Second Temple period smaller quantities of other substances were added to the incense mixture, as is reflected in the description by Josephus and in the relevant treatise in the Babylonian Talmud. The additional ingredients included myrrh, a gum-resin from camphor bushes; cassia, a cinnamon plant from which a perfumed oil was extracted; cinnamon bark; spikenard, another aromatic plant, also used for perfume; saffron, the yellow flowers of a type of crocus, also used for yellow dyes and for food flavouring; Cyprus wine; a pinch of salt from Sodom; *maaleh ashan* (literally 'smoke-raiser'), from an unknown plant; and *kipat ha-Yarden*, probably a species of cyclamen from the banks of the river Jordan.

Palestine lay on the enormously lucrative spice routes from Arabia, eastern Africa and India. Spices and aromatic oils for incense and perfume were of great value, and it was a costly item on the annual budget of the Temple, which used an estimated 600 pounds of incense a year. The incense was burnt twice daily, at the times of the morning and evening sacrifices, on the small golden altar that stood inside the sanctuary near the doorway to the Holy of Holies. When the high priest entered the Holy of Holies once a year on the Day of Atonement, he bore with him a censer of incense. In the later Second Temple period this fact gave rise to one of the many points of dispute on ceremonial details. The Sadducees held that the high priest's censer had to be lighted before he entered, lest he should inadvertently see the face of the Lord. The Pharisees pooh-poohed this ruling.

The exact prescription for the Temple incense was a closely guarded secret of one family, the priestly house of Avtinas, and it was prepared only in their home. In order to demonstrate that the incense was not diverted to improper use the ladies of the household wore no perfume.

Associated with the incense was the 'holy anointing oil'. The Book of Exodus gives its ingredients – olive oil blended with myrrh, cinnamon, aromatic cane and cassia – and directs that it be used to consecrate the Tabernacle, the Ark, the altars and the sacred utensils, and for the ordaining of Aaron and his sons as priests.

In the Second Temple period this special oil was used to anoint kings and high priests in the Temple when they assumed office, hence the term 'Messiah', which means 'the anointed one'. The residue of the oil was said to have been hidden by King Josiah (640–609 BC) and the oil was not used in the Second Temple period.

Large funds were required for the upkeep of the Temple – its maintenance and repairs, its numerous priests and attendants, and the cost of those sacrifices and offerings that were communal, therefore provided at the expense of the Temple itself. The most regular source of income was the half-shekel due, a kind of tax levied on all Jewish males from the age of twenty, collected in the diaspora communities as well. Some individual rulers, Persian or Seleucid, provided subsidies to the Temple as part of a policy of supporting religious shrines in their domains. The Temple was also endowed with generous gifts and bequests from wealthy individual donors. For instance the Nicanor Gate of burnished copper was presented by a rich Alexandrian Jew of that name. The treasury furthermore acted as a kind of bank or trust fund for widows, orphans and well-to-do families. All in all, with its stores of gold and silver, vessels and furniture, its revenues from Judea and abroad, and its deposits, the Temple was a well-endowed institution.

The Temple Scroll

The Temple Scroll, acquired for Israel by Professor Yigael Yadin in 1967, is considered to be one of the Dead Sea Scrolls from the caves in Qumran. It is longer than any of the others, measuring over 28 feet, and its date is estimated at about 100 BC.

A good part of the contents is devoted to aspects of the Temple, hence the name by which it is now known. Other sections deal with a variety of subjects: a collection of laws and rulings on ritual cleanliness, burials and other matters; rules for sacrifices and celebrating festivals; and a section on military arrangements, such as the composition of the royal bodyguard and mobilization plans in an emergency.

The section on the Temple gives a plan following that for the Tabernacle in the Book of Exodus. The sanctuary is surrounded by three square courts, one within the other. The middle and outer courts each have twelve gates, named after the twelve tribes of Israel.

The particulars in the scroll do not correspond to those in the accepted sources, notably Josephus and the *Mishna*. Presumably the sect to whom the scroll belonged was not concerned with an accurate description of the existing Temple and its cult, but with its own traditions and beliefs as to what should exist.

13 The Destruction

Under the Roman procurators the cycle of repression and reprisal brought Judea to the edge of open revolt. Within the Jewish community there was a spectrum of attitudes ranging from open collaboration with the authorities to an activist call for armed resistance. In between, the bulk of the populace felt a sullen but passive resentment. The most extreme group was the Zealots, whose religious fervour drove them to violence against the foreign rulers, and even against the Jewish moderates. Unrest was fanned by the Messianic expectations in the air. The recurrent famine conditions, the poor crops and heavy taxes increased the endemic brigandage with its nationalist overtones.

The last of the Herodian dynasty, Agrippa II, tried to act as an intermediary between the authorities and the turbulent population, especially on touchy problems concerning the Temple and religion. Although his political status was only that of tetrarch of the north-eastern part of the country (to which he was appointed in AD 54), he had been given authority to supervise the Temple and appoint the high priest. His complete loyalty to his Roman masters made him suspect in the eyes of the Judean dissidents. He lacked the personality of his father Agrippa I or of his great-grandfather Herod, and was dominated by his sister Berenice – in fact there was persistent scandal concerning the relations between them. His task was made no easier by the Jewish factional disputes over the appointment of the high priest.

Agrippa himself fell foul of the Temple authorities. When in Jerusalem he used as his residence the old Hasmonean palace facing the Temple Mount across the Tyropean valley. He built an addition to the palace from which one could see into the inner court of the Temple. The priesthood objected to this, and erected a wall to block the view. At Agrippa's request the procurator Festus ordered the wall to be knocked down. The Jewish leaders appealed to the Emperor Nero in Rome, and won their point through the sympathy of the Empress Poppaea.

Agrippa reacted by dismissing the high priest and appointing a more amenable one. When the revolt broke out Agrippa and Berenice identified themselves completely with the Roman side and were eventually given political asylum in Rome.

The simmering discontent came to a head under the procurator Gessius Florus (AD 64–6). A venal and heavy-handed colonial governor, he assumed that any local trouble could be dealt with by a show of firmness. Neither he nor his superiors in Antioch or Rome sensed how close Judea was to open revolt, and they were taken off guard when it came.

Florus confiscated 17 talents of silver from the Temple treasury, apparently to cover arrears in the annual Judean tribute to Rome. This action caused a storm of protest. Street demonstrators ridiculed him by going among the crowd with begging baskets to collect small coins for the penurious procurator. Enraged at this public insult, Florus led a body of troops to Jerusalem from Caesarea, and demanded that the Sanhedrin produce the culprits. When the council was unable to comply the Roman soldiers destroyed the market place in the Upper City, killing hundreds of people. The reinforcements Florus despatched to the Antonia garrison were driven back by rioters, who based themselves on the Temple Mount and smashed the colonnade giving access to the Antonia. The alarmed procurator withdrew most of his troops from Jerusalem. Agrippa proposed to the Sanhedrin a compromise whereby the arrears of tribute would be collected and spent on repairing the damaged Temple colonnade. But the situation had now got out of hand. Agrippa exhorted the crowd to keep order, but was hissed and had stones flung at him. He too left Jerusalem, never to return.

Trouble broke out also in the provincial capital, Caesarea. For some time there had been communal tension in the city between the Jewish and the Greek (Hellenist) inhabitants. Florus accepted a large sum of money from some of the wealthier Jews and promised them his support, but was conveniently absent when a pogrom broke out against the local Jewish community. A number of them were killed and the rest fled, causing a shock-wave through the country.

Younger and more militant elements among the Temple priesthood forced through an act of political defiance – suspension of the sacrifice that was regularly offered in honour of the emperor.

Exciting news was received in the city – a band of Zealots, led by one Menachem, had captured the rock fortress of Masada by overwhelming the small Roman garrison in a surprise attack. Menachem and his men entered Jerusalem. The rebels gained control of the Temple Mount and the Lower City, took the Antonia fortress by storm, overran the Upper City and penned up the remaining Roman soldiers in the citadel. The Romans surrendered on condition that they would be spared, but were killed by the mob after they had laid down their arms.

RIGHT Pompey and his troops defile the Temple by entering the Holy of Holies; from a fifteenth-century manuscript illustrated by Fouquet.

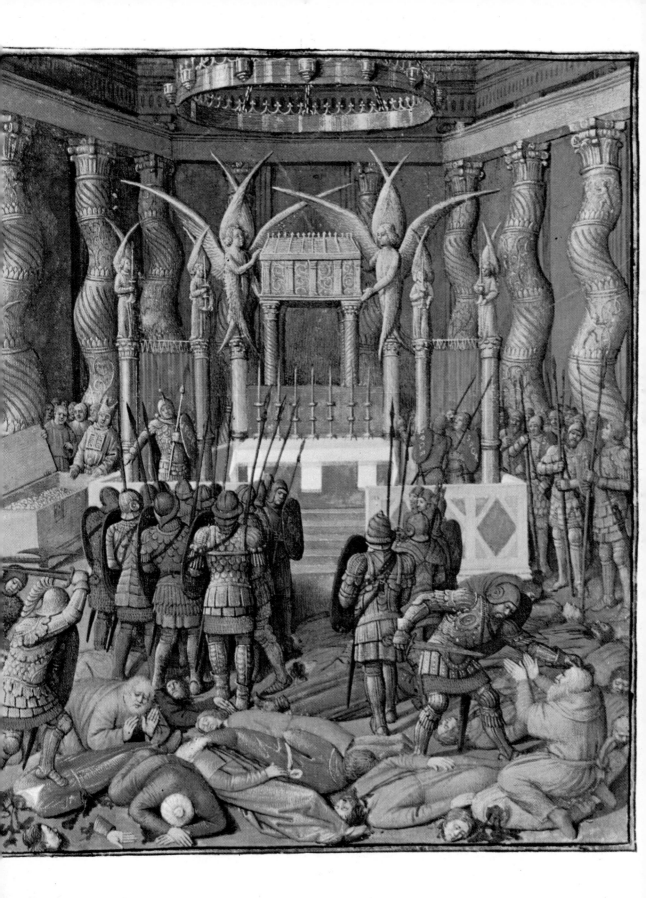

Disorder spread through the countryside. It was early in AD 66. The Jewish War against Roman rule had started. It was to end in disaster five years later.

It was clear to Rome that its rule in Judea had collapsed. Cestius Gallus, the legate in Syria, was sent marching southward with a substantial force. He reached Jerusalem and laid siege to it, but the defenders showed no inclination to surrender, and he did not have the means to take the strongly fortified city by assault. After six months he withdrew. In the pass of Horon, where Judah the Maccabee had won his first major victory against the Seleucid army, the Roman forces were ambushed by the Judean insurgents. Their retreat turned into a rout and all their baggage and siege equipment was lost.

Judea had regained its independence under a revolutionary leadership in Jerusalem, answerable to an assembly of citizens that met in the Temple court. New coins were struck – shekels, half-shekels and smaller bronze money – and stamped 'Year One', 'Year Two' and so on. Preparations were made to withstand a Roman invasion. The country was divided into military districts, and work was speeded up to strengthen the fortifications of Jerusalem and strong-points elsewhere.

It would be pleasant to record that this newly won freedom was accompanied by national unity and harmony. The actual story, as reported by Josephus in great detail, was a melancholy one of in-fighting, intrigue and violence among the Jews themselves.

Imperial Rome was not prepared to swallow defeat and indignity at the hands of its Judean subjects. The Emperor Nero placed in command one of his top generals, Vespasian, who had distinguished himself in the campaigns in Gaul and Britain. Vespasian marched south from Antioch with a large and well-equipped army of seasoned troops and auxiliaries. His son Titus brought up a legion from Egypt to join him. The Roman plan of operation was to subdue the Judean countryside piecemeal, thereby isolating Jerusalem and leaving the assault on it to the last.

The first area to be attacked was the Galilee, in the spring of AD 67. The Jewish defence had been put in the charge of a remarkable thirty-year-old priest sent from Jerusalem – Joseph ben Matthias, later known to the world by his Latin name of Josephus Flavius. He held out for two months in the fortress of Jotapata, then surrendered, went over to the Roman side and became labelled as a traitor by his own people.

By the beginning of the autumn rains all the strongholds in the Galilee had been overcome. During the winter Vespasian reconquered the area east of the Jordan, the coastal region and Idumea in the south. Except for a few isolated strong-points, only Jerusalem and a small enclave round it were left in Jewish hands.

The assassination of Nero in AD 68 plunged the Roman empire into a crisis of leadership. When the news reached Vespasian in Caesarea he

The leaders of the first revolt had new coins struck to commemorate their newly-won independence. This shekel is stamped 'Year Three'.

LEFT A fourteenth-century French miniature of the Crusaders storming the walls of Jerusalem.

decided to wait out the political convulsion and in the meantime suspended his military campaign. He was proclaimed emperor in AD 69 and
departed for Rome. Titus, then twenty-nine years old, was left to resume
the Judean campaign.

During the respite the dissension in Jerusalem grew sharper. At the
beginning of the revolt the Temple precincts had been occupied by a
group of Zealots led by Eleazar ben Simon. A respected former high
priest, Ananas, rallied the more moderate citizens in an effort to oust
Eleazar's men by force. Eleazar appealed for support to the Idumeans,
charging that Ananas planned to betray the city. A large contingent of
Idumeans gained entry to Jerusalem and joined the Zealots.

John of Gischala (*Gush Halav*), a redoubtable partisan leader in the
Galilee, escaped from the Roman operations there, reached Jerusalem
and became the dominant commander in the city. The Temple services
had continued, and the Zealots who held the Temple Mount allowed
access to worshippers. Taking advantage of this, John of Gischala
smuggled in a number of his men and gained control, absorbing
Eleazar and his group.

John's position was now challenged by a Zealot leader more radical
than himself, Simon ben Giora. He gathered a partisan force in the
south, and entered the city in April AD 69. After more confused strife
Simon was left in command of the Upper City, the western part of
Jerusalem; and John of the eastern ridge, including the Temple compound and the Antonia fortress. Only with the arrival of Titus before the
gates would they co-operate against the common foe.

Conditions in the city had deteriorated. Its population was swollen by
streams of refugees from the country areas, and by the thousands of
fighting men who gathered in the capital from elsewhere. Food supplies
were running short. Political control had passed into the hands of the
more militant factions. All the elements suspected of being willing to
negotiate a surrender were crushed. Many of them were executed after a
hasty trial before special tribunals, in a manner that was to be repeated in
the Jacobin phase of the French Revolution eighteen centuries later.
Facing the threat of famine and weakened by internal conflict, the Holy
City turned in the spring of AD 70 to meet the delayed Roman assault. It
did so with a heroism and a fortitude that has few parallels in history.

The Siege   Titus' army numbered 80,000 men, as against 25,000 Jewish fighters
within the city. The backbone of the Roman force was the four crack
Roman legions that converged on Jerusalem. The Tenth marched up
from Jericho in the east and camped on the Mount of Olives, where it
was held in reserve. The Twelfth approached from the west. Titus himself led the Fifth and the Fifteenth along the mountain road from the
north, together with the bulk of the auxiliary troops. From the top of
Mount Scopus he gazed down on the famous city he had studied from

staff reports and maps but not seen until now. On the eastern edge of Jerusalem the Temple platform was a gleaming, sunlit square, with the sanctuary surrounded by its courts and porticoes. Beyond it stretched the dense fabric of houses. With the trained eye of a soldier, Titus traced the city's topography and defences. On the north-western side the New Quarter of Bezetha was enclosed by the so-called Third Wall; it had been built but left incomplete by King Agrippa I, and the present defenders had hurriedly filled the gap. The wall ran northward from Herod's Citadel (where the Jaffa Gate now stands), looped round to the east and back along the edge of the Kidron valley to the corner of the Temple Mount. The Second Wall was a shorter one, from the citadel round the head of the Tyropean valley to the Antonia fortress. The citadel and the Antonia fortress were again linked by a section of the First Wall, which contained the older parts of the city.

Titus decided to launch his main thrust from the north-west at Agrippa's Wall into the New Quarter. The next phase would be to break through the Second Wall. After that he would develop a two-pronged assault. One force would swing eastward to take the Antonia fortress and the Temple Mount. Titus had not failed to note that (as the Roman historian Tacitus later described it) 'the Temple itself was a strong fortress in the nature of a citadel. The fortifications were built with consummate skill, surpassing in art as well as labour all the rest of the works. The very porticoes that surrounded it were a strong defence.' The rest of the Roman troops would turn southward to attack Herod's citadel, the key to the Upper City.

The main Roman force was concentrated in a camp west of the Third Wall. The sappers laboured on the platforms of earth and timber that would enable the battering rams to be brought up to the wall. Covering fire for these works was provided by archers and spearmen, while the ballistas or giant slings acted as heavy artillery, hurling rocks of over 100 pounds up to 500 yards into the city. The defenders fought back fiercely; they made repeated sorties and showered down arrows, stones and fire-brands. But by the seventeenth day the Third Wall had been breached and the Roman troops poured into the New Quarter. Four days later they had broken through the Second Wall and occupied the area behind it by fierce hand-to-hand fighting in the narrow alleyways.

Reluctant to sustain or inflict heavier casualties, Titus sent messages urging surrender. They were rejected. Simon ben Giora in the Upper City, and John of Gischala in the Antonia fortress and the Temple Mount, prepared to fight to the bitter end. Again Titus moved up his siege engines and constructed platforms for them. Again the defenders fought like tigers to disrupt the preparations and to prevent the battering rams doing their deadly job. Fire was the most potent Jewish counter-weapon. At the Antonia fortress John's men dug a tunnel under the

The siege of Jerusalem, AD 70. After four months Titus' forces broke into the city and the Temple was set on fire. This engraving illustrates the episode in an eighteenth-century English edition of Josephus' *Works*.

Roman platform and supported it with bitumen-coated logs. When the tower with the battering ram was moved into position, the logs were set on fire and the tunnel collapsed. In minutes the battering ram and tower were enveloped in flames. At the citadel end of the wall two rams were brought into action, but a suicide squad of three Zealots rushed out with firebrands and set the two battering rams alight before they were themselves killed.

After this double setback Titus called a halt and took counsel with his senior officers. The strength of the defences and the fanatical courage of the men defending them made it a difficult and costly affair to press on with the assault. On the other hand, time was on the side of the Roman besiegers. Conditions in the city were grim indeed, judging by the hundreds of corpses flung over the walls, the pitiful stories of deserters and the emaciated citizens who were caught venturing out at night to look for edible plants. Hunger and disease were powerful allies for the Romans; Titus would now encourage them to do their fearful work. His soldiers constructed a siege wall $4\frac{1}{2}$ miles long round the still defended part of the city, thus tightening the blockade around it.

In mid-summer, when the plight of the defenders was desperate and they still stubbornly refused to surrender, a fresh attack was thrown against the Antonia fortress. This time it was successful. Four battering rams were brought up and breached the wall. Roman shock-troops fought their way through and drove the Jews back into the Temple compound where they blocked themselves in against access from the fortress. John had strengthened the inner defences of the Mount by constructing four additional towers. By this time Temple sacrifices had been abandoned – there were no animals left to sacrifice.

Tacitus the Roman historian, like Josephus before him, was clearly reluctant in his account to blame Titus (who later succeeded his father as emperor) for the destruction of the Temple. After the capture of the Antonia fortress, writes Tacitus, 'Titus had now gained an eminence from which his war-like engines could play with advantage on the enemy. The approaches to the temple lay exposed to the valour of the legions. To save the sanctuary and even to protect the people in the exercise of a religion which with every Roman he condemned as a perverse superstition, was still the wish of his heart. ...' Again a demand for the surrender of the garrison was rejected. Before attacking the Temple Mount Titus called another council of his senior staff and commanders, and put to them the question of whether the Temple should be destroyed. Opinions were divided: 'Several thought it was not right to tear down a sacred edifice, renowned among the works of man; by sparing it they would leave a witness of Roman moderation; in destroying it they would mar the Roman name with a lasting blemish of cruelty.' But these scruples were rejected by a tough-minded majority of the council.

The principal officers [reports Tacitus] were of the opinion that nothing less than the utter destruction of the Temple would secure a lasting peace. A building which the Jews themselves had made a theatre of blood, ought not, they contended, to be any longer considered as a place of worship. It was rather a citadel in which the garrison remained in force and, since the proffered capitulation was rejected, ought to be given up to the fury of an enraged soldiery.

The battering rams were again pushed forward. After six days of pounding they had not damaged the wall of the Temple Mount, nor had attempts to scale it by building a ramp succeeded. The Romans managed to set the gates alight, and picked commandos battled their way in. The break-through is described by another Roman historian, Dio Cassius:

Though a breach was made in the wall by means of engines, nevertheless, the capture of the place did not immediately follow even then. On the contrary, the defenders killed great numbers who tried to crowd through the opening, and they also set fire to some of the buildings nearby, hoping thus to check the further progress of the Romans, even should they gain possession of the wall. In this way they not only damaged the wall, but at the same time unintentionally burned down the barrier around the sacred precincts, so that entrance to the temple was now laid open to the Romans. Nevertheless, the soldiers because of their superstition did not immediately rush in; but at last, under compulsion from Titus, they made their way inside.

Fighting every inch of the way, the Zealots were pressed back into the inner courts of the Temple enclosure and prepared to sell their lives dearly. Dio Cassius dramatically describes the last stand:

Then the Jews defended themselves much more vigorously than before, as if they had discovered a piece of rare good fortune in being able to fight near the temple and fall in its defence. The populace was stationed below in the court; the senators (the members of the Sanhedrin) on the steps, and the priests in the sanctuary itself, and though they were but a handful fighting against a far superior force, they were not conquered until part of the temple was set on fire. Then they met death willingly, some throwing themselves on the swords of the Romans, some slaying one another, others taking their own lives, and still others leaping into the flames, and it seemed to everybody, and especially to them that so far from being destruction, it was a victory and salvation and happiness that they perished along with the temple.

The end came when the sanctuary itself was set alight. Soon, in the words of Josephus: 'The flames of fire were so violent and impetuous that the mountain on which the Temple stood resembled one large body of fire, even from its foundations.' Through the pall of smoke the Roman soldiers ran amok, looting and killing. Titus and his entourage managed to enter the sanctuary before it was destroyed and carried off some of the vessels and furnishings that later reached Rome. It was the ninth day of the month of Av, the anniversary of the date on which Nebuchadnezzar's Babylonian soldiers had destroyed the First Temple and sacked Jerusalem more than six centuries earlier.

The two Zealot leaders and the remnant of their followers held out for another month in Herod's citadel in the Upper City, until it fell. On the orders of Titus the city was razed, except for the three towers of the citadel and the western section of the city wall, left as protection for the Tenth Legion, which remained on as a garrison.

Those inhabitants who were not butchered were hauled off to be thrown to wild animals in the arenas of Caesarea, Antioch and Rome, or were sold as slaves. A number of the young men were taken in chains to Rome and paraded in the triumphal processions of Vespasian and Titus. The captured Temple vessels were displayed as trophies in the official triumph, notably the great golden seven-branched candelabrum from the Holy Place of the Temple. Simon ben Giora was forced to march in the triumphal procession with a rope round his neck, then publicly executed at the forum, the fate custom demanded for captive enemy generals. Coins were struck to commemorate the occasion, showing a woman in a posture of mourning and the words *Judaea capta*. Titus had a great triumphal arch built that still stands in Rome, with scenes from his victory procession depicted on it in bas-relief. A conspicuous place is taken by the candelabrum carried by Judean captives. As personal souvenirs, Titus kept in his own palace the curtain that had hung before the entrance to the Holy of Holies and a copy of the Hebrew Scriptures. In this fashion the world's greatest power boasted of the crushing of a little freedom-loving nation, and the wiping out of an historic city and a sacred shrine.

Vespasian's *Judaea capta* coin, AD 70.

Chronology of the siege of AD 70

early April	Titus takes up position and starts preparations
8 May	attack launched
25 May	Third Wall breached
30 May	Second Wall breached
16 June	assault on Antonia fortress and citadel
20 July	renewed assault
28 August	destruction of Temple
28–30 August	Lower City sacked
about 30 September	citadel taken, Upper City sacked

The End of the Revolt

After the fall of Jerusalem three strongholds in the south-eastern part of the country remained in Zealot hands: Herodium, Macherus and Masada. Herodium, east of Bethlehem, was taken soon after by the new Roman legate, Lucilius Bassus. Macherus, on the plateau east of the Dead Sea, fell in AD 72, after a sharp siege. The toughest nut to crack was the Masada rock fortress, invested by Bassus' successor, Flavius Silva. In May AD 73 his troops broke through to the top, having built a ramp on a saddle on the western side. Before they could be captured alive, the nine hundred and sixty men, women and children who had held out on Masada for three years took their own lives on the urging of their commander, Eleazar ben Yair. The account by Josephus is one of the most poignant stories in the annals of warfare. With the fall of Masada the last embers of the great revolt were stamped out.

Josephus

But for one man, little would have been known today about the end of the Jewish state and with it the end of the Second Temple.

After his surrender in the Galilee Josephus was taken in chains to Vespasian's headquarters and jailed. In AD 68, after news had been received that Nero had died in Rome, Josephus shrewdly won Vespasian's regard by quoting an alleged Messianic belief that the master of the world would come out of Judea. The captive was released when Vespasian became emperor a year later. He attached himself to the Roman general, then to his son Titus, after Vespasian had returned to Rome. Josephus was with Titus during the siege of Jerusalem and on several occasions was used as an interpreter when the Roman commander tried to persuade the Jewish defenders to surrender.

It is hard to imagine what emotions went through the mind of the defector, as he witnessed from the enemy lines the death agony of his city and his nation. He obviously was out of sympathy with the Zealot leadership and thought further resistance as futile as it would be disastrous. There were other important Jews who identified themselves with the Roman rulers in the conflict. For instance King Agrippa II raised a force to fight with them, while Tiberius Alexander, the apostate nephew of Philo of Alexandria and a former procurator of Judea (AD 46–8), served as chief-of-staff to Titus during the siege. Still Josephus had no official post to justify, and some strange compulsion must have kept him on the scene as a first-hand observer of the tragic events. It may be that he had already resolved to record them for posterity.

After the war was over Josephus was well rewarded. He was granted Roman citizenship, permitted to settle in Rome, allotted a court pension and given facilities for writing a history of the conflict. He died about thirty years later without returning to his native land.

The first of two major works published by Josephus in Rome was *The Jewish War*. He wrote the original version, as he himself states, 'in my vernacular' Aramaic, but this has not been preserved. He was then en-

ABOVE An eighteenth-century French engraving of the siege of Masada.

BELOW The Zealot synagogue at Masada excavated by Professor Yigael Yadin.

couraged by Vespasian and Titus to adapt and translate it into Greek, and this is the version that has come down to us. It had on the whole a pro-Roman bias and was sharply critical of the Jewish leaders of the revolt, especially the Zealots.

Josephus then settled down to compile a monumental history in Greek of the Jewish people, published in AD 93 as *The Antiquities of the Jews*. The first part is a summary of the Old Testament, probably based on the Septuagint. The narrative ends in AD 66, on the eve of the Jewish War. Two shorter works are extant: *The Life of Josephus Flavius*, an auto-biographical memoir; and *Against Apion*, a defence of the Jewish faith and nation in reply to anti-Semitic propaganda of the time.

Some Greek copies of the writings of Josephus have survived from the Middle Ages and two versions in Latin translation from the fourth century AD. The works were translated into English and published in 1737 by the Reverend William Whiston, an eccentric mathematician and clergyman who succeeded Newton as a Cambridge professor.

The Copper Scroll

Was the accumulated wealth of the Temple treasury split up and buried in a number of hiding places before the siege of Jerusalem? This is one of the fascinating theories about the Copper Scroll, one of the Dead Sea Scrolls. It was found in 1952 in the earthen floor of Cave Three at Qumran. Physically there were two scrolls, as one piece had come away from the rest and been rolled up separately. The metal was too corroded for unrolling; by a very delicate operation it was cut up and peeled off strip by strip. When the strips were assembled most of the text inscribed on them was legible. It was in colloquial Hebrew that could be dated to the first century AD – that is, to the period of the destruction of the Second Temple.

The contents of the Copper Scroll purport to be an inventory of sixty-four caches of treasure deposited in different places in the Jerusalem–Jericho area. The directions and clues given in the scroll are so obscure that no single place has been definitely identified, and no portion of the treasure discovered. The scroll was no doubt composed so that it could be understood only by persons who were party to the secrets.

Another puzzling feature of the scroll is the fabulous quantity and value of the treasure listed in it. The gold and silver alone would add up to about 200 tons. This has suggested to some scholars that the list is fictitious, or maybe just a collection of legends about buried treasure-trove. If so it would be hard to explain why the author or authors should have gone to the great trouble and cost of inscription on copper, a material rarely used for documents, and only when a permanent record was wanted. Maybe the quantities were inflated and falsified on purpose, as part of the 'cover-up'. On the other hand if the contents were meant to be a secret, why was the document originally designed as a wall plaque before it was rather crudely rolled into two scrolls? The whole matter

remains a puzzle to which no convincing solution has been found.

It was thought at first that this was one of the Dead Sea Scrolls belonging to the nearby Qumran monastery which was occupied by a sect akin to the Essenes. However this is doubtful, as there is nothing in the text to connect it with Qumran. It has also been suggested that the scroll was hidden by Zealots operating in the locality during the war against the Romans. Particular items listed, such as quantities of incense and jars for tithes, tend to bear out the surmise that the treasure, or some of it, came from the Temple in Jerusalem.

ABOVE The revolt and the destruction of the Temple were recorded by Josephus in *The Jewish War*. This portrait of the historian is a frontispiece to the eighteenth-century English edition of his *Works*.

PART IV

AFTER THE TEMPLE

14 The Jews Remember

Yochanan ben Zakkai, a pupil of the great Hillel, was one of the most renowned sages in Jerusalem. He had served as co-president of the Sanhedrin, and his discourses in the Temple court drew large crowds. A man of peace, he was pessimistic about the outcome of the revolt against Rome and disapproved of the uncompromising spirit with which the Zealot leaders pursued it. He must have asked himself how the community and the faith could be preserved once the rebellion was crushed.

Some time before the final siege of Jerusalem, Yochanan decided to leave the city with a group of his more gifted pupils. According to a Talmudic legend, he escaped by having his disciples carry him out in a coffin. He made his way to Vespasian, who was flattered at being addressed as Caesar by the venerable rabbi. Yochanan obtained a promise that a number of other religious leaders would be spared. He was given permission to settle in Yavne, a village on the coastal plain south of Joppa, where there was already a *bet din* (religious court) and a seminary for *Torah* study. After the destruction of Jerusalem and the Temple Yochanan ben Zakkai devoted himself to developing the religious centre at Yavne, and attracting scholars to the academy he conducted there.

Fortunately for the survival of the Jewish identity, institutions and practices had evolved before AD 70 that could exist independently of the Temple. There was the Written and the Oral Law as a basis for a Jewish way of life; the moral authority of the rabbis who interpreted and expounded the Law; the synagogues as local places for worship and study; the Sanhedrin as a central body exercising authority in religious and judicial matters; and the position of *nasi* (prince or leader) held by Hillel and his descendants. The Jewish population of Judea outside Jerusalem had remained fairly intact, while large and autonomous diaspora communities existed in other countries. All these were foundations on which the future could be built.

Yochanan first revived the Sanhedrin, with Yavne as its new seat. It was now wholly a council of rabbis, since the Temple priesthood and the aristocratic Sadducee families formerly represented on it had been swept away.

Yochanan sought out Rabbi Gamaliel, a direct descendant of Hillel, and persuaded him to assume the office of *nasi* as Gamaliel II. He presided over the Sanhedrin and exercised other Jewish functions, such as fixing calendar dates and sending emissaries to maintain contact with the diaspora communities. The *nasi* became recognized by the Roman authorities as the patriarch or official head of the community. The office continued to be held by the descendants of Hillel until it was abolished in AD 425 by Roman edict.

It was of crucial importance to clarify and strengthen the Law. In the centuries to come it was the Law that would hold the Jewish people together as a community of faith without a political framework or a central sanctuary. Thirty years after the destruction of the Temple the Sanhedrin in Yavne finalized the canon of the Hebrew bible and the arrangement of its thirty-nine books in three sections: the Pentateuch (*Torah*), the Prophets (*Nevi'im*) and the Writings (*Ketuvim*). (The Hebrew word for the Old Testament, *Tanach*, is made up of the initials of the three sections.) At the same time the rabbis remained actively engaged in the Oral Law – the development and adjustment of the biblical precepts to meet contemporary needs, in the tradition of Hillel and Shammai. The task was started of sifting and collating this corpus of rulings and opinions.

A passage in the apocryphal Book of Baruch reflects how the Law had come to be the life-raft of the marooned Jewish people:

> She is the book of the Commandments of God,
> and the law that endures for ever.
> All who hold her fast will live,
> and those who forsake her will die.
> Turn, O Jacob, and take her;
> walk toward the shining of her light.
> Do not give your glory to another,
> or your advantages to an alien people.
> Happy are we, O Israel,
> for we know what is pleasing to God.

Baruch was the disciple and secretary of the prophet Jeremiah in the sixth century BC. The book that bears his name is a composite work, containing elements produced at different times. The passage quoted above is from a part of the book probably written down some years after the destruction of AD 70.

Though Judaism carried on, the loss of the Temple remained a searing memory. The rabbis tried to point out that their rational and ethical teaching had its own compensations. It is related that Yochanan ben Zakkai was once gazing on the Temple ruins with Rabbi Joshua, who said: 'Woe is us that this has been destroyed, a place where atonement was made for the sins of Israel.' Rabbi Yochanan replied: 'No, my son, do you not know that we have a means of making atonement that is like it. And what is it? It is deeds of love, as it is said: "For I desire steadfast love and not sacrifice . . ."' (Hosea 6:6).

Yet for centuries the tillers and herdsmen of Judea had brought their first fruits to the Temple, mingling on the great annual festivals with their diaspora brethren from many lands. They had made their peace with God through the traditional sacrifices; and they had been excited and uplifted by the splendour of the sanctuary and its colourful rites. The mystery and order of the universe had been expressed for the Jews through time-hallowed rituals and tangible symbols connected with the Temple. Now the focus of their national and religious life had been removed. The transition to a life without the Temple was a painful one.

Some quarters of Jerusalem were repopulated by small numbers of Jews; but the Temple site remained a square of blackened debris, overgrown with weeds. Many Jews clung to the belief that their freedom would be regained and their Temple rebuilt. Among them was Rabbi Akiba (*c.* AD 50–135), a man of strong personality and the leading Jewish scholar of his time. According to a story preserved in the Babylonian Talmud, Akiba, the patriarch Gamaliel II and two other sages came up to Jerusalem, looked down upon the city from Mount Scopus and tore their clothes in mourning. At the Temple site they saw a jackal slinking out of the rubble where the Holy of Holies had stood. The others wept at this sign of desolation, but to their bewilderment Rabbi Akiba smiled. He explained to them: 'The prophets foretold both the destruction of Jerusalem and its restoration to glory. Now I have seen the first prophesy come to pass, and I know the second will also be fulfilled.'

The Bar-Kochba Revolt

In AD 115, while the Emperor Trajan was involved in another war with the Parthians in the east, a Jewish revolt broke out in Cyrenaica, and spread to the communities in Egypt, Cyprus and Mesopotamia. It was subdued with great cruelty. The next emperor, Hadrian (AD 117–38), imposed a number of restrictions on the practice of the Jewish faith. At one point Rabbi Akiba travelled with the patriarch Gamaliel II on a mission to Rome to plead for religious freedom. Some of the rabbis urged submission to Roman policy in order to ease their lot. Akiba flung back at them the parable of the fox who urged the fish to come up on dry land in order to escape the fisherman's net. The fish replied: 'If we are afraid in the element in which we live, how much more should we be afraid when we are out of that element. We should then surely die.'

In AD 132 rebellion flared up again in Judea. Since there was no chronicler at hand like Josephus, the origins and course of this second

LEFT A bronze coin of Simon Bar-Kochba, AD 135.

Jewish war against Rome remained blurred. Little is known about its charismatic leader, Shimeon bar-Kosiba, who became known as Bar-Kochba (Son of a Star). He was given the powerful moral support of Rabbi Akiba, who hailed him as an 'anointed king'.

The uprising had been carefully planned and was at first successful. The Tenth Legion, which had remained stationed in Jerusalem, was hurriedly withdrawn to prevent it from being cut off. Bar-Kochba's guerillas joyfully occupied the city. Once again Judea was declared independent, and that year was proclaimed as Year One of the Redemption. Special coins were issued carrying the words 'Shimeon, Prince over Israel'. Bar-Kochba set up an administration in the capital and appointed local governors in the provincial districts. Plans were made to restore the Temple; and in the meantime sacrifices were resumed at an altar erected on the Temple site.

Hadrian resolved to crush the Judean revolt at all cost, lest the disaffection spread to other parts of the empire. A strong army was assembled and placed under the command of the leading general, Julius Severus, then governor in Britain. During the campaign the emperor himself spent some time in Judea to follow operations on the spot.

The strategy of Severus was closely modelled on that of Vespasian sixty-five years earlier. The Roman military machine relentlessly won control of the rest of Judea, town after town and village after village, then closed in on Jerusalem. Bar-Kochba and his troops were forced to abandon the city and retreated to the fortress of Bethar, a few miles to the south-west. In the summer of AD 135 it was captured. Bar-Kochba himself was slain in the battle. Rabbi Akiba and others who had been identified with the rebellion were rounded up and tortured to death.

Hadrian was now determined to curb the national aspirations of his Judean subjects, and to suppress what he regarded as their obscurantist and fanatical faith. Harsh anti-Jewish measures were introduced, reminiscent of those imposed by Antiochus Epiphanes before the Maccabean revolt three centuries earlier. They included a ban on circumcision and on *Torah* teaching, on pain of death. The name of the province was changed from Judea to Syria Palestina, though it continued to be administered by a procurator in Caesarea.

The word Jerusalem also disappeared from official documents. Hadrian had the site of the ruined Jewish city cleared and in its place constructed a small Roman town, covering roughly the area of the present Old City within its Turkish walls. He called it Aelia Capitolina, derived partly from his own full name, Hadrian Publius Aelius, and partly from Jupiter Capitolinus, one of the names of the chief Roman god. Following the layout of a typical Roman camp, there were two main thoroughfares intersecting at right angles in the centre of the town. The north–south axis lay between the present Damascus and Zion Gates.

The Muristan Bazaar on the site of the forum of Aelia Capitolina.

The east–west axis, between the citadel and the Temple area, followed the line of what is now David Street and the Street of the Chain. On the Temple Mount he erected a temple to Jupiter with an equestrian statue of himself in front of it. A small temple to Venus stood where the Church of the Holy Sepulchre now is, and in the open space before it (now the Muristan Bazaar) was the forum. Aelia had the usual recreational facilities that were part of the Roman way of life – public baths, and a theatre and hippodrome. The Tenth Legion, as the permanent garrison, had its barracks in what is today the Armenian Quarter.

Judaism Carries On

Organized Jewish life in the country slowly recovered from the calamity of the Bar-Kochba revolt, and the executions, devastation and economic distress that were its aftermath. The main area of Jewish activity shifted to the Galilee, especially to the towns of Sepphoris and Tiberias. The work of codifying the rabbinical *responsa* (rulings) and traditions was methodically carried out by a team of scholars under the direction of the greatest of the patriarchs, Judah ha-Nasi, in the late second and early third centuries. Over fifty years of this labour produced the code known as the *Mishna*, completed about AD 220. The compilation became in itself a point of departure for fresh discussion and development, covering both *halachah* (the legal sections) and *aggadah* (ethics and legends). From this mass of material the Jerusalem Talmud was compiled in Palestine by the fourth century, and the larger and more complete Babylonian Talmud by the sixth century. By then the Palestinian community had declined in numbers and influence, and the real centre of Jewish life had become the large and flourishing Babylonian community.

During these centuries Jews continued to visit the Temple site or its vicinity whenever they could. The sanctuary may have been demolished by a pagan conqueror, but it was believed that the *Shechinah*, the Divine Presence, had not departed. In claiming that the sanctity of the site was eternal, the rabbis relied on a number of biblical passages. For instance, as was said in Psalm 132:

> For the Lord has chosen Zion;
> he has desired it for his habitation:
> This is my resting place for ever;
> here I will dwell, for I have
> desired it [Psalms 132: 13–14].

The monumental work on Jerusalem by the Dominican Fathers Hughes Vincent and F.M. Abel (1926) describes the situation after the sack of the city:

> While the schools discussed the questions of the purity or impurity of the Temple Mount, of the legitimacy of sacrifice in a violated sanctuary ... the Jews of Palestine did not fail to visit their unfortunate capital which remained holy by virtue of its former consecration. At the site of the ruins of the sanctuary from which occasionally a jackal furtively made its escape, the pilgrims would tear their garments and having reached the foot of the gates and the crumbling walls, gave vent to their sorrow and lamentations. ...

The reverence required of Jews on the Temple site is stated in a passage in the *Mishna*: 'No man shall behave frivolously when standing near the eastern gate, which looks to the Holy of Holies; he shall not enter the Temple Mount with his cane, his shoes, his purse or the dust on his feet, nor shall he use it as a short cut, still less shall he spit there' (Berachot 9: 5).

In Hadrian's Aelia Capitolina Jews were at first forbidden on penalty of death to enter the city. The ban was applied even to Jews converted to Christianity. Later they were allowed in once a year in the summer on the ninth day of Av (Tisha b'Av) to mourn the destruction of the Temple. The earliest Christian witness to this custom was the so-called Pilgrim from Bordeaux, who visited Jerusalem in AD 333 and recorded that 'not far from the statues of Hadrian there is a perforated stone to which the Jews come every year and anoint it, bewail themselves with groans, rend

While openly contemptuous of the Christian faith, Julian the Apostate was the most tolerant of the Roman emperors toward the Jews. 'The Emperor Julian amused by quarrelling Christian Scholars' painted by Edward Armitage, 1875.

their garments, and so depart'. The stone he mentioned was probably the Stone of Foundation on which the altar of burnt offering of the Temple had stood, now enclosed in the Dome of the Rock Mosque.

Jewish access to the Temple area was eased during the reign of the Emperor Julian (AD 361–3). He had an open contempt for the Christian faith and sought to revive the old pagan beliefs and the principles of Greek philosophy – hence the Church historians dubbed him Julian the Apostate. To the Jews he was the most sympathetic of all the Roman rulers. He issued a letter headed 'To the Jewish Congregations', claiming credit for abolishing anti-Jewish taxes and promising to visit and rebuild Jerusalem and the Temple. It was a tragedy for his Jewish subjects when his brief reign ended on the battlefield.

Numbers of Jewish pilgrims must have visited the Temple site during this period. In the early stage of the current excavations round the south-western corner of the Temple Mount a Hebrew inscription dating from this time was disclosed. Beautifully chiselled into one of the stones in the wall was a quotation from Isaiah: 'You shall see, and your heart shall rejoice; your bones shall flourish like the grass ...' (Isaiah 66: 14). The words that occur in the Bible immediately before this quotation are: 'You shall be comforted in Jerusalem.'

When the Temple still stood the pilgrim festivals had been joyful occasions, with great throngs in festive garb and mood. In contrast, such pilgrims as still came to the site of the ruined Temple were dejected mourners. Their appearance drew a biting comment from the early Church Father, St Jerome (AD 342–420). He settled in 386 in Bethlehem as abbot of a monastery, and produced from the Hebrew original the Latin translation of the Bible known as the Vulgate, officially adopted by the Roman Catholic Church. Although a Hebrew scholar, Jerome shared the biased attitude against the Jews and the *Torah* that was common among the Christian churchmen of his time. This prejudice shows up clearly in the feelings aroused in his mind by the sight of the Jews at the Temple Mount on Tisha b'Av:

> Until this very day faithless inhabitants are forbidden to enter Jerusalem, and that they may weep over the ruins of their state, they pay a price, purchasing their tears ... so that not even weeping is free to them. You see on the day of the destruction of Jerusalem a sad people coming, decrepit little women and old men encumbered with rags and years, exhibiting both in their bodies and their dress the wrath of the Lord. A crowd of pitiable creatures assembles and under the gleaming gibbet of the Lord and his sparkling resurrection, and before a brilliant banner with a cross waving from the Mount of Olives, they weep over the ruins of the Temple; and yet they are not worthy of pity. Thus they lament on their knees with livid arms and dishevelled hair, while the guards demand their reward for permitting them to shed some more tears ... [from Jerome's *Commentary to Zephaniah*].

In the reign of the Emperor Constantine the Great (AD 306–37) Christianity was legalized and then given official status in the Roman empire. At the same time anti-Jewish restrictions were tightened, including the ban on Jews entering Jerusalem. The city now became increasingly a centre of Christian pilgrimage. The pagan name of Aelia Capitolina was abandoned; nothing more is heard of the sanctuary to Jupiter on the Temple Mount and it was no doubt demolished and the stones used for other buildings, in the time-honoured fashion. The small temple of Venus was certainly pulled down to make room for Con-

'You shall see and your heart shall rejoice; your bones shall flourish like the grass.' The quotation from Isaiah inscribed on one of the stones of the Temple Mount wall.

stantine's great new basilica, the Church of the Holy Sepulchre, on what was regarded as the site of Golgotha or Calvary, where Jesus was cruci-fied. Constantine's lavish building programme in Jerusalem was en-couraged by his mother Helena, an ardent convert to Christianity.

Constantine established his capital on the Bosphorus Straits and named it Constantinople after himself. In the middle of the fourth century AD the newly-elected Emperor Valentinian divided the empire with his brother Valens. Valentinian kept the western empire – Gaul, Italy and Illyria. The eastern empire, called Byzantium after the original name of Constantinople, extended from the Danube, Greece and Sicily eastward to the borders of Persia, including Palestine. The Christian faith underwent a corresponding partition. It became divided between the Roman Catholic (Latin) Church in the west, under the Pope, and the Eastern (Orthodox) Church under its own patriarch in Constantinople.

In his famous Law Code the Emperor Theodosius II (AD 401–50) defined the status of the Jews in the Byzantine empire. They were made second-class citizens, deprived of many civil rights and forbidden to build new synagogues. On the death of the Jewish patriarch in Palestine, Gamaliel IV, in 425, the emperor abolished the office and transferred the title to the Orthodox bishop of Jerusalem. Ironically, the widow of Theodosius, the Empress Eudocia – a wealthy, pious and very active lady – came to reside in Jerusalem, and through her influence Jews were allowed to settle freely again in the city.

Echoes of the lost Temple continued to be heard in the worship of the dispersed Jewish people wherever they were. All synagogues were oriented so that the *aron kodesh*, the ark containing the Scrolls of the Law, was on the wall facing in the direction of Jerusalem. Jews standing at prayer faced the same way. On every continent the pilgrimage festivals were observed in accordance with the agricultural seasons in the Holy Land, when the products of field and flock were brought as Temple offerings in the days of old. Some features of the synagogue service survived from Temple rituals – for instance, the blowing of the *shofar* (ram's horn) on the holy days; the blessing given by the *cohanim*, the descendants of the Temple priests; and the use on *Succot*, the Feast of Tabernacles, of the *ethrog* (citron) and the *lulav* (a palm branch decorated with three other species of plants common in Palestine).

The order of prayers in the synagogue had become a substitute for the Temple sacrifices and followed a roughly similar pattern: the *Shachrit* service instead of the morning *Tamid* sacrifice; the *Minchah* service instead of the afternoon *Tamid* sacrifice; and the *Mussaf* service instead of the additional sacrifices on feast days. A certain ambivalence crept into the recollection of the former animal sacrifices. The rabbis in the Talmudic period carefully preserved the sacrificial details, no doubt to provide a manual of ritual practices when the Temple would be restored. Later sages, and in particular the school of medieval cabbalism, tended to explain and justify these sacrifices as mystic symbols of a spiritual relationship with God. It took the powerful rationalism of Maimonides in the twelfth century AD to reject the idea of animal sacrifices in principle, and to describe them as having been distasteful to the Lord. The early Hebrews, he wrote, had shared in what was then a universal practice. In moving them towards a purer faith God had not made them break too abruptly with familiar and deeply rooted customs. Animal sacrifices as part of Judaism had first been restricted to the Temple in Jerusalem and then ceased altogether with its destruction. To Maimonides this was a step forward in the spiritual development of the Jews.

After the end of the Temple music in synagogues was forbidden, and the only instrument to remain in use was the *shofar*. The rabbis thought it unseemly to get pleasure from song and music after the national calamity. These elements were in any case important in pagan and afterwards Christian worship, and therefore were influences to be resisted by Jews. It was the reform movement of the nineteenth century that adopted organ music and choir singing from the church. Children's choirs are now general, though Orthodox congregations still shun the organ or other musical instruments. From the Middle Ages melody and harmony came back into synagogue liturgy through the office of the *chazzan* or cantor, who led the chanting of prayers. In modern times the leading *chazzanim* became as famous as top operatic singers.

OPPOSITE The Greek Orthodox Chapel of Calvary in the Church of the Holy Sepulchre.

15 The Mosques on the Mount

The last Byzantine emperor to hold the Holy Land was Heraclius (AD 610–41). He was intolerant of the Jews and ordered them to be baptized. It was small wonder that they welcomed a Persian occupation in AD 614. Jews from the Galilee aided the invading Persian army as auxiliaries. The Persians treated the Christian inhabitants harshly. Fifteen years after he had lost Palestine, Heraclius reconquered it. Revenge was taken against the Jewish citizens of Jerusalem, who were again either killed or expelled.

Restored Byzantine rule did not last long. A new and militant faith had sprung up in Arabia. Its prophet, Mohammed, died in Medina in AD 632. His followers swarmed out of Arabia, fighting with the zeal of a holy war in which paradise awaited the fallen. They overran Persia, defeated a Byzantine army in Syria, occupied Damascus and invaded Palestine. Soon only Jerusalem and Ramla were left in Christian hands. The Byzantine commander withdrew his forces into Egypt. The Caliph Omar laid siege to Jerusalem in AD 638. Fearful of what the Moslem soldiers might do to the city, the Christian patriarch Sophronius would surrender it only to Omar in person. The caliph entered Jerusalem on foot as a mark of respect. (Another conqueror, the British general Allenby, was to do the same nearly thirteen centuries later.) Omar guaranteed that the Christian citizens could carry on their affairs unmolested. He also allowed the Jews to return to the city.

Mohammed had attacked the Jewish tribes in Arabia when they spurned his religious ideas. But the faith he had launched was imbued with reverence towards the Jewish and Christian prophets, especially Moses and Jesus. In fact the Arabs accepted Abraham as their own forefather, through Ishmael. Basically Islam, like Christianity, was the offspring of Hebrew monotheism. It was natural for Omar to respect a city that was holy to the adherents of the two older religions. It was soon to become holy to Islam as well.

A passage in the Koran was interpreted by the faithful as linking the prophet Mohammed with Jerusalem and the Temple Mount. The seventeenth Sura, 'The Night Journey', relates that in a dream or vision Mohammed was carried by night 'from the sacred temple to the temple that is more remote, whose precinct we have blessed, that we might show him of our signs . . .' (Everyman's Library translation 1909). Moslem belief identifies the two temples mentioned in this verse as being in Mecca and Jerusalem.

According to tradition, Mohammed's mystic journey was in the company of the Archangel Gabriel, and they rode on a winged steed called El Burak, meaning lightning (the Hebrew word is *barak*). They came to the Temple Mount in Jerusalem, and from there ascended through the seven heavens into the presence of Allah. The Koran itself makes no reference to El Burak; it is first mentioned in the *Hadith*, the collection of oral traditions compiled in the ninth century, some two centuries after Mohammed's death. Various spots on the Temple Mount or next to it were later indicated as the traditional place where El Burak was tethered before the ascent to heaven.

One account of the night journey is that given in a life of the prophet by Ibn Hisham (died 834) in the name of Al-Hassan, a contemporary of Mohammed:

> The Prophet of God said: 'While I was sleeping within the wall of the Kaaba, came to me Gabriel and kicked me with his foot, so I sat up, but not seeing anything, I lay again on my bed. He kicked me then once more, and I sat up and did not see a thing, so I lay back on my bed. He then kicked me a third time and I sat up, whereupon he pulled me by the arm and I rose, and went to the door of the temple. There was standing a white beast, between a mule and an ass in size, with two wings on its thighs, digging its hind legs in and placing its forelegs as far as it can see. Gabriel carried me on the beast, and we went together at the same speed.' So the Prophet of God journeyed, and with him also Gabriel, until they reached the temple in Jerusalem. He found there Abraham, Moses, and Jesus, among other prophets, and he led them in prayers. Then he was given two vessels, one filled with wine and the other with milk, so the prophet of God took the vessel with milk and drank it, leaving the vessel of wine. Seeing that, Gabriel said to him: 'You were guided to the true religion [Isla'm] and so was your nation, for wine is forbidden unto you.'

When Mohammed had fled to Medina he thought for a time of abandoning Mecca altogether. At that stage he called on his followers to make Jerusalem the *kiblah* (the direction to be faced during prayers) as was the Jewish tradition. It was only in the second year of the *hegira* (flight), after Mohammed had quarrelled with the Jews of Medina, that Mecca

The ascent of Mohammed into heaven on his horse, El Burak; from a Persian
manuscript of the sixteenth century.

was made the *kiblah* for Moslems. In the second Sura of the Koran, called 'The Cow', the prophet insists on this change from Jerusalem to Mecca.

There is an interesting comment on this question in the travel diary of a Persian Moslem, Nasir-l-Khusrau, who visited Jerusalem in AD 1047, half a century before the Crusader conquest. Referring to the rock over which the Dome of the Rock was built, he says:

> This stone of the Sakhrah is that which God commanded Moses to institute as the Kiblah. . . . Then came the days of Solomon – upon him be peace! – who seeing that the Rock was the Kiblah point built a mosque around it. . . . So it remained down to the days of our Prophet Mohammed, the Chosen One – upon him be blessings and peace! –who likewise at first recognized this to be the Kiblah, turning towards it at his prayers; but God – be He exalted and glorified – afterwards commanded him to institute, as the Kiblah, the House of the Ka'abah [at Mecca] [Palestine Pilgrims' Text Society 1893].

This Persian traveller, commenting on Jerusalem as the third holy city for Moslems after Mecca and Medina, gives the precise degrees of holiness of each:

> The doctors of religion concur in saying that a single prayer offered up here in this Holy City, has vouchsafed to it the effect of five-and-twenty thousand prayers said elsewhere; just as in Medina, the City of the Prophet . . . every single prayer may count for fifty thousand, while to each that is said in Mecca, the Venerable . . . will pass for a hundred thousand. And God give grace to all His servants, that they may one day acquit themselves of such prayers.

There is an old story that when Omar entered Jerusalem he insisted on being taken to the Temple site by the Christian patriarch. He was disgusted to find it was used as the city refuse dump, and made the prelate crawl through the filth on hands and knees as a punishment for polluting a hallowed place of another faith. Another version shows Omar setting a lead by starting to gather up the refuse in his cloak.

Omar constructed a large temporary mosque on the Temple platform, of a rectangular shape. The French bishop, Arculf, spent some time in the Holy Land thirty years after the Moslem conquest, and wrote: 'In that renowned place where once the Temple had been magnificently constructed, placed in the neighbourhood of the wall from the east, the Saracens now frequent a four-sided house of prayer, which they have built in a rough manner, by raising planks and great beams on some remains of ruins; and it is said that this house can hold three thousand men at once.'

In AD 691 the Caliph Abdel Malik replaced the improvised structure

Omar directs the construction of a temporary mosque on the Temple platform. A fifteenth-century French miniature.

with the dazzling Dome of the Rock (*Kubbat es-Sakhra*), popularly but erroneously called the Mosque of Omar. The mosque was designed by Byzantine architects engaged by the Caliph. It was an octagonal structure enclosing the rock (*es-Sakhra*) with a golden dome above it. 'At the dawn, when the light of the sun first strikes on the cupola and the drum catches the rays, then is this edifice a marvellous site to behold and one such that in all Islam I have never seen its equal; neither have I heard tell of aught built in pagan times that could rival in grace this Dome of the Rock' (Mukadassi, the famous Moslem traveller born in Jerusalem, writing about AD 985).

Malik's objective was political and economic as much as religious. The seat of his caliphate was Damascus, and Jerusalem fell within his territory. The two Arabian cities holy to Islam, Mecca and Medina, however, were controlled by a rival caliph. Malik wanted to build up the importance of Jerusalem as a centre in his own domain for Moslem worship and pilgrimage. The rock outcrop on the Temple Mount was already richly laden with holiness in Jewish tradition, and had been the site of

OPPOSITE The Dome of the Rock.

the main altar in the Temple courtyard. Now Moslem belief identified the same rock as the exact spot from which Mohammed's horse had sprung up to heaven. A cup-like indent towards one side was later pointed out as the imprint made by the heel of the prophet.

An Arabic inscription in the mosaics on the outer wall of the mosque states that the rock is from the Garden of Eden. Moslem tradition holds that all the fresh water in the world originates underneath it.

Hollowed out below the rock is a cavern reached by a flight of steps. Praying niches within it are named for Abraham, David, Solomon, Elijah and the Angel Gabriel.

It is said that the gold leaf with which Abdel Malik covered the dome cost the total revenues he derived from Egypt for seven years. To protect this investment from the weather he had an enormous covering woven for it from camelhair, wool and cotton; but it afforded no protection against despoilers. By modern times none of the gold leaf remained and the dome was left with only its lead cover. The lead was recently replaced by an aluminium bronze alloy from Italy that has the appearance of pale gold. This weighs only 35 tons, as against the hundreds of tons of lead.

There are forty-five thousand ornamental tiles used in the mosque and on its outer walls, most of them installed by Suleiman the Magnificent. The eight graceful arches facing the sides of the mosque, at the top of the steps leading up to it, are known as Mawasin, i.e. scales. The belief is that on Judgement Day the souls of Moslems will be weighed on them.

To the south of the Dome of the Rock Mosque, close to the edge of the Temple platform, Malik's son and successor, the Caliph Waleed, erected a larger rectangular mosque with a silver dome over its centre. It was called El Aksa, 'the far distant place', from the passage in the Koran about Mohammed's dream.

The Jews called it 'Midrash Shlomo', that is, 'Solomon's House of Study', which was said to have been located at this spot. Because of earthquakes, little remains of the original structure. The present mosque dates from the eleventh century, with various reconstructions since then. Extensive repairs and alterations were carried out between 1938 and 1943, including the addition of the white marble columns imported from Italy. The splendid inlaid pulpit donated by Saladin was destroyed in the fire of 1969.

Just east of the Dome of the Rock Mosque, and resembling it in shape, stands a small building called the Dome of the Chain. It was built in the eighth century and served as the treasury of the two mosques. The Arabs also call it 'The Tribunal of the Prophet David'. The legend is that King David gave judgement here, and a large chain suspended from the dome served as a lie-detector. If a witness held the chain and gave false testimony a link would fall out.

The whole Temple platform was given the Arabic name it still bears,

OPPOSITE The Dome of the Chain, built as a treasury in the eighth century.

Plan of Temple Mount

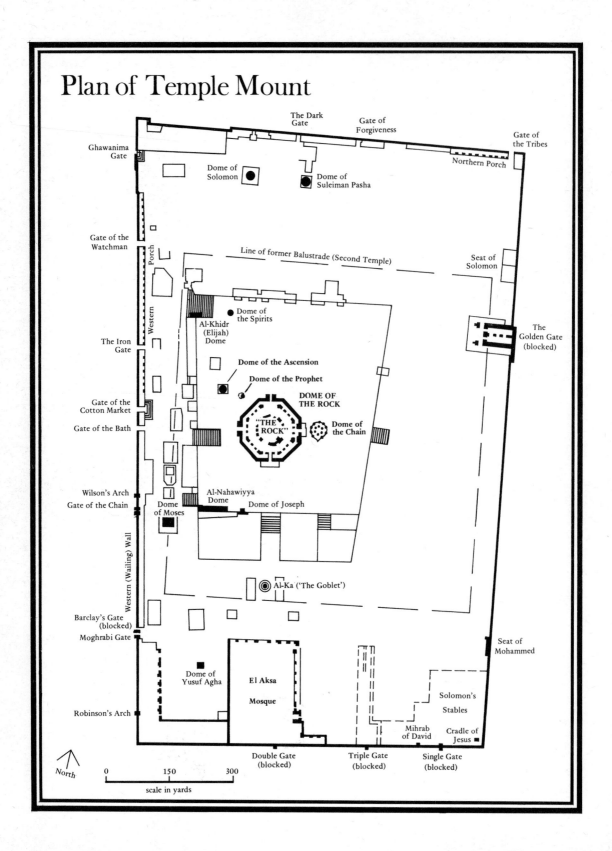

The Dark Gate

Gate of Forgiveness

Gate of the Tribes

Ghawanima Gate

Dome of Solomon

Dome of Suleiman Pasha

Northern Porch

Gate of the Watchman

Line of former Balustrade (Second Temple)

Seat of Solomon

Porch

Western

Dome of the Spirits

Al-Khidr (Elijah) Dome

The Iron Gate

The Golden Gate (blocked)

Dome of the Ascension

Dome of the Prophet

DOME OF THE ROCK

Gate of the Cotton Market

Gate of the Bath

"THE ROCK"

Dome of the Chain

Western (Wailing) Wall

Wilson's Arch

Gate of the Chain

Al-Nahawiyya Dome

Dome of Joseph

Dome of Moses

Al-Ka ('The Goblet')

Barclay's Gate (blocked)

Moghrabi Gate

Seat of Mohammed

Dome of Yusuf Agha

El Aksa Mosque

Solomon's Stables

Robinson's Arch

Mihrab of David

Cradle of Jesus

North

0   150   300

scale in yards

Double Gate (blocked)

Triple Gate (blocked)

Single Gate (blocked)

Haram esh-Sharif (Noble Sanctuary). In the course of time the *Haram* acquired a number of small shrines and fountains as gifts from pious benefactors. Today there are about a hundred structures in the compound, large and small.

The Jews in Arab Jerusalem The transition from Byzantine to Arab rule was a relief for the Jews. Officially allowed to live in the city, they seem to have concentrated in two quarters: one on the high ground facing the Western Wall of the Temple Mount (the present Jewish Quarter) and the other inside the northern city wall. In these areas there were several synagogues and an academy for the study of the *Torah*.

On feast days the Jews would go in procession round the walls of the Temple Mount and pray at the gates. It was also customary to ascend the Mount of Olives and offer prayers there while looking down on the Temple site. There are indications that on certain holy days Jews were permitted into the *Haram esh-Sharif*.

At the place of prayer next to the Western Wall, a small synagogue and study house stood against the Wall. An open space in front of the Wall was referred to by travellers as the Azarah, the term that had been used for the forecourt to the Temple while it stood.

Several inscriptions have recently been found at the gates to the Temple Mount that must have been put there by Jewish pilgrims in the early period of Arab rule. One such inscription at the northern end reads in translation: 'Thou Lord of Hosts build this House in the lifetime of Jacob ben-Joseph, Theophylactus, and Sisinia and Anistasia. Amen and Amen, Selah.' The names indicate that these were the names of Jewish pilgrims from a Greek-speaking country. Other inscribed names suggest Arabic-speaking pilgrims, while one couple state clearly that they came from Sicily.

According to a tenth-century document, one condition for the right to pray at the gates of the Temple Mount was that the Jewish community should be responsible for sweeping the *Haram esh-Sharif* and keeping it clean. Some accounts state that Jewish attendants were employed in the mosque area, and that Jewish craftsmen provided lamps for the mosques.

16 *The Crusaders*

In the eleventh century Palestine reverted to its age-old role as a pawn in the struggle between the Nile and Euphrates river basins. In this case the rivalry was between two Moslem dynasties claiming the caliphate: the Abbasids in Baghdad and the Fatimids in Cairo. Power in Baghdad was seized by Seljuk Turks, members of a central Asian Moslem tribe that had served the Abbasid caliphs as mercenary soldiers and officials. When they defeated a Byzantine army and threatened Constantinople the Byzantine emperor sent emissaries to appeal for help from his fellow-Christians in western Europe. Various factors stimulated a positive response. The knights of France and Germany had already gained experience in fighting Moslems during the attempts to oust the Moors from Spain. Wandering preachers like Peter the Hermit stirred up religious sentiment with stories of atrocities against Christians in Palestine and desecration of the Holy Places. Colour was lent to these stories by the memory of the 'mad caliph', Hakim of Egypt, who earlier in the century had banned non-Moslem pilgrimages and ordered the demolition of churches and synagogues alike. The Church of the Holy Sepulchre had been seriously damaged at that time.

In 1095 Pope Urban II launched the first Crusade, with the avowed aim of regaining the Holy Land from the Moslem infidels. There were indeed brave and pious men among those who sewed the cross of red on their shoulders. But others were a rough and unruly lot, drawn by the promise of adventure and gain. In their progress across Europe, the Crusaders were joined by a huge rabble of landless peasants and toughs. Egged on by bigots, they attacked the hapless Jewish communities along the way, killing thousands, looting their property and burning their synagogues.

In July 1099 the Crusader forces broke into Jerusalem. The Moslem commander surrendered in the Tower of David, on condition that he and his bodyguard would be allowed to withdraw to Ashkelon. 'The Crusaders, maddened by so great a victory . . . rushed through the streets and

The Crusaders before Jerusalem; a nineteenth-century engraving.

into the houses and mosques, killing all that they met, men, women and children alike. All that afternoon and all through the night the massacre continued ...' (Sir Steven Runciman, *A History of the Crusades* 1951). A number of Jews took refuge in their main synagogue, which was set alight, and its trapped occupants were burned to death.

Many of the Moslem garrison retreated to the Temple Mount and tried to make a last stand in the El Aksa Mosque. Pursued by one of the Crusader commanders, Tancred, they surrendered to him, promising a large sum of money as the price for their lives. Tancred hoisted his banner over the mosque as a sign of protection and his men then pillaged the nearby Dome of the Rock Mosque. The banner was of little avail. Another band of Crusaders forced their way into the El Aksa and slaughtered everyone in it. 'When Raymond of Aguilers later that morning went to visit the Temple area he had to pick his way through corpses and blood that reached up to his knees' (Runciman, *A History of the Crusades*).

The Jews who survived the pogrom were taken captive by Tancred and sold as slaves, or were taken to Ashkelon and ransomed by the Egyptian Jews. Not a single Jew remained in Jerusalem. Other Jewish communities such as those in Ramla, Jaffa and Haifa, also disappeared.

The Crusade had been over three years on the way, but nobody had worked out what they should do with the Holy Land when they regained it. Some now proposed that it should be a papal state, under the direct jurisdiction of the Church. The Crusader leaders, however, wanted one of their own number as ruler. Their army was a loose alliance of feudal nobles, each with his own knights and retainers. The total is estimated at about four thousand horsemen and fifteen to twenty thousand foot soldiers, plus an unknown number of retainers and camp followers. In the capture of Jerusalem the main commanders were four French counts: Raymond of Toulouse, Godfrey of Lorraine, Robert of Flanders and Robert of Normandy. Another leader of Norman blood, Bohemond of Tarranto (southern Italy), had made himself Prince of Antioch along the way and abandoned the march on Jerusalem. His nephew, the dashing Tancred, was prominent in the taking of the city and later became Prince of Galilee. (Benjamin Disraeli was to write a romantic historical novel about him.)

In Jerusalem, Godfrey was elected to rule. He piously refused to call himself king, maintaining that he could not wear a crown where Jesus had worn a crown of thorns, and took instead the title of Advocatus Sancti Sepulchri (Defender of the Holy Sepulchre). After his death his brother and successor felt no such scruples. On Christmas Day 1100 the patriarch crowned him in the Church of the Nativity at Bethlehem as King Baldwin I of the Latin Kingdom of Jerusalem. The kingdom extended from the Negev desert in the south to the coast of Lebanon.

Further north lay the smaller Crusader principalities of Tripoli, Antioch and Edessa.

A ban was imposed on the entry of non-Christians to Jerusalem. Later a few Jewish cloth-dyers were allowed to live in the city, as that was an exclusively Jewish craft. Apart from the Christian quarter round the Church of the Holy Sepulchre three-quarters of the city was left derelict. It gradually filled up with native Christians from across the Jordan, and with churches and religious establishments. Some of the churches were converted mosques.

The Temple Mount

The Dome of the Rock Mosque became the Templum Domini (Temple of our Lord) and the crescent surmounting its dome was replaced by a cross. The mosque-turned-church figures on coins of the Crusader kingdom. Its shape inspired several circular churches in Europe, such as those at Aix-la-Chapelle, Metz and Laon, and the Temple Church in London. In painting New Testament scenes medieval and Renaissance artists tended to depict the Temple in the form of the Templum Domini of the Crusader period – that is, the Dome of the Rock Mosque. A famous example is Raphael's 'Marriage of the Virgin', hanging in the Brera Gallery in Milan.

The Russian Abbot Daniel, who made a pilgrimage to the Holy Land in 1106, shortly after the Crusader capture of Jerusalem, describes the Moslem Dome of the Rock Mosque before it was converted into the Christian Templum Domini. In setting out the associations the site had with Jesus, he states: 'There are still seen in the rock the footsteps of our Lord . . .' (Palestine Pilgrims' Text Society 1893). The same volume of the Pilgrims' Text contains the travel diary of the Persian Moslem traveller Nasir-l-Khusrau in 1047, before the Crusader invasion. He states that on the rock 'there is an appearance as though a person had walked heavily on the stone when it was soft like clay, whereby the imprint of his toes had remained there on. ... I heard it stated that Abraham was once here with Isaac when he was a boy, and that he walked over this place and that the footmarks were his.' This comment by an erudite Moslem, four centuries after Mohammed, indicates that the mark on the rock had not yet been identified as made by the heel of the prophet on his visionary night journey to heaven, via the Temple Mount. In true ecumenical spirit, the indentation suggesting a footmark has thus been linked with Abraham, Jesus and Mohammed.

At first the Temple area was looked after by the Canons of Templum Domini, a religious house established for the purpose by Godfrey. The abbot and some of the canons had their dwelling-place and garden on part of the Temple Mount. The El Aksa Mosque was converted into royal quarters and a wing added on its western side. Later King Baldwin made part of these premises available to Hugh of Paience, a French knight from Champagne, who with eight companions founded the

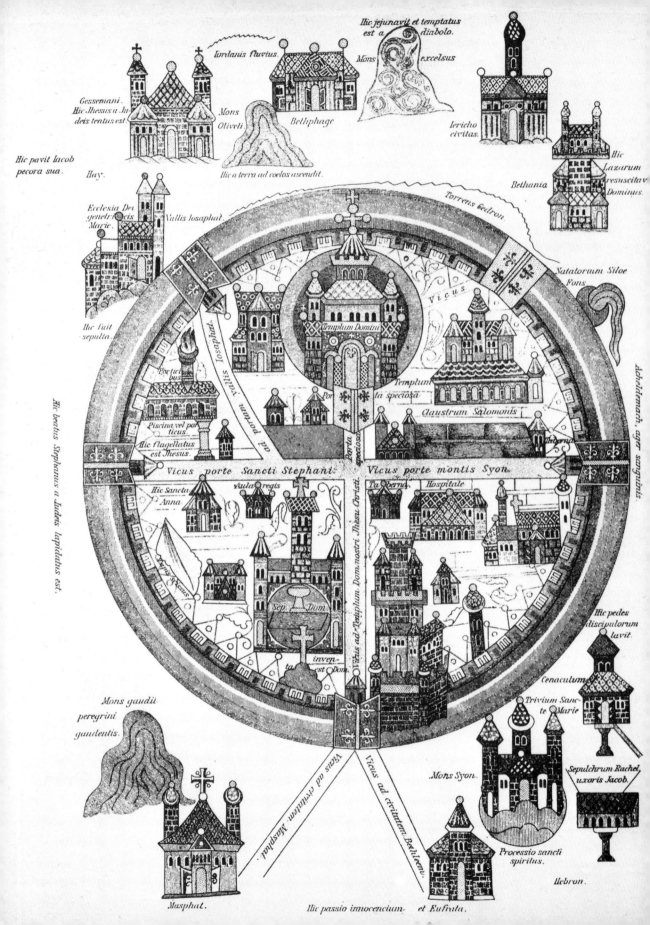

Hic jejunavit et temptatus
est a diabolo.

Iordanis fluvius.

Mons excelsus

Gessemani.
Hic Jhesus a Iu-
deis tentus est.

Mons
Oliveti.

Bethphage

Iericho
civitas.

Hic pavit Iacob
pecora sua.

Hay.

Illic a terra ad coelos ascendit.

Bethania

Hic
Lazarum
resuscitav
Dominus.

Ecclesia Dei
genetricis
Marie.

Vallis Iosaphat.

Torrens Cedron

Hic fuit
sepulta.

Natatorum Siloe
Fons

Porticus

Vicus

Templum Domini

Piscina vel por-
ticus.

Hic flagellatus
est Ihesus.

Porta speciosa

Templum

Claustrum Salomonis

Acheldemach, ager sanguinis.

Hic beatus Stephanus a Iudeis lapidatus est.

Vicus porte Sancti Stephani.

Vicus porte montis Syon.

Hic Sancta
Anna

Aula regis

Taberna

Hospitale

Mons Pilatus

Sep. Dom.

inven-
ta est Dom.

Titus ad Templum Dom. nostri Jhesu Christi.

Porta speciosa

Hic pedes
discipulorum
lavit.

Cenaculum

Mons gaudii
peregrini
gaudentis.

Vicus ad civitatem Masphat.

Vicus ad civitatem Bethleem.

Mons Syon.

Trivium Sanc-
te Marie

Sepulchrum Rachel,
uxoris Jacob.

Masphat.

Illic passio innocencium

et Eufrata.

Processio sancti
spiritus.

Hebron.

Order of the Knights Templar. When the order grew it was allowed to take over the royal wing as well. Other extensions were made to the mosque: it gained a large arcaded porch in front and vaulted galleries at the sides. The building served as the headquarters of the order, with its refectory in the main hall of the mosque. The Templars named it Templum Solomonis, as they believed that Solomon's palace had stood on Mount Moriah at this location. The present El Aksa Mosque contains remains of the Crusader additions, the rose window for example.

The subterranean vaults holding up the south-eastern part of the Temple platform were used by the Crusaders for stabling their horses, and called Solomon's Stables. The animals were tethered to the pillars, of which there are eighty-eight divided into twelve rows. Remains of the mangers can still be seen. The horses were brought in and out through the Single Gate in the southern wall near the eastern end. It is now visible only as an archway of stones in the wall. At the western end of the stables another series of vaults reveals the inner chambers of the Double and Triple Gates (the Gates of Hulda), which are also closed.

Also walled in is the imposing double portico of the Golden Gate, facing across the Kidron valley from the eastern wall of the Temple compound. The present gate is of Byzantine origin. Since it was never covered with gold its name is probably due to a verbal corruption. Herod's Beautiful Gate stood about here, and the Greek word for beautiful, *Oria*, may have been rendered in Latin as *aurea*, meaning golden. There is a Jewish tradition that the Messiah will come in through this gate, and Christians believe that Jesus entered by it on the Sunday before his death. Maybe for these reasons, or maybe for security, the gate was blocked off after the Arab conquest. The Crusaders reopened it twice a year – on Palm Sunday and on the feast celebrating the bringing to Jerusalem of the Holy Cross, which the Byzantine Emperor Heraclius claimed to have recovered from the Persians.

Adjacent to the northern end of the Temple Mount is the Crusader Church of St Anne, of mixed Norman and Arab architecture. It has remained in an excellent state of preservation.

The Order of the Knights Templar was the only international body ever to be born on the Temple Mount. It was preceded in time by the Order of St John in Jerusalem (the Hospitallers). The initial duty of the Templars was to police the pilgrim route from the coast to Jerusalem.

In course of time the two orders developed into powerful and autonomous organizations of fighting men that assumed much of the burden of defence of the Crusader states in the Near East. Their founders conceived of a type of community new in the annals of Christendom – a combination of the ideas of chivalry held by aristocratic medieval knights, with the vows of poverty, chastity and obedience taken by medieval monks. In the context of the Holy War proclaimed by Pope Urban to

OPPOSITE Jerusalem in the twelfth century. On the Dome of the Rock, renamed Templum Domini, the cross has replaced the crescent.

regain the Holy Land, fighting could thus become respectable in terms of the Christian ethic. As was laid down in paragraph 57 of the Rule of the Temple, the code of the Knights Templars: 'Knighthood should be admitted to religion and thus religion armed by knighthood should progress and kill the enemy without guilt.'

At the height of their power the two military orders were virtually independent of rulers and Church alike in 'Outremer' (the Crusader-occupied area of the Near East), and their grand masters owed allegiance directly to the Pope. They were based on chains of massive castles that controlled the border areas and the main routes – such as the Templar stronghold at Athlit, built on a rocky promontory south of Haifa; the gigantic Krak de Chevaliers of the Hospitallers in northern Syria; and Montfort (Starkenberg) in western Galilee, belonging to the Teutonic Knights, a third military order that came into existence during the late Crusader period. The Templars also controlled Gaza, which guarded the approach from Moslem Egypt. Each of the two main orders could put into the field about three hundred knights and a couple of thousand foot-soldiers – together the equivalent of all the forces raised directly by the local rulers. In battle the warriors most feared by the Moslem enemy were marked by the red crosses on white tunics worn by the Templars, and the white crosses on black tunics of the Hospitallers.

Through grants and bequests of land and villages the orders became the biggest single landowners in the Crusader states, while their branches in Europe disposed of extensive feudal estates there. In addition, they had their own churches and ecclesiastical properties. With their huge surplus revenues and the international ramifications of their order the Templars developed a type of corporate business far removed from their founding ideology. They became bankers and money-lenders to a number of princes in Outremer, in European countries and even in Moslem lands bordering on the Crusader kingdoms. The order had developed into a unique blend of private army, monastic commune, philanthropic association and high-level finance house.

When the fall of Acre in 1291 ended the Crusader occupation of the Holy Land, Cyprus remained in Crusader hands and the Templars established their permanent headquarters there. The Hospitallers, too, remained in Cyprus for a while, then gained a new home by invading and seizing the island of Rhodes, and in a later period took over Malta. The Teutonic Knights withdrew to their widespread holdings in the Baltic region, especially Prussia.

The Templars fell into disfavour and made many enemies, notably King Philip IV of France. The image of the order had been damaged by their money-lending transactions (never a popular role), their Moslem ties, their quarrels with the Hospitallers and stories that they indulged in secret heresies and orgies. Philip could not tolerate the order being a

OPPOSITE The Crusader Church of St Anne adjacent to the Temple Mount.

state within a state and a church within a church. Nor could he tolerate repaying a large sum he had borrowed from the French Templars. He enlisted the support of the Pope, a Frenchman, to smash the order.

A number of leading Templars were arrested on the testimony of hired informers, tortured into 'confessions' and then burnt at the stake. The main formal charge against them was spitting on the cross in their hidden rituals. In 1312 a papal decree abolished the order altogether and ruled that its wealth and property should be used to reimburse the costs of the trials, with the balance handed over to the Hospitallers. Two years later the grand master of the Templars was publicly burnt in Paris. That rang down the final curtain on the remarkable organization that had started so humbly on the Temple Mount nearly two centuries earlier. All that survives in modern times of this medieval power and pageantry is the Freemason Order of the Temple. Its lodges (mainly in the United States) devote themselves to masonic rites and charitable works.

In their heyday the Knights Templars had an important branch in London. The founder of the order, Hugh of Paience, left Jerusalem with four of his original brethren on a recruiting tour of Europe. He arrived in England in 1128 and was well received by King Henry I. There were Englishmen among the three hundred knights he took back with him to the Holy Land. The local order started in Holborn, in London, then moved to their monastery complex at New Temple in a meadow sloping towards the Thames next to the present Follet Street. When their round Temple Church, inspired by the Templum Domini (Dome of the Rock) in Jerusalem, was completed in 1185, the patriarch came from the Holy Land to consecrate it, in the presence of King Henry II and his court. Henry politely declined the patriarch's offer that he should assume the crown of Jerusalem.

The English Temple became so wealthy and powerful that its master was among the barons who obtained the Magna Carta from King John in 1215. But when the order was smashed by King Louis of France, with the co-operation of the Pope, the English Temple was also wound up. Its buildings were handed over to the rival Order of St John, the Hospitallers. They were leased to and later acquired by two guilds of City lawyers that then became the Inns of Court, still known as the Middle Temple and the Inner Temple. They still retain some old customs that are echoes from their Templar predecessors. The walls of the banqueting halls are hung with the heraldic shields of their treasurers. The legal title of 'sergeant-at-law' derives from the sergeants-at-arms who were the yeomen who fought with the Crusaders. Even the waiters are called 'panyer men', from the *pannarius* of the Templars. But the vocation of the bewigged judges and barristers belonging to these Inns of Court has little in common with that of the fighting men in armour who once occupied these beautiful buildings.

Jewish Pilgrims

Twenty or thirty years after the Crusader occupation the attitude towards the Jews became more tolerant in the Latin kingdom, although anti-Jewish atrocities continued to stain the annals of later Crusades on their way through Europe. Outside of Jerusalem Jewish life started reviving in Palestine, with the main community in Acre. In the stream of Christian pilgrimage there was a growing number of Jewish pilgrims and travellers. In the later Crusader period they were allowed to enter Jerusalem and pray in the vicinity of the Temple area, though residence was still barred to them.

The most illustrious Jewish visitor to the Holy Land in this period was the scholar, philosopher and medical authority Rabbi Moses ben Maimon (the Rambam), generally known as Maimonides. In 1165, when he was thirty years old, he escaped from Moslem persecution in Fez with his father and family. They reached Acre, where they remained with the local community for five months. One of the communal leaders took them on a tour round the Holy Land, during which, Maimonides recorded in one of his commentaries, he entered the site of the 'great and holy house' and prayed there. Maimonides endorsed the belief that the Temple Mount remained holy after the sanctuary had been destroyed: 'Although because of our sins the Temple is desolate today, everyone is in duty bound to reverence it even as though it were established ... even though it is desolate it retains its sanctity' (*Hilkhoth Bet ha-Beherith*). From Acre the family moved to Cairo, where Maimonides became the leader of the Jewish community and the physician to the vizier (governor) appointed by Saladin.

The Saracen leader, Saladin, who defeated the Crusader forces at the Horns of Hittin and recaptured Jerusalem.

Pilgrims travelling to Jerusalem; from a seventeenth-century German travel book.

Rabbi Pethaliah of Regensburg (Ratisbon) came to Palestine in about 1180, and found the Jews there to be poor and limited in number compared to the vigorous Babylonian community he had visited on the way. He located only one Jew living in Jerusalem, a cloth-dyer called Abraham, who showed him the Mount of Olives and the gates to the Temple Mount.

The most renowned Jewish traveller in the Middle Ages was Benjamin of Tudela, a town in northern Spain. In the course of a journey throughout the Mediterranean and the Near East that lasted some fourteen years, he reached the Holy Land about 1167. In Jerusalem he found a little Jewish colony of two hundred souls living together near the Tower of David, and operating a dye-house for which they paid a tax to the king. In his factual style Benjamin noted down the details of the buildings on the Temple Mount, and stated that 'in front of this place is the Western Wall, which is one of the walls of the Holy of Holies. This is called the Gate of Mercy, and hither come all the Jews to pray before the Wall

in the open court.' Benjamin mentions the custom for Jewish pilgrims to write their names on the stones of the Wall.

Benjamin also described other Jewish holy places, such as Rachel's Tomb and the Cave of Machpelah (the Tombs of the Patriarchs) at Hebron. He visited the other towns in the country where there were Jews – Acre, Haifa, Caesarea, Nablus, Bethlehem, Ashkelon and Tiberias.

The Saracens   The Latin kingdom of Jerusalem lasted ninety years. In 1187 the Crusader forces were defeated at the Horns of Hittin in the eastern Galilee by the brilliant Saracen leader, the Sultan Saladin (Salah-ed-din), an Armenian Turk by birth. (Saracen was an old Graeco-Roman name for desert Arabs. It was used by the Crusaders for their Moslem foes in general.) Saladin entered Jerusalem on the anniversary of the day in the Moslem calendar when, according to legend, Mohammed had ascended to heaven from the Temple Mount in his dream. Saladin protected the Christian inhabitants and churches from harm with a chivalry that was in striking contrast to the barbaric behaviour of the Crusaders when the city fell to them. All the Franks (as the Crusaders and other western Europeans were called in the Levant) were obliged to leave, on redeeming themselves at the rate of 10 dinars per man, 5 for a woman and one for a child. A lump sum was accepted for the poor, who could not afford these payments. They departed for Antioch in three long convoys. The Orthodox Christians were allowed to remain on the payment of an extra head tax. In 1190 the Jews were officially invited to settle again in Jerusalem.

One of Saladin's first acts in the city was to Moslemize the Temple Mount again. The Templum Domini Church reverted to being the Dome of the Rock Mosque by the symbolic act of removing the cross on top of it and putting back the crescent. The plaster covering the Arabic inscriptions was scraped off. Every reminder of Templar occupation was removed from the El Aksa, and it was once more equipped and dedicated as a mosque. Both buildings were sprinkled with rose water in a rite of purification.

The Crusaders kept a foothold at Tyre on the coast, together with control of the sea. In 1191 a fresh Crusader army landed, led by King Philip of France and King Richard the Lion Heart of England. After Acre had fallen to them Philip returned home and Richard advanced down the coastal plain to Jaffa. But he was unable to develop an offensive against Jerusalem. The following year he concluded a treaty with Saladin confirming the territory held by each, with access to Jerusalem for Christian pilgrims.

Forty years later Frederick II of Germany was ceded Jerusalem by the then Egyptian sultan, in exchange for a promise of Crusader help against the caliph in Baghdad. However the Temple Mount with its mosques remained in Moslem hands. This time the Crusaders kept Jerusalem for fifteen years, when it was retaken and sacked by the troops of the Mameluke Egyptian sultan. The city would not be under Christian rule again for seven centuries.

The kingdom of Acre lasted until 1291, when the Mameluke regime overran the city, as well as the other Crusader towns along the coast – Tyre, Sidon and Haifa. The two centuries of the Crusader story in the Holy Land had come to an end.

In the western mind the Crusaders linger as legendary knights in shining armour riding off to redeem the holy places. For the Jews the Crusades were a blood-soaked chapter in their saga of suffering in medieval Europe. Modern historians tend to see the Latin kingdoms in Palestine as the first venture in European colonialism – the force that was to dominate the world from the seventeenth to the twentieth century.

Under Saracen rule the Jewish community in Jerusalem revived. Access to the Temple area was once more permitted and a growing

RIGHT The excavation of the southern wall of the Temple Mount by Professor Mazor exposed vast blocks of Herodian masonry.

OVERLEAF 'The Wailing Wall' by Isaac Snowman, painted in 1922.

number of Jews came to Jerusalem from the countries of dispersion.

In 1210 Rabbi Samuel ben Samson arrived from France with a group of Jewish settlers. In a long report to his congregation back home he described how they rent their garments as prescribed when they came in sight of the Holy City, and burst into tears of emotion. On the Sabbath they were allowed on to the Temple Mount for the afternoon prayers: '... on the spot where the uncircumcised [the Gentiles] had time and again set up a sanctuary ... the Ishmaelites [Arabs] venerate this spot.'

In the following year another three hundred of the Jewish devout arrived from France and England to live in Jerusalem. During the next few decades the Jewish population of the city reached a total of some four thousand. They were nearly wiped out in the capture of the city by the Mamelukes in 1250, and its sack by Mongol invaders a decade later. When the great Spanish scholar Nachmanides – Rabbi Moses ben Nachman, known as the Rambam – came to settle in the city in 1267, he found seventy Jewish families in all. He reconstructed a synagogue and brought back the Scrolls of the Law from Shechem, where they had been taken for safe keeping by Jewish refugees. Nachmanides noted that the pilgrimages to the Temple area were resumed, and expressed the hope that 'he who has been privileged to see Jerusalem in its ruin will be privileged to see it restored to its glory'.

The Ottoman Turks

The Mamelukes were a Moslem dynasty founded by former Turkish and Circassian slaves. They ruled Egypt and Palestine for over 250 years. In 1516 the Ottoman Turks overthrew the Mameluke regime and annexed Syria, Palestine and Egypt. They were warlike nomads from the central Asian steppes who had been converted to Islam. In the middle of the fifteenth century they surged westward, captured Constantinople and put an end to the Byzantine empire. Constantinople became the capital of the new Ottoman empire and the Turkish sultan proclaimed himself Caliph of Islam.

Many of the Jews expelled from Spain and Portugal found refuge in Turkey and prospered there. When the Turks acquired Palestine this religious tolerance was extended to its Christian and Jewish inhabitants by Sultan Selim I. Both the numbers and the intellectual level of the Palestine Jewish community were raised by an influx of Sephardim – Spanish Jews. Selim's son and successor, Suleiman the Magnificent, took a special interest in Jerusalem. He reconstructed the splendid walls and gates which still enclose the Old City and did much to improve and adorn the *Haram esh-Sharif*. After Suleiman there followed over three centuries of corrupt and inefficient Turkish rule in Palestine, which was virtually controlled by a succession of semi-autonomous pashas as governors.

Ottoman rule lasted almost exactly four centuries, until the country was occupied by the British army in the First World War. The Holy

LEFT The gates of Hulda the prophetess in the southern wall of the Temple Mount. A watercolour by William Simpson, 1873.

Land was once more under a Christian power – this time neither Byzantine nor Latin, but Protestant. Thirty years later, in 1948, Britain's League of Nations Mandate ended, and the state of Israel was proclaimed. For the first time in two thousand years the Jews were again an independent nation in their ancient homeland. It was a situation previously unknown in the history of either Christianity or Islam. One of the first acts of the Jewish state was to guarantee the holy places and religious interests of all three world faiths.

17 The Western Wall

As early as the third and fourth centuries AD there were rabbis who referred to the Western Wall of the Temple Mount as being especially sacred, because it was close to the Holy of Holies of the demolished Temple, where the Divine Presence was thought to linger. To quote the fourth-century rabbi, Acha: 'The Shechinah has never departed from the Western Wall, as it is written, "Behold, He standeth behind our Wall".' There was no suggestion at that stage that a particular section of the Western Wall was an exclusive holy place. In the succeeding centuries Jews were at times allowed on to the Temple Mount itself. They also prayed and lamented at the different gates of the mount, and from the Mount of Olives.

It is unclear when the part that became specifically defined as *Ha-Kotel Ha-Ma'aravi* (the Western or Wailing Wall) was accepted as a fixed and regular place of worship. That usage must have crystallized in the early medieval period. A synagogue already stood at this spot in the eleventh century. In the twelfth century Benjamin of Tudela mentions the prayer meetings in the Azarah, the open space before this part of the Wall. Certainly from the Middle Ages onwards the *Ha-Kotel Ha-Ma'-aravi* served as the most holy shrine of the Jewish faith, and the symbol of the destroyed First and Second Temples.

Under Ottoman rule the Jewish prayers at the *Kotel* were a regular and tolerated practice. Moses Hagiz, a noted seventeenth-century scholar, records a Moslem story of how Sultan Selim, the conqueror of Jerusalem, recovered the Wall. It had been buried under ordure emptied on it by Christians. The Sultan threw money over the heap and in digging out the coins the poor people of the city started to clear the Wall. A similar story is attributed to Selim's son, Suleiman the Magnificent.

The Nineteenth Century

In the nineteenth century the Jewish community in Palestine started to expand, and a growing stream of settlers, pilgrims and visitors came from western lands. For Gentiles too, the country was no longer just a holy land for religious pilgrims but a target for travellers, tourists, explorers and archaeologists. The Jews praying at the Western Wall, especially on the eve of the Sabbath or on a festival, were one of the regular sights for visitors to Jerusalem. It was treated as such in the first guide-books, such as Murray's *Handbook to Syria and Palestine* (1858), the *Joanne Guide* (1861) and Baedeker's *Palestine and Syria* (1894). It was only in the late nineteenth century, incidentally, that the Turkish authorities permitted Christians to visit the Temple Mount.

A typical Sabbath scene at the Wall is described in 1894 by the French archaeologist and scholar Philippe Berger:

> In the broad sunshine we followed little unpaved lanes hemmed in by wretched hovels. As we went on we met men and women dressed in a sort of big white shroud, who were taking the same road as we were. The crowd became more and more dense walking side by side jostling one another. At last at the corner of a little alley jammed with people we came to the wall of the Jews ... you are in a narrow passage so crowded with people that you must use your elbows to get through. There is a procession today, it is the first of Nisan, and it is hardly possible to pass. Some children led by the cantor sing with extraordinary energy. The Jewish women are in white, the men dressed in robes of purple or blue velvet, fur hats on their heads, long beards, their curls of hair combed in front of their ears hang on their temples, in the hands are old worn Bibles bound in black [*Notes de Voyage* 1895].

The unfeeling behaviour of some of the sightseers at the Wall offended Captain (later General Sir Charles) Warren, when he was surveying the Temple Mount in the 1860s for the Palestine Exploration Fund. It appears that his professional interest in the masonry of the Wall was combined with a human interest in the worshippers. In *Underground Jerusalem* (1876), he notes:

> ... many of the stones are very much worn, and the people in prayer thrust their hands into the interstices, and also push, as far into the crevices as they can, prayers they have written to God, thinking that they will be carried from thence up to heaven. If afterwards they come and find these paper scraps gone, they think their prayers will be answered. On one occasion, I met a Frank diligently (when no Jews were by) collecting as many of these letters as he could to send home as curiosities; such documents, I think, ought to have been looked upon as worthy of remaining in their places. ...
>
> It is a most remarkable sight; these people all thronging the pavement, and wailing so intensely that often the tears roll down their faces. It was also a great rendezvous for Frank visitors, who walked

about laughing and making remarks, as though it were all a farce, instead of realizing that it is perhaps one of the most solemn gatherings left to the Jewish church.

Warren curiously refers to European Christians as 'Franks', a term going back to the Crusades.

The efficacy of prayer at the Wall was a matter of general belief. Prayers for rain would be requested by the authorities in times of drought. In the Russo-Turkish War of 1878 the Jews were asked to offer a prayer at the Wall for the success of the Turkish army, and groups of rabbinical students went there with a military guard of honour. In 1871, when the Prince of Wales was critically ill, Sir Moses Montefiore sent a cable from London to the Chief Rabbi of Jerusalem, requesting prayers for his recovery. They were promptly held in all the synagogues. In the telegram of reply to Sir Moses the Chief Rabbi states that 'we ordered a congregation of pious and learned men to call upon our God at the Western Wall of the ancient Temple from which spot, we are told by our ancestors, the Divine Glory never departed'. Whether for this reason or not, the Prince recovered, and thirty years later succeeded his mother Queen Victoria as King Edward VII.

Indeed the Jews of Jerusalem had a personal interest in the welfare of the Prince of Wales. He had visited the Holy Land in 1862, and by special arrangement had met the Chief Rabbi and the heads of the community at the Western Wall. He asked the Chief Rabbi whether the Wall was a relic of Solomon's Temple, and the affirmative reply 'evidently impressed the Prince, for he raised the covering from his head in token of the sincere veneration which he felt for the sacredness of the spot' (*Jewish Chronicle*, London, 2 May 1862). At the Prince's request prayers were offered in Hebrew for his mother, the Queen, and the soul of his father, the late Prince Consort.

Sir Moses Montefiore was a very devout Jew who maintained a synagogue at his home in Ramsgate, England. He regularly prayed at the Wall when he visited Palestine, and noted that fact in his diary. He made altogether seven pilgrimages to the Holy Land, the first in 1839 and the last in 1875 at the age of ninety-one (he lived to be over a hundred). As the leading Jewish figure of his age, Sir Moses used his prestige to ameliorate the primitive conditions at the Wall. In 1866 he reported that the Governor of Jerusalem, Izzet Pasha, had given him permission to erect an awning at the Wall to afford shelter and protection from the rain and heat for the worshippers. He also asked the Pasha to stop the Arabs throwing refuse and dung on to the pavement in front of the Wall.

James Finn, who served as the first British consul in Jerusalem from 1845 to 1862, constantly tried to relieve the Jews from the money exactions of the Turks and the Arabs. In the record of his mission, *Stirring*

Times (1878), he noted that the Jewish community had to pay

> ... the sum of £300 a year to the effendi whose house adjoins the
> Wailing Wall for permission to pray there; £100 a year to the villagers
> of Siloam for not disturbing the graves on the Mount of Olives; £50 a
> year to the Ta'amra Arabs for not injuring the Sepulchre of Rachel
> near Bethlehem, and about £10 a year to Sheikh Abu Ghosh for not
> molesting their people on the high road from Jaffa, although he was
> highly paid by the Turkish government as warden of the road.

Finn referred to these bribes as 'disgraceful to the Turkish government'.

Finn's role as protector of the local Jews had a remarkable background.
He owed his appointment as consul to the great social reformer of early
Victorian England, the Earl of Shaftesbury. An extremely pious man,
Shaftesbury was convinced that the millennium could be brought forward by two events – the acceptance of Christ by the Jews and their
restoration to the Holy Land. England was destined to be the chosen
instrument for fulfilling these aims. Shaftesbury headed the London
Society for Promoting Christianity among the Jews; it had a glittering
committee, but the results were negligible. He also put forward a plan
to settle Jews in Palestine, with British sponsorship and support. Under
his pressure his kinsman Lord Palmerston, the powerful foreign secretary, made a half-hearted approach to the Sultan about the settlement
project, but nothing came of it.

Palmerston did, however, obtain two important concessions from the
Sultan, for the stationing in Jerusalem of an Anglican bishop and a
British consul. Both were Shaftesbury's nominees. The first Anglican
Bishop of Jerusalem was a converted Jew called Alexander, a professor
of Hebrew in London. As the choice for consul, James Finn shared the
views of his aristocratic patron. In Palestine he made a rough census of
the Jewish population and found there were less than ten thousand –
mostly very poor. In the years to come Finn spent much of his time and
his own money trying to promote Jewish settlement on the land. (He
also made an abortive attempt to establish near Bethlehem a village of
Jewish converts to Christianity.)

It is not surprising that Finn should record in his memoirs: 'I have
experienced many acts of kindness from Jews in the Holy Land. Among
other affecting tokens of gratitude, individuals have on several occasions
resorted to the Western Wall of the Temple to pray for my children and
also for myself in times of sorrow and sickness.'

**The British
Mandate**

At the end of the nineteenth century Jewish settlement in Palestine
was given a fresh impetus through the Zionist movement. The Western
Wall became a symbol of national hopes for the future and not just of
religious memories from the past.

At the beginning of December 1917 Jerusalem was taken by General

Allenby, commander of the British forces in the campaign in Palestine against the Turks. On 11 December he officially entered the city on foot as a mark of respect, following the example of the Caliph Omar thirteen centuries earlier. Allenby caused the following proclamation to be read to the inhabitants:

> Since your city is regarded with affection by the adherents of three of the great religions of mankind, and its soil has been consecrated by the prayers and pilgrimages of multitudes of devout people of these three religions for many centuries, therefore do I make known to you that every sacred building, monument, holy spot, shrine, traditional site, endowment, pious bequest, or customary place of prayer, of whatsoever form of the three religions, will be maintained and protected, according to the existing customs and beliefs of those to whose faiths they are sacred.

Palestine remained under British military rule until 1920, when a civil administration was set up and Sir Herbert Samuel, an Anglo-Jewish statesman, was appointed as the first high commissioner. In 1922 the League of Nations formally conferred the Mandate for Palestine on Great Britain, and it came into force the following year when Turkey signed the Treaty of Lausanne.

The Palestine Mandate made special provisions for religious interests. Under Article 13 the mandatory power was responsible for 'preserving the existing rights and of securing free access to the holy places, religious buildings and sites and the free exercise of worship, while ensuring the requirements of public order and decorum'. The League of Nations remained the final authority in these matters.

To preserve 'existing rights' was easier said than done, since many religious places were subject to conflicting claims by different religions and sects. Article 14 of the mandate instructed the mandatory power to set up a special commission 'to study, define and determine the rights and claims in connection with the holy places and the rights and claims relating to the different religious communities in Palestine'. It proved impossible to get agreement among all concerned even for the setting up of this commission, and it never came into existence. The Palestine administration was left to deal with each dispute that arose, and to keep the peace among the different sects. In doing so, the administration clung to one magic formula – the *status quo*.

Historically the *status quo* referred first and foremost to the struggle that had gone on through the centuries for control of the main Christian shrines – the Church of the Holy Sepulchre in Jerusalem and the Church of the Nativity in Bethlehem. The rival Christian camps were the Orthodox (eastern) Rites that had been associated with the Byzantine empire and the Catholic (Latin) Rites subject to the authority of the Pope in

OVERLEAF Worshippers at the Western Wall, 1900.

Rome. The main eastern churches were the Greek Orthodox, the Armenian, the Syrian Orthodox and the Coptic.

The Crusader occupation meant that the Roman Catholic Church had taken from the Orthodox control of the Christian holy places. As soon as Saladin had restored Moslem rule in Jerusalem the Byzantine emperor sent a delegation to gain his favour.

During the four centuries of Ottoman rule, from the sixteenth century, the balance of influence over the Christian holy places shifted back and forth. In 1757 the Sultan issued a firman (decree) setting out in intricate detail the rights of the chief claimants in the two shrines. The firman dealt with such seemingly trivial particulars as the use of parts of an altar, the right to hang a lamp or picture, the cleaning of steps and the timing of processions and services. Even the driving of a nail into a disputed wall or pillar might be construed as an assertion of ownership. As a result, parts of the two churches remained in chronic disrepair because there was a stalemate over the right to repair them.

In the nineteenth century the Christian shrines were caught up in the conflicts between the major European powers. A weak and corrupt Ottoman empire had become 'the sick man of Europe', and was propped up by western countries to block the southward expansion of Czarist Russia. As part of this struggle Russia made herself the protector of Orthodox claims in the Holy Land. (The Russian Orthodox Church had also entered the picture.) In 1852 the Sultan issued another firman, reaffirming that of 1757. It was favourable to the Orthodox and unacceptable to the others.

The controversy over the holy places was one of the causes of the Crimean War of 1854–5. At the conclusion of peace the *status quo* was guaranteed, without the points in dispute being resolved. At the end of the Russo-Turkish War of 1878 it was laid down that the Sultan's firmans should be observed in practice, though disputes continued. Britain was relieved to inherit from the Turks the firmans that constituted a ready-made *status quo* for the main Christian holy places.

This background is relevant to the British handling of the Jewish-Moslem dispute over the Western Wall. The mandatory authorities were well aware that in Palestine religious issues tended to become highly political, and that disputes focused on what might appear unimportant details. The administration sought to apply blindly to the Western Wall the principles of the *status quo* relating to the Christian shrines. In practice, that increasingly meant that the Jews should not be allowed to do anything at the Wall to which the Moslem Arabs strongly objected.

The first test case came on the Day of Atonement in 1925, when the narrow pavement in front of the Wall was crammed with Jewish worshippers. Acting on complaints from the Moslem authorities of the *Haram esh-Sharif*, the British police entered the lane and removed a few benches and seats that had been placed there for the use of the aged and infirm on this day of fasting. The British government justified this action on the ground of the *status quo*, though the facts about past practices were uncertain. When the Zionist Organization protested to the League of Nations, that body prudently refrained from expressing an opinion on the merits of the dispute, but urged the mandatory authorities to get Jewish-Moslem agreement.

A similar incident occurred on the Day of Atonement in 1928. During the service at the Wall the police forcibly removed a light screen temporarily placed there to separate men from women. In the scuffle that took place some of the worshippers were injured. This action caused an uproar in the international press, and a debate in the House of Commons in London.

The government issued a White Paper (policy statement), again invoking the *status quo* in support of the act of the police at the Wall. The League once more appealed for agreement between the two communities, but the White Paper held that 'public opinion had definitely removed the matter from the purely religious orbit and had made it a political and racial question'. The document then laid down the principles by which official policy was governed:

> ... having in mind the terms of Article 13 of the Mandate for Palestine, [the Government] have taken the view that the matter is one in which they are bound to maintain the 'status quo', which they have regarded as being, in general terms, that the Jewish community have a right of access to the pavement for the purposes of their devotions, but may bring to the Wall only those appurtenances of worship which were permitted under the Turkish regime.

The use of benches, chairs and screens was forbidden, since it was not proved that they had been permitted by the Turks. The White Paper also laid down that the Wall and the pavement in front of it were Moslem property, subject to the Jewish right of access.

The Jewish reaction was that no such restrictions had been enforced under the Ottoman regime. In any case, it was argued, that question no longer applied, since the mandate had guaranteed the Jewish community complete freedom of worship, which included prayers at the Wall.

The Moslem side hailed the British White Paper of November 1928 as a victory, and were encouraged to step up a campaign of pressure and harassment in connection with the Wall. Propaganda charges were spread through the Arab population and the Moslem world, alleging that the Jews planned to usurp the Wall and then to attack and take over the mosques on the Temple Mount. A society was formed for the 'defence' of the El Aksa Mosque and other Moslem holy places, and branches were opened round the country. The Western Wall was for the first time

defined as a place holy to Islam in its own right, because of the legendary connection with Mohammed's steed, El Burak. New entrances were made at both ends of the pavement in front of the Wall, so that a larger number of Arabs came passing through with their donkeys and other animals while the Jews were at prayer. On a rooftop at the southern end of the lane a muezzin was stationed, loudly calling the Moslem faithful to prayer five times a day. Behind the Wall at the northern end the Zikr ritual was incessantly performed; it consisted of praising Allah with a great clamour of shouting, banging and playing of instruments. The Wall was lowered along the access lane so that the Jews were no longer screened from observation during their devotions. A private house at the southern end of the pavement was converted into a *zawiyah*, a Moslem place for prayer and Koran readings. Most disturbing of all to the Jewish community was the new building being constructed at the edge of the Temple platform overlooking the Jewish place of prayer, and adding 4 feet to the height of the Wall. All these innovations were deliberate changes in the *status quo*, and most of them were obviously designed to harass and annoy the Jews who came to the Wall.

The Jewish leadership protested strongly to the government, but with little result. At the same time the Jewish authorities tried to allay the Moslem fears that had been incited. In its petition to the League of Nations, the Zionist Executive stated that 'we wish emphatically to repudiate as false and libellous the rumours that are circulated that it is the intention of the Jewish people to menace the inviolability of the Moslem Holy Place which encloses the Mosque of Omar and the Mosque of El Aksa'. For its part, the Supreme Moslem Council headed by the Mufti of Jerusalem submitted a memorandum stating that 'Moslems believe that the Jews' aim is to take possession of the Mosque of El Aksa on the pretence that it is the Temple, by starting with the Western Wall ...'. The traditional Jewish right to pray at the Wall was dismissed in the Moslem memorandum as 'a mere favour granted by the inhabitants of the quarter to visitors of all communities and creeds'. In other words, it was denied that the Jews had any rights at all.

The Moslem campaign was undoubtedly being inspired by the sinister figure of the Mufti, Haj Amin el-Husseini. At the beginning of the mandate he had been involved in the 1920 riots, and then fled to Syria to escape trial. In a short-sighted bid to overcome Palestinian Arab resistance to the mandate, the high commissioner, Sir Herbert Samuel, had not only pardoned him, but had appointed him as president of the newly formed Supreme Moslem Council in Palestine. The Mufti had exploited this position to make himself the leader of militant Arab nationalism in Palestine, and the most dangerous foe of the British, the Jews and the more moderate Arabs alike. He was now fanning Moslem religious sentiment over the Western Wall dispute for more far-reaching

OPPOSITE The narrow pavement in front of the Wall before 1967.

political aims of his own. (Even after the 1929 disturbances the British authorities would still cling to the delusion that the Mufti wanted to co-operate with them, and was a restraining influence on his own people. That naive belief was laid to rest only when he led the Arab rebellion that broke out in 1936, and when he fled to Germany and collaborated with the Hitler regime during the Second World War. He died in Beirut in 1974.)

In August 1929 Jewish anger mounted over the changes made by the Moslems and the unwillingness of the government to maintain the *status quo* as far as Jewish rights to the Wall were concerned. Stabbing attacks by Arabs on individual Jews at the Wall inflamed feelings still more. On 15 August, which was Tisha B'Av – the ninth day of Av, commemorating the destruction of the Temple – several hundred Jews belonging to a right-wing Zionist party marched in procession to the Wall, where they displayed the Zionist flag and sang the Zionist anthem, *Hatikvah*.

The following day an excited Moslem crowd of about two thousand, headed by the sheikhs of the El Aksa Mosque, surged to the Wall and were roused by inflammatory speeches. Jewish petitions inserted in the crevices were taken out and burnt, as well as the prayer books found there. The only Jew present at the Wall was the beadle, who was roughed up and had his clothes torn.

During the next few days a number of Jews were injured by Arab attacks in Jerusalem, and one Jewish boy was stabbed to death. On

Haj Amin el-Husseini, the Mufti of Jerusalem, instigated the Arab riots of 1936.

23 August a huge crowd of Arabs, many of them brought in from the surrounding villages, assembled at the *Haram esh-Sharif* and were incited by their leaders. Armed with heavy clubs, sticks and swords, they swarmed out of the Jaffa and Damascus Gates and into nearby Jewish quarters, yelling with frenzy. There followed a wave of Arab attacks and local disturbances all over the country.

The authorities were taken off guard and had woefully inadequate police and military forces available. Royal Air Force contingents were rushed in from Trans-Jordan, and naval vessels were hurriedly despatched from the British base at Malta. By the time order was restored 113 Jews had been killed and 339 wounded. There were nearly as many Arab casualties, mostly inflicted in clashes with British security forces.

The most murderous Arab attack was on the small and pious Jewish community in Hebron. That massacre, in which over a hundred Jews were killed and wounded, wiped out a community that had lived in the town from medieval times. Only forty years later did Jews again take up residence in the Kiriyat Arba quarter on the edge of the town.

What had started as an apparently minor dispute about the 'appurtenances of worship' at the Western Wall had developed into widespread disorders and bloodshed, and a major political crisis. The mandatory government appointed the Shaw Commission to investigate the disturbances. Its report, at the beginning of 1930, marked the start of a British retreat from the policy of the Jewish National Home in Palestine, as first set out in the Balfour Declaration of 1917. The Shaw Report stressed that the Arab attacks were an expression of hostility against Zionist colonization in the country, and suggested restrictions on Jewish immigration and land purchase.

The report was endorsed by the British government in the Passfield White Paper, named after the colonial secretary of the time. It provoked a political storm, and the prime minister, Ramsay MacDonald, somewhat modified the policy in a letter to the Zionist president, Dr Chaim Weizmann.

One result of the 1929 disturbances was that, at the request of the League of Nations, the British government appointed an international commission 'to determine the rights and claims of Moslems and Jews in connection with the Western or Wailing Wall at Jerusalem'. The commission had three members, all non-British: a former Swedish minister for foreign affairs, a Swiss judge and a former Dutch colonial governor. It arrived in Jerusalem in June 1930, and heard extensive evidence from the administration and the two communities concerned. The Jewish memorandum to the commission ended with a moving plea:

We would ask you, in the first place, to view this Wall as the most ancient of the sacred places in Jerusalem, and as one which would, by

ABOVE The tense days of July 1936; police were posted in every quarter of the city in an effort to keep the peace.

BELOW British troops attempt to control a rioting crowd, 1936.

its imposing character and its great history, interest every civilized man. It would be natural that such a unique monument of antiquity, to put it only upon that plane, be so cared for and so placed that it could be approached by all with a feeling of reverence, and that its proportions and beauty might be seen. What do you behold? A narrow lane, 3·6 metres wide and 28 metres long, serving also as the entrance to a series of alms-houses and hovels through which men, donkeys and sometimes even camels pass at any time of the day – such is the approach to an historic monument nearly 3000 years old. Upon this ground, in the first instance, we submit that your honourable body should request the Mandatory to see to it that the approaches to this Wall are decent and respectable, and that the site in front of the Wall itself should cease to be a thoroughfare such as it is now claimed to be. If such considerations apply with regard to any ancient monument, how much more are they applicable when the ancient monument is also a place of sacred resort to a whole people, which has seen almost all of its sacred places in its old land handed over to others, and craves for the privilege of worship before this place in order, and in decency, and in respect, and without interruption, and without nuisance. For the claim laid before you is simply for the continuation under conditions of decency and decorum of a sacred custom which has been carried on by us for many centuries without infringement upon the religious rights of others.

The commission's main conclusions were: a) that the Moslems had sole ownership of the Western Wall, of the pavement in front of the Wall and of the adjacent Moghrabi Quarter. All of these were Waqf properties, that is, religious or charitable trusts. On the other hand the Moslems were not entitled to carry out any construction or demolition on these properties which would encroach on the pavement, impair the access of Jews to the Wall or interfere with Jewish prayers there. It was also pointed out that the Wall was registered as a historical site under the Antiquities Law, and therefore under government control; b) that the Jews had a right of free access to the Western Wall for the purpose of devotions at all times, subject to the restrictions laid down by the government; and c) that for their part the Moslems were to refrain from creating a disturbance during times of Jewish prayers – for instance, by keeping the gates open, by driving animals through or by conducting the noisy Zikr ceremony.

These rules were given statutory effect by a British Order-in-Council. The text of the law shows to what Alice-in-Wonderland absurdity the right to pray at the Wall had been reduced. The heading to the document is like a flourish of heraldic trumpets:

PALESTINE (WESTERN or WAILING WALL)
ORDER IN COUNCIL, 1931
At the Court at Buckingham Palace
the 19th day of May, 1931
The King's Most Excellent
Majesty in Council

WHEREAS by treaty capitulation grant usage sufferance and other lawful means His Majesty has power and jurisdiction within Palestine: ...

The end of the Order-in-Council is a schedule laying down the exact height, width and depth in centimetres of the objects that the Jews were permitted to use at the Wall, namely, an ark, a table for the ark, a table for the scrolls, a small stand for prayer-books, ritual lamps and stand, a portable washstand, a water-container and a prayer mat. Sitting on a bench or stool, separating the women with a screen, stretching an awning to protect the worshippers from the sun's heat and blowing a *shofar* had all become breaches of the law punishable by imprisonment or fine. (After that it was to become a tradition to smuggle in a *shofar* on the Day of Atonement, blow it at the appointed time and be arrested.)

The Order-in-Council was in effect His Majesty's firman, laying down the fine print of a *status quo* for the Western Wall, in the way the Sultan's firmans of 1757 and 1852 had done for the Church of the Holy Sepulchre and the Church of the Nativity. This *status quo* for the Wall did not survive the end of the mandate, and was swept away by two Israel-Arab wars: the War of Independence in 1948–9, and the Six-Day War in 1967.

The Wall Area   The surroundings of the Wall underwent a marked change after 1967. This is how old-timers remember it during the mandatory period.

The length of the entire Wall which bounded the western side of the Temple Mount is 1,580 feet long, running from north to south; but most of it is hidden by structures built against it through the centuries. The exposed section, known traditionally as the Western Wall (*Ha-Kotel Ha-Ma'aravi*), is the southern part, lying near the south-western corner of the Temple Mount. It is only 30 metres, less than 100 feet, in length. During two thousand years the Tyropean valley outside the Wall had filled up to such an extent with debris and rubbish that the foundations were about 70 feet below ground level, and nineteen courses of the huge stone blocks were buried. Only five courses of the Herodian structure were still visible above ground at the Wall. On top of these courses later layers of smaller stones were added in Roman, Mameluke and Turkish times. The top of the Wall was 58 feet above the pavement.

The pavement in front of the Wall was 11 feet wide. It was hemmed in by the wall of the Moghrabi (Moroccan) Quarter, the Arab inhabitants of which often used the pavement as a passage. Behind the patch of crowded dwellings that formed the Moghrabi Quarter, the ground rose to the edge of the Jewish Quarter.

The regular access to the Wall for worshippers and visitors was by a narrow lane that led from David Street and joined the northern end of the pavement, at right angles to it. To the north, across an open courtyard, was the Sharia (Moslem religious) Court. Above the courthouse was the residence of the president of the Supreme Moslem Council (the Mufti). From its windows one could look down on the Jews praying in front of the Wall.

At the southern end of the pavement were steps, houses and a courtyard. Above them was the Moors' Gate of the *Haram* platform, also known as the Gate of the Prophet. Set inside this part of the Wall was a small chamber, used as a mosque and named after the steed, El Burak, who had been tethered at this spot according to one version of the legend. The entrance to the El Burak Mosque was by steps from the inside of the *Haram esh-Sharif*.

The Moghrabi Quarter

The word *moghrabi*, corresponding to the Hebrew word *ma'aravi*, means 'westerner'. It was the name used in medieval times for the Arabs in North Africa and Spain, at the western end of the Arab world. (The term 'Moor' is derived from it.) The huddle of small slum dwellings belonged to a charitable trust (Waqf) set up in the thirteenth century by a wealthy Moroccan Arab called Abu Midan to house pilgrims and poor people from his country.

From the middle of the nineteenth century there were various Jewish attempts to reach agreement on rehousing the occupants and demolishing the quarter, in order to create an open space in front of the Western Wall and to facilitate the access to it.

In 1877 Baron Edmond de Rothschild, the great benefactor of early Jewish settlement in Palestine, offered to buy the Moghrabi Quarter from the Waqf authorities, who could use the funds to provide better housing for the inhabitants in another location. The proposal was acceptable to the then Mufti of Jerusalem, the father of Haj Amin el-Husseini. Baron Edmond made the transaction subject to the approval of the leaders of the Sephardi community, under whose auspices a new trust would be created for the property. Negotiations took place over a period but were not concluded, one of the obstacles being the differences of opinion within the Sephardi community itself about the nature and control of the proposed trust.

In the years before the First World War several more Jewish efforts were made to acquire the Moghrabi Quarter. There were abortive soundings through the Anglo-Palestine Bank. Again, in 1912, the matter was raised during a visit to Jerusalem by the well-known American Jewish philanthropist Nathan Straus. He was accompanied by Dr Judah Magnes (later the first president of the Hebrew University), who asked

Straus whether he would be prepared to put up the money for such a purchase. However Straus's interest lay in health services and he was busy establishing a child health centre and a soup kitchen for the Jewish poor of Jerusalem. In any case, it is not known whether there was at the time a serious prospect of an agreement with the Arabs.

A genuine opportunity presented itself from a totally unexpected quarter. After the outbreak of the war in 1914 Jamal Pasha, the powerful Turkish governor of the Syria-Palestine region and commander of the Turkish Fourth Army, moved from Damascus to Jerusalem in the autumn of that year. He received assurances of loyalty from the heads of the local Jewish community, and agreed to visit the Western Wall in the company of Albert Antebi. A Damascus-born Jew, Antebi spoke good Turkish and served as the contact man between the Palestine office of the Zionist Organization and the Ottoman authorities.

At the Wall Jamal Pasha was offended by the dilapidated state of the thirty or so dwellings that made up the Moghrabi Quarter, and the sight of several of his soldiers emerging from cheap brothels in it. There and then he proposed to Antebi that the Jewish community should buy the property for £20,000: £2,000 in cash to rehouse the inhabitants and an undertaking to pay the balance after the war. Antebi immediately reported the offer in a confidential letter to Chaim Nahum Effendi, the *haham bashi* or chief rabbi in Constantinople, asking him to enlist the help of Henry Morganthau Sen., then United States Ambassador to Turkey. He also referred the matter to Dr Arthur Ruppin, the head of the Palestine office.

Looking back, it seems incredible that the transaction should not have been concluded at once. But Dr Ruppin had neither the money nor the authority to do so. Moreover the war had plunged the Zionist Movement into total disarray. Its headquarters in Berlin had ceased to function. A provisional office was being operated in neutral Copenhagen by one member of the Zionist Executive, Victor Jacobson. Relations with the Turkish government in Constantinople were being maintained by another Zionist official, Richard Lichtheim. The funds of the organization had dried up. The files of the Central Zionist Archives in Jerusalem contain the long and frustrating correspondence (in German), in the course of which the opportunity dwindled away.

On 15 November 1914 Ruppin wrote to Lichtheim on the subject and explained that what Jamal Pasha had in mind was that the part of the cleared area near the Wall would extend the Jewish place of worship and the remaining space would be a public garden. He stressed that the money could be found only with American help and that 'if the thing is publicized it will be ruined and Jamal Pasha will be extremely annoyed'. Lichtheim sent on the letter to Jacobson, who wrote back asking for proposals about the body that would figure as the registered owner of the

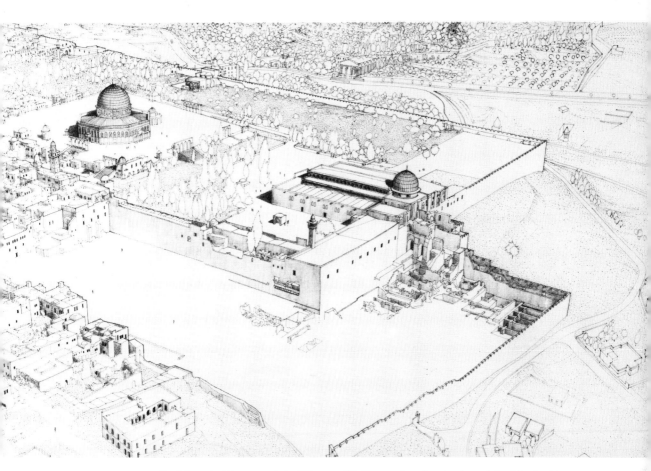

The Temple Mount and the Western Wall area after the clearing of the Moghrabi Quarter in 1967.

ground. He also complained that the price was high and asked that Ruppin should try to reduce it. Jacobson also wrote to the American Zionist leader Louis Brandeis (about to be appointed to the United States Supreme Court), asking for his help on the financial side.

In August 1916, nearly two years after Jamal Pasha's visit to the Wall, Ruppin wrote sadly that Antebi was no longer prepared to pursue the matter and no one else was in a position to do so. The story had in any case already been published in the Polish-Jewish press. By that stage of the war the Turkish authorities suspected the Palestine Jews of pro-Allied sympathies, and Jamal was expelling the active Zionist settlers – including David Ben-Gurion and Yitzhak Ben-Zvi, who more than thirty years later would be prime minister and president respectively of a Jewish state. Antebi himself was exiled to Damascus; before the end of the war he was conscripted into the Turkish army and died of typhoid.

At the beginning of 1918, after Jerusalem had been captured by the British forces under General Allenby, Dr Chaim Weizmann arrived in Palestine at the head of a Zionist commission. On 30 May he wrote to the British foreign secretary, Arthur Balfour, describing the disheartening picture facing the commission. He appealed for Balfour's support on three concrete proposals: a start with the Hebrew University project on Mount Scopus, a plan for reviving some of the Jewish farm settlements and 'the handing over of the Wailing Wall to the Jews'. On the latter question Dr Weizmann wrote that up against the Wall was 'a group of miserable, dirty cottages and derelict buildings which make the whole place, from the hygienic point of view, a positive danger, and from the sentimental point of view a source of constant humiliation to the Jews of the world'. An amicable arrangement might be reached with the Moslem trust concerned and liberal compensation would be paid. He assured Balfour that a satisfactory settling of this matter 'would help to rally the Jews, especially the great masses of orthodox Jewry in Russia, Galicia and Roumania, as well as in England, Germany and America round the platform which we have created, namely, a Jewish Palestine under British auspices'. Again, this appeal produced no tangible results.

The proposal about the Moghrabi Quarter was made once more in the Jewish memorandum submitted to the International Commission on the Western Wall in 1930. The document argued that under the existing conditions of the Moghrabi Quarter official policy was not being carried out, since it was not possible to conduct services at the Wall in such a way as to satisfy 'normal liturgical requirements and decencies'.

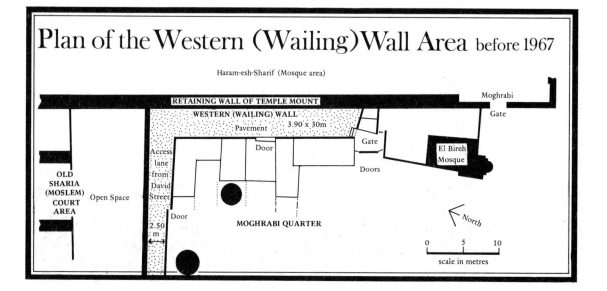

Plan of the Western (Wailing) Wall Area before 1967

Haram-esh-Sharif (Mosque area)

RETAINING WALL OF TEMPLE MOUNT

WESTERN (WAILING) WALL

Pavement   3.90´ x 30m

Moghrabi Gate

Door   Gate

El Bireh Mosque

Doors

OLD SHARIA (MOSLEM) COURT AREA

Open Space

Access lane from David Street

Door

2.50 m

MOGHRABI QUARTER

North

0   5   10

scale in metres

After this long history it is hardly surprising that the Moghrabi Quarter should promptly have been demolished with the Israel occupation of the Old City in the Six-Day War in 1967. It is already difficult to recall how the worshippers at the Wall were hemmed in on a narrow pavement before 1967.

The Western Wall plaza; an architect's model showing a possible future development for the area.

18 The State of Israel

In 1947 Britain brought the 'Palestine question' before the United Nations, the body that had replaced the League of Nations after the Second World War. In November of that year the United Nations General Assembly adopted a partition plan. Independent Jewish and Arab states would be set up in Palestine. The Jerusalem area would remain for ten years a separate enclave or *corpus separatum* under an international regime that would supervise the holy places. This proposal, it was hoped, would partly satisfy the political aspirations of both Jews and Arabs, while giving the world organization control over Jerusalem with its religious interests.

The Jewish side reluctantly accepted the partition proposal, but the Arabs rejected it out of hand and claimed the whole of Palestine. Their armed forces invaded the country in May 1948, when the British Mandate terminated and the state of Israel was proclaimed. The partition proposal was, therefore, stillborn – and with it the international regime for Jerusalem.

In the fighting the Arab Legion of Trans-Jordan cut off and shelled Jerusalem, then launched an attack to capture it. The legion occupied the eastern half of the city, including the walled Old City. The inhabitants of its Jewish Quarter were killed or taken captive and the quarter itself was laid waste. All its fifty-eight synagogues were destroyed, or used as stables or latrines. Most of the ancient Jewish cemetery on the Mount of Olives was uprooted and desecrated.

The Israel-Jordan armistice agreement of 1949 guaranteed free access for Jews to their holy places on the Jordanian side of the armistice line. That undertaking remained a dead letter. For the next nineteen years no Jew set foot in the City of David, nor prayed at the Western Wall. It was the first time since the Roman occupation that Jews had been completely cut off from the Wall.

On Monday morning, 5 June 1967, the Six-Day War started with

The ruins of the Jewish Quarter after the fighting of 1948.

heavy fighting between Israel and the Egyptian forces in the Sinai desert. The question was whether King Hussein of Jordan would join in and open a second front. Only five days previously he had flown to Cairo and with much fanfare concluded a military pact with the Egyptian president, Gamal Abdel Nasser.

Early that Monday morning Premier Levi Eshkol of Israel sent the king a message through the head of the United Nations Truce Supervision Organization, urging him to keep out of the hostilities. The appeal was rejected. Jordanian artillery opened a bombardment along the armistice line. In Jerusalem, Jordanian troops occupied the United Nations headquarters in the neutral Government House zone on the Hill of Evil Counsel. Jewish Jerusalem was lightly held by an infantry brigade of reservists. They managed to evict the Jordanians from Government House. The battle for Jerusalem was on.

A paratroop brigade of reservists was rushed up from the coastal plain. With heavy losses they broke through the Jordanian positions just north of the Old City and reached Mount Scopus. Here they were joined by an armoured brigade that had fought its way through the hills, and cut the road between Jerusalem and Ramallah. Then the paratroopers captured the Mount of Olives in a bold daylight assault. Their commander, Colonel Mordecai (Motta) Gur (later the Israel Chief of Staff), looked down from the hill at the walled city lying below, the gold and silver domes of the two mosques on the Temple Mount shining in the strong light. Grabbing the microphone of the signals' transmitter on his jeep, he called out the following message to his unit commanders: 'The Temple Mount, the Western Wall, the Old City. For two thousand years our people have prayed for this moment. Let us go forward to victory.' He then raced down the hillside and was one of the first soldiers to smash through the Lions' Gate (St Stephen's Gate), near the north-eastern corner of the *Haram esh-Sharif*. At 9.50 am he sent a signal to HQ Central Command: 'The Temple Mount is ours: repeat, the Temple Mount is ours.'

The Israel troops poured through the broken gate, driving the Jordanians through the narrow alleys and winkling out snipers. Soon a paratrooper yelled: 'The Western Wall! I can see the Wall!' His comrades rushed to join him. The exhausted soldiers, who had been in action for thirty-two hours, leant their faces against the hallowed stones of the Wall and wept. Fifteen minutes later a jeep dashed up with Rabbi Goren, the chief chaplain to the Israel forces. He recited a Hebrew prayer of thanksgiving and produced a *shofar* on which he gave a long blast.

For the first time in nineteen centuries the city of Jerusalem and the Temple site were in the hands of a Jewish state. A wave of intense excitement swept through Israel and the whole of the Jewish world. In the reunited city complete freedom of access to their holy places was ensured for the adherents of the three faiths. That included access to the Church of the Holy Sepulchre and the *Haram esh-Sharif* for the Israel Arabs, Christian and Moslem, and unrestricted access to the Western Wall for the Jews.

The inhabitants of the Moghrabi Quarter were evacuated, subject to compensation and other arrangements. The dwellings, most of them in disrepair, were then demolished and the area converted into the present paved plaza in front of the Wall. This demolition enabled the exposed part of the Wall to be extended a little southward, where it was bounded by a stone ramp constructed to lead up to the Moors' Gate.

On Wednesday, 14 June, just one week after the capture of the Old City, there occurred the Jewish pilgrim festival of *Shavuot*, the Feast of Weeks. From all over Israel people streamed to the capital in a spontaneous mass pilgrimage. All day a crowd estimated at a quarter of a million people pushed through the Dung Gate in the southern wall of the Old City and thronged into the space that had been cleared in front of

Rabbi Goren sounds the *shofar* at the Wall after the recapture of the Temple Mount, 1967.

the Wall. Some prayed in rapture; others, even the non-religious, felt this was a hallowed day.

Day by day numbers of Jews also went up on to the *Haram esh-Sharif* and visited the mosques that occupied the Temple site. For the orthodox the age-old doctrinal problem of whether it was permissible for Jews to set foot on the Temple Mount was revived. After the destruction of the Temple the general opinion of the rabbis – including Maimonides – had been that the previous rules for entry to the Temple area remained in force. But that view was difficult to apply in practice. No one had been allowed to enter the Holy of Holies except the high priest, and even he only on one day in the year, Yom Kippur. But its exact site could no longer be defined with certainty, and so anyone walking on the Temple Mount might inadvertently step into the holy area. Moreover the entire Temple and its immediately adjacent courts were banned to the ritually unclean. But once the sacrificial rites of purification had been swept away with the Temple, it was hard to tell who was clean and who unclean according to the letter of the *halachah* (the religious laws). The rules had been stricter for the inner enclosure than for the outer court – but this dividing line was no longer known. The majority of orthodox Jews believed that they should refrain from entering the Temple compound.

That view was endorsed in the twentieth century by the renowned Chief Rabbi Kook. There were, however, dissenting opinions. Clearly in the Six-Day War and after, the ban did not apply to soldiers on duty, because of the venerable and elastic doctrine of *pikuach nefesh*, which means that religious laws can be broken when human life is at stake. Rabbi Goren maintained that the southern portion of the Temple Mount was not subject to the ban, but that opinion was not accepted by the religious authorities. In practice, Orthodox Jews refrain from walking on any part of the mount, though other Jews do so.

The Fire in the El Aksa Mosque

The extraordinary affair of the El Aksa fire in 1969 illustrated how deeply the Temple Mount remained embedded in the politics of the Israel-Arab conflict.

At seven o'clock on the morning of 21 August the sun had already risen above the Mount of Olives, and shone down on the platform of the *Haram esh-Sharif*. The Moslem faithful, who had performed their dawn prayers in the mosque, had already left, and the sacred area was empty of visitors. A lean young man with cropped hair and glasses, and a haversack on his back, entered the enclosure. He had been hanging about off and on for ten days, and his odd behaviour and lavish tips had caused derision among the Moslem attendants and guides. In front of the entrance to El Aksa he met one of the guards, having previously given him money to be let into the mosque before it opened to visitors at 8 am, ostensibly to take some photographs – which was forbidden except with special

The interior of the El Aksa Mosque before the fire.

permission. Once inside he lifted bottles of kerosene and petrol from the haversack, poured their contents on to the wooden steps of the magnificent *minbar* (the pulpit installed by Saladin nearly eight centuries earlier), lit a scarf placed in the fluid and left. When someone shouted that the mosque was on fire, he broke into a run and disappeared through a different gate.

In response to the alarm Jewish and Arab fire-engines dashed towards the Temple Mount from Jerusalem, and then from nearby towns. Within an hour the fire had been controlled and by 10.30 the last embers extinguished. It was then seen that the pulpit had been destroyed, and the roof above it gutted.

The Israel police acted swiftly. From the descriptions given by two of the Moslem guards they drew up an 'identikit' picture, and with it went the rounds of the hotels. That night, in kibbutz Emek Hasharon on the coastal plain, they arrested a twenty-nine-year-old Australian Christian tourist named Michael Denis William Rohan, who was attending an *ulpan* (Hebrew language course) in the kibbutz. He immediately admitted to the crime and gave the police a statement.

It was clear from the first moment that there would be sweeping emotional and political reactions to this act of vandalism in the third holiest shrine of Islam, which had come under Israel rule little more than two years earlier. The Israel premier, Mrs Golda Meir, immediately issued a statement expressing her sense of outrage, and called an emer-

21 August 1969; smoke rises from the El Aksa Mosque as firemen fight to control the blaze.

gency meeting of the cabinet. The Jordan television and radio put out a story that the Israel cabinet had earlier decided on the burning of the mosque. In Jerusalem the Moslem authorities called for a one-day protest strike and a demonstration march to the mosque, which the police controlled with difficulty. A campaign of incitement spread throughout the Moslem world.

The Israel government set up a committee of inquiry, headed by a Supreme Court judge, and including two Arab notables: a Moslem judge from Nazareth and the Greek Orthodox mayor of that city. The committee found that Rohan's unauthorized entry into the mosque had been made possible by the slackness and greed of the guards concerned, as well as by the inadequate security arrangements, which were entirely an internal Moslem responsibility. The Moslem religious authorities appointed a former Arab army officer to improve the arrangements for protecting the mosque area.

By now it was obvious that this irrational act had been committed by a mentally unbalanced person. Rohan's pathetic story emerged from his own statements to the police, and from the evidence produced at his trial in Jerusalem at the beginning of October. He had had an unhappy childhood in Sydney, Australia, had been a school drop-out at fifteen, and had then drifted from one job to another. He was seduced by a woman older than himself, who left him soon after. Rohan then developed symptoms of mental illness and was treated for a while in a mental home, where he was diagnosed as a paranoiac, suffering from hallucinations and religious delusions. On recovering somewhat, he got a job and saved some money. He became religious, joined a fundamentalist sect called 'Church of God', and was told by his 'inner voices' to leave the country on an undisclosed mission. After wandering through other countries he came to Israel. There he received signs and revelations, and became convinced that he was a descendant of King David, destined to be King of Judea and to build the Third Temple. In order to make way for the Temple, the El Aksa Mosque had to be demolished. Rohan obtained some kerosene, climbed over the wall at night and made an unsuccessful attempt to destroy the mosque by setting the door alight. He spent the next ten days planning the second effort.

At his trial Rohan was a perplexing figure. Well-dressed, relaxed and attentive, he seemed to the layman completely normal. But the substance of his beliefs, and the testimony of the psychiatrists who were called, led to the inevitable judgement by the court that he was mentally ill and could not be held legally responsible for his actions at the time of the fire. He was remitted for treatment and five years later, in 1974, was repatriated to Australia.

A week after the fire an urgent meeting of the United Nations Security Council was requested by twenty-five member-states – fourteen of them

The Arab demonstration march to the El Aksa after the fire.

Arab and the rest Asian and African states with predominantly Moslem populations. The debate extended over six sessions of the council. Some Arab representatives charged that Israel had deliberately caused the fire, then impeded the fire-fighting operations by cutting off the water supply. Such allegations were not taken seriously, and the real issue that emerged was Israel's control of Jerusalem since the Six-Day War. A resolution was carried by a majority vote, linking the El Aksa fire with this broader political question.

In the course of the debate the Israel representative put on record his government's position about the rebuilding of the Temple. He said that the Temple Mount was so holy to the Jewish people that 'the devout amongst us would not even tread on it'. However, 'According to the *halachah*, the Temple will be rebuilt when the Messiah will have come. It is, therefore, inconceivable that we ourselves should make any plans for the rebuilding of the Temple.'

OVERLEAF The ninth day of Av, 1967. For the first time in nineteen years, Jewish pilgrims were able to visit the Wall on the day commemorating the destruction of the Temple in AD 70.

The Temple of the Spirit

The rebuilding of the Temple of Jerusalem nineteen hundred years after it was demolished is not a political reality. Yet pious Jews continue to plead in their synagogue services (to quote an English prayer-book), 'that the Temple be speedily rebuilt in our days ... and there we will serve Thee with awe ... then the offering of Judah and Jerusalem will be pleasant unto the Lord as in the days of old'.

They cling to the mystical three-thousand-year memory of the great sanctuary that once stood on Mount Moriah and project it into the Messianic future. In God's good time, the universal vision of the Hebrew prophets will be fulfilled. A kingdom of righteousness and peace will arise in a troubled world, and at its centre the Temple will shine again on the platform:

> It shall come to pass in the latter days that the mountain of the house of the Lord shall be established as the highest of the mountains, and shall be raised above the hills; and all the nations shall flow to it, and many peoples shall come, and say: 'Come, let us go up to the mountain of the Lord, to the house of the God of Jacob; that he may teach us his ways and that we may walk in his paths.' For out of Zion shall go forth the Law, and the word of the Lord from Jerusalem [Isaiah 2: 3].

Selected Reading List

AHARONI, Yohanan, *The Land of the Bible* (London, 1967)

ALBRIGHT, William Foxwell, *From the Stone Age to Christianity* (New York, 1957)

ALBRIGHT, William Foxwell, in *Bulletin of American School of Oriental Research*, 85 (1942)

AVIGAD, N., in *Beth Mikra*, 8 (1964)

AVI-YONAH, M., ed. *Sefer Yerushalaim* (1956)

AVI-YONAH, M., and AHARONI, Y., *The Macmillan Bible Atlas* (New York, 1968)

BRIGHT, John, *A History of Israel* (New York, 1960)

CLEMENTS, R. E., *God and Temple* (Oxford, 1965)

COMAY, Joan, *Who's Who in the Old Testament* (London and New York, 1971)

COMAY, Joan, *Who's Who in Jewish History* (London and New York, 1974)

DE VAUX, R., in *Kedem*, 2 (1948)

Encyclopaedia Judaica (Jerusalem, 1972)

Encyclopaedia of Islam, 2nd ed. (1954–68), s.v. 'El Kuds'.

FINN, James, *Stirring Times* (London 1878)

GOITEIN, S. D., *Studies in Islamic History and Institutions* (Jerusalem, 1966)

HOLLIS, F. J., *The Archaeology of Herod's Temple* (1968)

ISRAEL EXPLORATION SOCIETY, *Jerusalem through the Ages* (1968)

JONES, A. H. M., *The Herods of Jerusalem* (Oxford, 1938)

JOSEPHUS, *The Jewish War* (Harmondsworth, 1959)

KAUFMANN, Yehezkel, 'The Biblical Age', in *Great Ages and Ideas of the Jewish People* (New York, 1956)

KENNEDY, A. R. S., in *Hasting's Dictionary of the Bible* (Edinburgh, 1909), s.v. 'Temple'

KLAUSNER, Joseph, *History of the Second Temple Period*, Hebrew (Jerusalem, 1949)

KOLLEK, Teddy and Pearlman, Moshe, *Jerusalem* (London, 1968)

MAZAR, B., in *Eretz Yisrael*, 9 (1969)

Palestine Pilgrims' Text Society, 1–17 (London, 1890–97)

PARKES, James, *A History of Palestine* (New York, 1949)

PARROT, A., *Le Temple de Jerusalem* (Neuchchâtel, 1954)

PEARLMAN, Moshe, *The Maccabees* (London, 1974)

PRAWER, Joshua, *The Latin Kingdom of Jerusalem* (London, 1972)

ROTH, Cecil, *Short History of the Jewish People* (London, 1948)

RUNCIMAN, Steven, *A History of the Crusades* (Cambridge, 1951)

SMITH, George Adam, *Jerusalem, from the Earliest Times to A.D. 70* (London, 1907)

VINCENT, L. H., *Jerusalem de l'Ancien Testament* (Paris, 1954–56)

VINCENT, L. H. and Abel, F. M., *Jerusalem* (Paris, 1926)

WARREN, Charles, *Underground Jerusalem* (London, 1876)

WILSON, Charles, *The Recovery of Jerusalem* (London and New York, 1971)

WILSON, Charles, ed. *Picturesque Palestine*, I (London, 1880)

WRIGHT, G. E., in *Biblical Archaeologist*, 4 (1941)

WRIGHT, G. E., and Filson, F. V., *The Westminster Historical Atlas to the Bible* (Philadelphia, 1956)

YEIVIN, S., in *Beth Mikra*, 8 (1964).

ZEITLIN, Solomon, *The History of the Second Commonwealth* (Philadelphia, 1933)

Chronology

PART I: BEFORE THE TEMPLE

BC *c.* 1800–1700   The Patriarchs
          c. 1250   The Exodus
  c. 1220–1200   The Conquest
  c. 1200–1030   Period of the Judges
       1030–1010   King Saul
       1010– 970   King David

Capture of Jerusalem
Temple Site acquired

PART II: THE FIRST TEMPLE

BC   970–931   King Solomon

Building of Temple

DIVIDED MONARCHY: 931–587

931–721 Israel	931–587 Judah
Jeroboam I (931–910)	Rehoboam (931–913)
Ahab (874–853)	Athalia (841–835)
Prophet Elijah	Uzziah (781–740)
	Hezekiah (716–687)
Jeroboam II (783–743)	Prophet Isaiah
Fall of Samaria (721)	Assyrian Invasion (701)
	Josiah (640–609)
	Religious Reforms
	Jerusalem Surrenders (598)
	Prophet Jeremiah
	Jerusalem and
	Temple destroyed (587)

PART III: THE SECOND TEMPLE

BC	598–	Babylonian Exile
		Prophet Ezekiel
		Prophet Second Isaiah
	538	Edict of Cyprus
	538–520(?)	Zerubbabel Governor
	537	*Second Temple Foundations*
	520–515	*Second Temple built*
	445–425	Mission of Nehemiah
		Jerusalem Walls rebuilt
	458 (398?)	Mission of Ezra
		Religious Reforms
	323	Death of Alexander
	301–197	Judea under Ptolemaic (Egyptian) Rule
	197–142	Judea under Seleucid (Syrian) Rule
	175–163	Antiochus IV
	167	Start of Maccabean Revolt
	164	*Temple re-dedicated*
	163–37	Hasmonean Dynasty
	63	Pompey occupies Jerusalem
	34–4	Herod the Great
	19	*Temple rebuilt*
AD	6–41	Judea under Roman rule
	c. 30	Death of Jesus
	66–70	The Jewish War
	70	*Sack of Jerusalem and*
		Temple destroyed

PART IV: AFTER THE TEMPLE

70	Jochanan ben Zakkai at Yavne
132–135	Bar-Kochba Revolt
c. 212	Mishnah completed
c. 313	Christianity dominant in Roman Empire
4TH century	Jerusalem Talmud compiled
6TH century	Babylonian Talmud compiled
638–1099	*Arab Period*
638	Caliph Omar enters Jerusalem
691	Dome of the Rock completed
715	El Aksa Mosque completed
1099–1291	*Crusader Period*
1099	Capture of Jerusalem
1187	Saladin occupies Jerusalem
1291	Fall of Acre
1516–1917	*Ottoman Turkish Period*
1520–1566	Suleiman the Magnificent
1757, 1852	Firmans on 'Status Quo'
1882	Beginning of Zionist Settlement
1917	Balfour Declaration
1920–1948	*British Mandatory Period*
1917	Allenby enters Jerusalem
1929–1931	Crisis over Western Wall
1947	UN Partition Resolution
1948–	*State of Israel*
1948	Temple Mount occupied by Jordan
1967	Temple Mount recaptured by Israel

Photographic Acknowledgments

Photographs and illustrations are supplied by or reproduced by kind permission of the following :

Aldus Books (John Freeman) *230–31*; Associated Press 248 (above and below), 261, 263; Badisches Landesmuseum 49; Biblioteca Medicea-Laurenziana, Florence 103; Biblioteca National, Madrid 47; Bibliothèque Nationale, Paris 71, 118–19, *179*, 210; Bodleian Library 30, 169, 226, 227; Denise Bourbonnais 26; Y. Braun 120; Werner Braun *229*; British Library 55 (left), 126; British Museum 14, *38–9*, 59, 65, 66, 92, *153* (John Freeman), 181, 188; Mike Busselle 42, 43 (below), 75, 91, 130, 131, 156, 204, 211, 223; Archbishop of Canterbury and the Trustees of Lambeth Palace Library 90; Richard Cleave *40*; Cliché des Musées Nationaux 21; A. Glik 160 (above), 165 (above left), 203; Felix Gluck 41, 80, 220; David Harris *37*, 49, 77, 106, 110, 122, 140, 142, 165 (below), 244, 264–5; Herzog Anton Ulrich Museum 55 (right); Israel Department of Antiquities and Museums 77, 213; Israel Government Press Office 150, 259; Israel Museum 6, 122; Jewish Seminary of America 80; Keystone Press Agency 246; Arthur Kutcher 253; Leiden University Library 121; Louvre, Paris 43; Mansell Collection 52 (below left), 82, 89, 139, 147, 172–3, 190 (above), 201, 208; Manuscript Library of St Thoros, Armenian Patriarchate, Jerusalem 18; Mary Evans Picture Library 15, 53 (below), 67, 79, 100, 105, 217, 225; Middle East Archives 31; Musée Condé, Chantilly 26; National Gallery, London 149; Novaes, Lisbon *154*; Palestine Exploration Fund 163, 165 (above right), *232*; Photo Garo 260; Pierpont Morgan Library, New York *113*; Popperfoto 17, 87; Rheinisches Bildarchiv 52 (below right), 128 (left and right); Cecil Robert *180*; Moshe Safdie Architects Ltd., Jerusalem 255; Jorg Schmeissel 6; Ronald Sheridan 23 (below), 52 (above), 62, *116*, 159, 160 (bottom), 199, 240–41; Vatican Library, Rome 25, 108; Wells Cathedral (Eric Purchase) 96; The Dean and Chapter, Winchester (E. A. Sollars) 167; Yigael Yadin 190 (below), 197.

Picture research by Patricia Mandel
Maps by Edward MacAndrew Purcell
Numerals in italics indicate colour illustrations

Index